D1195404

AFRICAN HISTORICAL DICTIONARIES
Edited by Jon Woronoff

1. *Cameroon,* by Victor T. LeVine and Roger P. Nye. 1974
2. *The Congo,* 2nd ed., by Virginia Thompson and Richard Adloff. 1984
3. *Swaziland,* by John J. Grotpeter. 1975
4. *The Gambia,* 2nd ed., by Harry A. Gailey. 1987
5. *Botswana,* by Richard P. Stevens. 1975
6. *Somalia,* by Margaret F. Castagno. 1975
7. *Benin [Dahomey],* 2nd ed., by Samuel Decalo. 1987
8. *Burundi,* by Warren Weinstein. 1976
9. *Togo,* 2nd ed., by Samuel Decalo. 1987
10. *Lesotho,* by Gordon Haliburton. 1977
11. *Mali,* 2nd ed., by Pascal James Imperato.1986
12. *Sierra Leone,* by Cyril Patrick Foray. 1977
13. *Chad,* 2nd ed., by Samuel Decalo. 1987
14. *Upper Volta,* by Daniel Miles McFarland. 1978
15. *Tanzania,* by Laura S. Kurtz. 1978
16. *Guinea,* 2nd ed., by Thomas O'Toole. 1987
17. *Sudan,* by John Voll. 1978
18. *Rhodesia/Zimbabwe,* by R. Kent Rasmussen. 1979
19. *Zambia,* by John J. Grotpeter. 1979
20. *Niger,* by Samuel Decalo. 1979
21. *Equatorial Guinea,* by Max Liniger-Goumaz. 1979
22. *Guinea-Bissau,* by Richard Lobban. 1979.
23. *Senegal,* by Lucie G. Colvin. 1981
24. *Morocco,* by William Spencer. 1980
25. *Malaŵi,* by Cynthia A. Crosby. 1980
26. *Angola,* by Phyllis Martin. 1980
27. *The Central African Republic,* by Pierre Kalck. 1980
28. *Algeria,* by Alf Andrew Heggoy. 1981
29. *Kenya,* by Bethwell A. Ogot. 1981
30. *Gabon,* by David E. Gardinier. 1981
31. *Mauritania,* by Alfred G. Gerteiny. 1981
32. *Ethiopia,* by Chris Prouty and Eugene Rosenfeld. 1981
33. *Libya,* by Lorna Hahn. 1981
34. *Mauritius,* by Lindsay Rivière. 1982
35. *Western Sahara,* by Tony Hodges. 1982
36. *Egypt,* by Joan Wucher-King. 1984
37. *South Africa,* by Christopher Saunders. 1983
38. *Liberia,* by D. Elwood Dunn and Svend E. Holsoe. 1985
39. *Ghana,* by Daniel Miles McFarland. 1985
40. *Nigeria,* by Anthony Oyewole. 1987
41. *Ivory Coast,* by Robert J. Mundt. 1987

Historical Dictionary
of
THE IVORY COAST
(COTE D'IVOIRE)

by
Robert J. Mundt

African Historical Dictionaries, No. 41

The Scarecrow Press, Inc.
Metuchen, N.J., & London
1987

Library of Congress Cataloging-in-Publication Data

Mundt, Robert J.
    Historical Dictionary of the Ivory Coast
(Côte D'Ivoire).

    (African historical dictionaries ; no. 41)
    Bibliography: p.
    1. Ivory Coast--History--Dictionaries.
I. Title. II. Series.
DT545.57.M86 1987   966.6'8'00321   87-12724
ISBN 0-8108-2029-3

CONTENTS

ACKNOWLEDGMENTS

Financial support for the preparation of this work came from the Chancellor's Office at the University of North Carolina at Charlotte and the Southern Regional Education Board. Special thanks are due to Ms. Joanne Zellers, Area Specialist, African Section, Library of Congress, for her bibliographic assistance. Mme. Dankowska, documentarian at the Center for African Studies at the Maison des Sciences de l'Homme (Paris), went beyond the call of duty in making the collections available during the vacation months. Ms. Mary McGinnis helped get the manuscript in publishable form.

The author, and many of the authors cited herein, owe a large debt of gratitude to Claude Pairault, who, as Director of the Institut d'Ethnosociologie of the University of Abidjan in the late 1960s and early 1970s, gave unstinting assistance to visiting scholars. The magnitude of that assistance is brought home when compiling a bibliography of this sort by the frequency with which he was singled out for thanks.

A NOTE ON SPELLING

Orthography is always a matter of difficult choices in work on francophone African countries. The general principal here is to use the spelling under which the dictionary user is most likely to have encountered a term, with a cross listing from variations on that spelling. Thus, city names like Abengourou are found under the official (French) orthography. On the other hand, readers in English are as likely as not to read "Baule" as "Baoule," so the former is listed as primary.

There is even disagreement on the English spelling of the adjectival form of the country's name. Many authors use "Ivorian," derived directly from "Ivory Coast." Others use

Ivoirian, an anglicization as close as possible to the French ivoirien. The author prefers the latter, although it may be an irrational compromise, as esthetically more pleasing. Also, because the Ivoirian government proclaimed in 1986 that the country must be called Côte d'Ivoire in all languages, "Ivoirian" should carry the day.

EDITOR'S FOREWORD

In 1957, on the eve of African decolonization, two of the continent's aspiring leaders met in Abidjan: Kwame Nkrumah of Ghana and Félix Houphouët-Boigny of the Ivory Coast. On that occasion, they entered into a wager as to which would bring greater economic and political progress. At that time, the charismatic Nkrumah was the overwhelming favorite. In the end, the more conservative and pragmatic Houphouët managed to turn in better results. But it has taken a long time to realize that.

Where the success has been most convincing is the rapid development of what had been a very backward economy, one that achieved exceptional growth rates until the recent slowdown of the world economy. While some Ivoirians gained more than others, and Europeans were deeply involved, there was a vital contribution by the nation's farmers and traders. On the political side, the success is more questionable. Houphouët has remained in power from that day to this and the problem of succession has not been solved. Yet, in a continent known for political instability and military coups, things could have been much worse.

This makes the Ivory Coast one of the most intriguing, and also controversial, African countries. That becomes increasingly clear while reading through this dictionary. Professor Robert J. Mundt, Chairman of the Political Science Department of the University of North Carolina at Charlotte, has done an excellent job of tracing the political, economic, social, and cultural development of the country, not just since independence but well before.

Professor Mundt's interest in the Ivory Coast goes back to the early 1970s, when he wrote his dissertation on the Ivoirian Code Civil. Since then he has visited the country several times and written further. His knowledge is transmitted in a very readable and comprehensive guide to a country which is well known to the French-speaking public but frequently neglected in other parts of the world. Such an oversight is more than just unfortunate, given the crucial role of Houphouët and the Ivory Coast in African affairs. We are therefore pleased to help fill the gap with this historical dictionary.

Jon Woronoff
Series Editor

ABBREVIATIONS AND ACRONYMS

ADB	African Development Bank
ADIACI	Association pour la Défense des Intérets des Autochtones de la Côte d'Ivoire
AFI	Association des Femmes Ivoiriennes (Ivoirian Women's Association)
AOF	French West Africa (Afrique Occidentale Française)
ARSO	Southwest Region Development Authority (Autorité pour l'Aménagement de la Région du Sud-Ouest)
AVB	Autorité pour l'Aménagement de la Vallée du Bandama (Bandama Valley Development Authority)
BAO	Banque de l'Afrique Occidentale
BCEAO	Central Bank of West African States (Banque Centrale des Etats de l'Afrique de l'Ouest)
BIAO	Banque International pour l'Afrique Occidentale
BICICI	Banque Internationale pour le Commerce et l'Industrie de la Côte d'Ivoire
BNDA	Banque Nationale pour le Développement Agricole (National Agricultural Development Bank)
BOAD	Banque Ouest Africaine de Développement (West African Development Bank)
CCFOM	Caisse Centrale de la France d'Outre-Mer
CCI	Crédit de la Côte d'Ivoire
CEAO	West African Economic Community (Communauté Economique de l'Afrique de l'Ouest)
CEE (EEC)	Communauté Européenne Economique (European Economic Community)
CFA	Communauté Financiére Africaine (African Financial Community)

CFAO	Compagnie Française d'Afrique Occidentale
CFCI	Compagnie Française de la Côte d'Ivoire
CFCT	Compagnie Française pour le Développement des Fibres Textiles (French Company for the Development of Textile Fibers)
CFTC	Confédération Française des Travailleurs Chrétiens
CGT	Confédération Générale du Travail
CICA	Compagnie Industrielle et Commerciale de l'Afrique
CIDT	Compagnie Ivoirienne pour le Développement des Textiles (Ivoirian Textile Development Company) (Ivorian Company for Textile Development)
CRO	Center for Oceanographic Research
CROA	Comptoirs Réunis de l'Ouest Africain
CSSPPA	Caisse de Stabilisation et de Soutien des Prix des Produits Agricoles
CTFT	Centre Technique Forestier Tropical (Technical Center for Tropical Forestry)
ECOWAS	Economic Community of West African States
FAC	Fond d'Aide et de Coopération
FAO	Food and Agriculture Organization
FEANF	Fédération des Etudiants d'Afrique Noire en France
FED	Fond Européen de Développement (European Development Fund)
FIDES	Fonds d'Investissement pour le Développement Economique et Social
GEC	Groupe d'Etudes Communistes
ICCO	International Cocoa Organization
IEAOFT	Institut d'Emission de l'Afrique Occidentale Française et du Togo
IFAN	Institut Française (Fondamentale) d'Afrique Noir
IFCC	Institut Française pour le Café et le Cacao
IFRDC	Institut Français de Recherche pour le Développement en Coopération
IOM	Indépendants d'Outre-Mer
IRAT	Institut de Recherches Agronomiques Tropicales et des Cultures Vivrières (Institute

	for Research in Tropical Agriculture and Foodcrops)
IRCT	Institut de Recherches du Coton et des Fibres Exotiques (Institute for Research on Cotton and Exotic Fibers)
IRHO	Institut de Recherches des Huiles et Oléagineux (Institute for Research on Edible Oils and Oleaginous Products)
JRDACI	Jeunesse Rassemblement Démocratique Africain de Côte d'Ivoire
MOTORAGRI	Société pour le Développement de la Motorisation de l'Agriculture (Company for the Development of Agricultural Motorization)
OAMCE	Organisation Africaine et Malgache pour la Coopération Econoomique
OAU (OUA)	Organization of African Unity (Organisation de l'Unité Africaine)
OCAM	Organisation Commune Africaine et Mauricienne (African and Mauritian Common Organization)
OPEI	Office for the Promotion of Ivorian Enterprise (Office de Promotion de l'Entreprise Ivoirienne)
ORSTOM	Office de la Recherche Scientifique et Technique Outre-Mer
PCF	French Communist Party (Parti Communiste Française)
PDCI	Parti Démocratique de Côte d'Ivoire
PETROCI	Société Nationale d'Opérations Pétrolières de la Côte d'Ivoire
PPCI	Parti Progressiste de la Côte d'Ivoire (Progressive Party of the Ivory Coast)
RAN	Régie du Chemin de Fer Abidjan-Niger (Abidjan-Niger Railroad)
RDA	Rassemblement Démocratique Africain
SAA	Syndicat Agricole Africain
SATMACI	Technical Assistance Society for the Agricultural Modernization of the Ivory Coast. (Société d'Assistance Technique pour la

	Modernisation Agricole de la Côte d'Ivoire)
SCOA	Société Commerciale de l'Ouest Africain
SFIO	Section Française de l'Internationale Ouvrière (French Socialist Party)
SGBCI	Société Générale des Banques en Côte d'Ivoire
SIB	Société Ivoirienne de Banque
SOCATCI	Société des Caoutchoucs de Côte d'Ivoire (Ivory Coast Rubber Company)
SODE	Société de Développement
SODEFEL	Société pour le Développement des Fruits et Légumes (Fruit and Vegetable Development Company)
SODEFOR	Société pour le Développement des Plantations Forestières (Forestry Development Company)
SODEMI	Société pour le Développement Minier en Côte d'Ivoire (Ivory Coast Mining Development Company)
SODEPALM	Société pour le Développement et l'Exploitation du Palmier à l'Huile (Oil Palm Development Company)
SODEPRA	Société pour le Développement des Productions Animales (Livestock Production Development Company)
SODERIZ	Société pour le Développement de la Riziculture (Rice Development Company)
SODESUCRE	Société pour le Développement des Plantations de Cannes à Sucre, l'Industrialisation et Commercialisation du Sucre (Sugar Development Company)
SOGEFIHA	Société de Gestion Financière de l'Habitat (Company for the Financial Management of Housing)
SONAFI	Société Nationale de Financement (National Finance Company)
UAM	Union Africaine et Malgache (African and Malagasy Union)
UDAO	West African Customs Union (Union Douanière entre les Etats de l'Afrique Occidentale)
UDEAO	Customs Union of West African States (Union Douanière des Etats de l'Afrique de l'Ouest)
UDECI	Union for the Defense of Ivory Coast Economic Interests (Union pour la Défense des Intérets Economiques)

UFOCI	Union Fraternelle des Originaires de la Côte d'Ivoire
UGECI	Union Générale des Etudiants de la Côte d'Ivoire
UGTAN	Union Générale des Travailleurs de l'Afrique Noire
ULSC	Union Locale des Syndicats Confédérés CGT de la Côte d'Ivoire
UMOA	West African Monetary Community (Union Monétaire Ouest-Africaine)
UNECI	Union Nationale des Etudiants de la Côte d'Ivoire
UNTCI	Union Nationale des Travailleurs de Côte d'Ivoire
UOCOCI	Union des Originaires des Six Cercles de l'Ouest
UTCI	Union des Travailleurs de Côte d'Ivoire

CHRONOLOGY

c.1400   First Manding migrations into present-day
                Ivory Coast.

1469   Portuguese Soerio da Costa lands at Sassandra.

1490–1510   Second wave of (Diomandé) Manding migrations
                into Ivory Coast from Mali.

c.1600   Founding of Kingdom of Bouna.

1637   First attempt by French to establish a post
                at Assinie.

c.1650–1720   Akan migrations into Baule region.

1700   Settlement of Agni at Assikasso (Agnibilékrou).

1701   Asantehene Osei Tutu defeats Denkyera (Akan
                state in present Ghana); Denkyera refugees
                cross Comoé and Nzi, settle among Senufo,
                Guro and Malinké already there.

1720–1780   Further waves of Akan migration.

c.1740   Establishment of Agni kingdoms of Moronou
                and Indénié.

c.1750   Baule settle between Nzi and Bandama Rivers.

c.1760   Creation of Diarassouba (Bambara) state of
                Nafana.

1838   French re-establish post at Assinie.

1840s   Beginning of commercial production of palm
                oil.

1842	French make formal claim to Assinie and Grand Bassam.
1848	Creation of the Kabadugu kingdom at Odienné.
1860s	Establishment of the <u>Compagnie de Kong</u> by Arthur Verdier.
1878	Arthur Verdier named <u>Résident de France</u>.
1880	First cocoa plantation established.
1885	Verdier introduces coffee-growing to the Ivory Coast.
1887-89	Exploration by Louis Binger between the Atlantic and the Niger, and by Treich-Laplène from Assinie to Bondoukou and Kong.
1889	Meeting of Binger and Treich-Laplène at Kong.
1893	Proclamation of Ivory Coast as a French colony. Binger named first governor. Samory Touré establishes second empire at Dabakala.
1894	Telegraph line opened from Assinie to Grand-Bassam. Gbon Coulibaly becomes ruler of Tyembara Senufo, allies with Samory.
1897	Samory destroys Kong.
1898	Samory captured by French at Guélémou.
1899	Grand Bassam, colonial capital, devastated by plague and yellow fever epidemics.
1900	Transfer of capital to Bingerville.
1903	Beginning of railroad north from Abidjan.
1905	Félix Houphouët-Boigny born in Yamoussoukro.
1908	Gabriel Angoulvant named governor, begins final military campaigns against peoples resisting French rule.

1912	Railroad line reaches Bouake.
1913-1914	William Wade Harris in the Ivory Coast.
1915	Robusta cofee introduced. Road completed from Abidjan through Bingerville to Grand Bassam.
1916	First motorized vehicles in Ivory Coast.
1918	Completion of French "pacification."
1933	Merger of Ivory Coast and a large portion of Upper Volta.
1934	Transfer of capital from Bingerville to Abidjan. Railroad line reaches Upper Volta.
1944	Formation of the Syndicat Agricole Africain by Houphouët-Boigny and Auguste Denise, to seek equal treatment for indigenous planters.
1946	Ivory Coast becomes a territory in the French Union. Democratic Party of the Ivory Coast formed to participate in elections to French Constituent Assembly.
1947	Ivory Coast and Upper Volta redivided.
1950	PDCI ends affiliation with French Communist Party. Completion of Vridi Canal opens Abidjan to ocean-going shipping.
1956	Loi-cadre reforms passed in French National Assembly, introducing universal suffrage and a single electoral roll for Overseas France.
1958	Ivory Coast votes for membership in French Community. Anti-alien riots lead to expulsion of 18,000 foreign Africans.
1960	Independence from France under President Félix Houphouët-Boigny.
1962	Death of Gbon Coulibaly, chef superieur of the Senufo.

1963   Attempted overthrow of Houphouët reported, followed by many arrests, trials, and prison sentences for former party stalwarts.

1969   Construction begins on Kossou Dam.

1972   Electric production begins from Kossou Dam.

1973   Twelve junior army officers convicted of planning a coup.

1975   Third re-election of Houphouët as President.

1977   Three senior ministers dismissed from government as a result of unsatisfactory economic performance.
Ivory Coast becomes world's largest cocoa producer.

1980   Fourth re-election of Houphouët as President; first competitive National Assembly elections. Elimination of post of Secretary General of the PDCI; creation of post of vice-president.

1981   First structural adjustment loan from World Bank to Ivory Coast.

1983   Severe drought severely reduces hydro-electric production. Strikes by students and faculty at University of Abidjan. Yamoussoukro named political capital.

1985   Fifth re-election of Houphouët as President. Unfilled position of Vice-President abolished. Government resumes diplomatic relations with Israel.

1986   Government resumes relations with USSR, other Eastern bloc states; announces official name of country to be "Côte d'Ivoire" in all languages.

TABLES

Table 1: IVORY COAST POPULATION

Year	Total		Abidjan	Bouaké	Daloa
1912			1,400		
1920	1,540,000		5,400		
1934			17,000		
1945			45,000		
1955	3,000,000		127,000		
1961			212,000	45,000	18,000
1965	3,880,000		340,000		
1975	6,670,866	(census)	921,682	173,000	42,000
			951,215	175,264	60,837
1979	7,500,000	(est.)			
1980	8,189,549	(est.)	1,422,436	269,915	

1975 Population by Prefecture:

Abengourou	177,692	Danané	170,249
Abidjan	1,389,141	Dimbokro	475,023
Aboisso	148,823	Divo	278,526
Adzopé	162,837	Ferkéssédougou	90,423
Agboville	141,970	Gagnoa	259,504
Biankouma	75,711	Guiglo	137,672
Bondoukou	296,551	Katiola	77,875
Bouaflé	263,609	Korhogo	276,816
Bouaké	808,048	Man	278,659
Bouna	84,290	Odienné	124,010
Boundiali	132,278	Sassandra	191,994
Dabakala	56,230	Séguéla	157,539
Daloa	369,610	Touba	77,786

Table 2: IVOIRIAN ETHNIC GROUPS

Cultural Area	Group	As Named by Neighboring Groups	Location (Department, unless otherwise noted)
AKAN	Abron, Brong	Doma, Tchaman, Abron	Bondoukou
	Anyi, Agni	Ton, Kotoko	Bongouanou
	Béttié		Dimbokro
	Bini		Aboisso
	Bona		Abengourou
	Juablin		Bondoukou
	Moronou		
	Ndenye		
	Sanwi		
	Baule, Baoulé	Ton, Kotoko, Baba, Po	Bouaké
			Dimbokro
			Bouaflé
			S.P. of Tiassalé
VOLTAIC (GUR)	Senufo, Syénambélé	Siena, Bamana, Senefo	Katiola
			Dabakala
			Ferkéssédougou

Cultural Area	Group	As Named by Neighboring Groups	Location (Department, unless otherwise noted)
			Korhogo Boundiali Odiénné
	Kulango, Lorhon, Kulamo	Kulango, Nkoramfo, Ngwela, Nabé	Bouna, Bondoukou
	Lobi, Birifor, Téguessié	Lobi, Birifo, Lorhon, Touna, Tounbé	Bouna
	Gouin, Mbwèn, Kpen	Gouin	S.P. of Ferkéssédougou
	Siti, Kira	Sitigo, Paxala, Konosarala	S.P. of Bouna
	Dégha, Déya	Buru, Mmofo, Dyoma	S.P. of Bondoukou
	Gonja	Gonja	S.P. of Bondoukou S.P. of Mankono
	Samogho	Samogho	S.P. of Boundiali

Cultural Area	Group	As Named by Neighboring Groups	Location (Department, unless otherwise noted)
KRU	Béte, Magwé	Tsien, Bokya, Kpwe	Daloa, Gagnoa, Issia, Soubré
	Niaboua	Niaboua	S.P. of Zoukougbeu
	Niédéboua	Niédéboua	S.P. of Vavoua
	Kouya	Kouya	S.P. of Vavoua
	Kouzié	Kouzié	S.P. of Buyo
	Dida, Godié	Dida, Kwè, Gwedji	Divo, Lakota
	Kotrohou, Kodia	Kotrohou, Kodia	S.P.s of Guitry, Fresco, and Grand-Lahou
	Wobé, Wè	Wobé	S.P.s Kouibly, Fakobly, Logoualé, Bangolo
	Guéré, Wè	Gewo	Guiglo
	Kru, Wané, Grebo	Kru, Wané	Sassandra

Cultural Area	Group	As Named by Neighboring Groups	Location (Department, unless otherwise noted)
	Bakwé, Srigbé	Touwé, Bakwé	S.P.s of Soubré and San Pedro
	Ubi (Oubi)	Ubi	S.P. of Tai
	Neyo	Neyo	Sassandra
LAGUNAIRE	Abbey, Abé	Abé	Agboville
	Abidji, Ari	Abidji	S.P. of Sikensi
	Abure, Abouré	Agoua, Compa, Abonwa	S.P.s of Grand-Bassam, Bonoua, Aboisso
	Adjukru, Odjukru	Boubouri, Adjoukrou	S.P. of Dabou
	Ahizi, Aizi, Kpokpo	Ahizi	S.P. of Jacqueville
	Alladian, Nladja-wron	Alladian	S.P. of Jacqueville
	Atié, Akyé	Atié	Adzopé, S.P. of Alépé

Cultural Area	Group	As Named by Neighboring Groups	Location (Department, unless otherwise noted)
	Avikam, Brignan	Brignan, Gbanda, Lahou	S.P. of Grand-Lahou
	Ebrié, Kyaman	Ebrié, Gbon, Tchrimbo, Ebu	Abidjan
	Ega	Ega, Dïes	S.P.s of Guitry, Fresco
	Ehotilé, Mekyibo	Ehotilé, Vétéré, Ewutre, Byetri	S.P. of Adiaké
	Essouma	Essouma	S.P.s of Adiaké and Aboisso
	Krobou	Krobou	Agboville
	Mbatto, Gwa	Mbatto	S.P. of Bingerville
	Nzima, Zéma Appolonians	Nzima, Appolo, Assoko, Amanya	S.P.s of Grand-Bassam and Adiaké
SOUTHERN MANDE	Yacouba, Dan	Mebe, Samia, Gyo, Yacouba	Man, Danané, Biankouma

Cultural Area	Group	As Named by Neighboring Groups	Location (Department, unless otherwise noted)
	Toura, Wenmebo	Toura	Biankouma
	Guro, Gouro, Kouéni	Lo, Dipa, Kouen, Guro	Bouaflé, Zuénoula
	Mona, Mwanu	Mwa, Ganmu	Mankono
	Wan, Ouan, Ngwanu	Wan	S.P.s of Kounahiri, Béoumi, and Mankono
	Gagu, Gagou, Gban	Gagu	S.P. of Oumé
	Beng, Ngan, Nguin	Ngan, Nguin	S.P. of Mbahiakro
NORTHERN MANDE	Malinké, Maninka	Malinké	Mankono, Séguéla, Touba, Odienné
	Dyula, Dioula	Dyula, Va, Febe, Kangah	S.P.s of Kong, Satama-Sokoura, Bondoukou
	Bambara, Banmana	Banmana	S.P.s of Goulia, Tienko, Kaniasso

Cultural Area	Group	As Named by Neighboring Groups	Location (Department, unless otherwise noted)
	Assimilated Groups:	Fula, Huela, Goro, Gbin, Ligbi	Odienné, Bouna, Bondoukou

Source: J. N. Loucou, Histoire de la Côte d'Ivoire, 1984

Table 3: EXPORTS FROM IVORY COAST (In Metric Tons)

Year	Coffee	Cocoa	Bananas	Wood	Palm Oil	Cotton	Rubber
1893					5,442		77
1898					4,331		289
1903					4,863		1,166
1908					5,557		915
1913	10	42		42,651	6,014		962
1918	30	420		36,406	3,168		249
1933	1,699	30,914	196	41,935	3,102		
1938	14,076	52,720	12,271	65,683	2,971		
1943	22,992	543	2	2,418	2,942		
1963	182,100	99,700	133,400	1,478,000			400
1968	214,400	121,500	147,300	2,620,000	500	11,300	7,000
1973	212,600	143,000	145,000	3,497,000	49,800	17,000	14,900
1978	230,451	244,000	144,123	2,004,600	75,126	25,584	17,531
1981	231,187	494,087	111,391	1,788,798	62,821	38,856	22,304
1982	272,532	380,776	91,706	1,752,605	61,209	37,817	28,298
1983	223,072	338,493	79,834	1,769,414	52,650	49,849	29,309

INTRODUCTION

Location

The Ivory Coast is located on 340 miles of the West
African Atlantic coast between Ghana and Liberia. It also
has common borders with Guinea, Mali, and Burkina Faso.
The country's area totals 124,503 square miles (322,463 sq.
km.), about that of Italy or Japan. It is located between 4
and 10 degrees north latitude, and is bisected by the fifth
meridian west of Greenwich. Between 1932 and 1947 the Ivory
Coast colony also included a large portion of Upper Volta (now
Burkina Faso).

Climate

The climate of the Ivory Coast is transitional between
tropical and equatorial. The temperature range is narrow in
the southern part of the country (73-80 degrees Fahrenheit);
humidity averages 80-90 percent south of the fifth parallel,
70-80 percent between the fifth and eighth parallels, and less
than 70 percent north of that. The lowest monthly averages
are between 85 and 55 percent progressing north from the
coast to Bouake, and fall below 50 percent in the far north.
There is a mean annual rainfall of 80-120 inches. The primary rainy season extends from mid-May to mid-July.

Physical Features

The Ivoirian seacoast is marked by numerous lagoons
separating a sandy island from the mainland to the east of
the Bandama River estuary; west of the Bandama the coast
is more rocky, with picturesque bays, beaches, and cliffs.
There is a coastal plain extending inland about forty miles.

1

Republic of Ivory Coast

Thereafter the surface gradually rises to a plateau. Rolling countryside is found in the west and northwest, with mountains and waterfalls in the region of Man, near the border with Liberia. There are also hilly areas near Bongouanou, in the Baoulé chain, and the granite domes and inselbergs in the extreme northwest corner. The principal rivers are the Cavally, Sassandra, Bandama, and Comoé. None of these is navigable beyond a short distance from the coast. The northernmost region is drained by tributaries of the Niger.

About 46 percent of the country is covered with rain forest, of which the thickest portion is in the southwest region. The northern third is wooded savanna.

There are no major mineral deposits in the Ivory Coast, although oil has been discovered and exploited off shore.

Population

The total population was recorded in the 1975 census as 6,670,912. It was estimated by the United Nations at 7,500,000 in 1979 and 8,190,000 in 1980. The number of French citizens resident in the Ivory Coast has risen from about 15,000 at independence (1960) to 50,000 today. There are about 3,000,000 Africans from neighboring countries living there, drawn by the relative Ivoirian prosperity. (It is estimated that almost one fourth of the population of Burkina Faso actually lives and works in the Ivory Coast.) Over one third of the population now lives in cities of 10,000-plus population, and over one half are less than 20 years old. The population increased at an annual rate of 1.4 percent in 1945, 1.9 percent in 1955, 3.1 percent in 1965, and 4 percent in 1975.

The distribution of population in the Ivory Coast is determined more by history than by physical environment. Several areas of high density correspond to the first centers of settlement of major ethnic groups, especially the Maninka and Akan areas settled between the fifteenth and eighteenth centuries. By the early nineteenth century, these population distributions were fixed much as at present. At the end of the nineteenth century, Samory's (q.v.) campaigns greatly altered the population distribution in the north. The regions through which his armies swept are now thinly populated, as whole villages and towns were abandoned by fleeing peoples. On the other hand, the high densities around Korhogo and Bouake result from their diplomatic and military strengths in avoiding conquest, for they received the refugees from other areas. Colonial policy involved moving villages to centers of transportation, both to improve control of the population and to locate work forces convenient to the maintenance of the roads. The population is still linearly distributed along the main roads as a result of such resettlements, which continued into the 1930s in southwest Ivory Coast.

Peoples

Ever since Delafosse (q.v.) wrote of the "over 60

languages and dialects of Ivory Coast," observers have emphasized the country's ethnic fragmentation. In fact, there
are only four (Akan, Kru, Manding, and Voltaic) or eight
(Kru, southern Mandé, Manding, Senufo, Kulango, Lobi, Akan,
Lagoon) cultural zones, depending on the specificity of cri-
teria one uses to categorize cultures. The Baoulé, an Akan
subroup, is the largest single ethnic group, with a population
of about 765,000 (1971). In addition, as much as 30 percent
of the population are migrant workers from Burkina Faso, Mali,
and Ghana. Finally, there is a non-African population of
about 100,000 Lebanese and 60,000 French. There is great
cultural diversity, in a pattern more complex than any map
or list of groups can suggest. Most ethnic maps are based
on home areas as of the beginning of the colonial period.
Interregional migration and urbanization since then have resulted in a thorough mixing, with "lumps" remaining in the
original locations.

The population is about one-fourth Moslem and one-eighth
Christian, predominantly Roman Catholic. The remainder follow traditional beliefs. There is a great diversity of languages
spoken, but the official language is French.

History

The original inhabitants of the Ivory Coast are unknown;
no pre-Paleolithic remains have been found there. Some
fragments of arms and tools from the Paleolithic era have been
found west of the Bandama River in the "Baule V" (q.v.) and
at Abengourou. Neolithic remains, such as polished axes,
are more numerous. There are many sites of residue of iron-
working north of the lagoons and in the savanna region.
Piles of shells along the lagoons have been carbon-dated to
between 1500 B.C.-1500 A.D. Some sources suggest negrillos
or pygmies as the first inhabitants, based largely on reference
to "little red men" in oral tradition of the origins of several
Ivoirian cultures.

The Ivory Coast is the home of several major ethnic and
linguistic groups that arrived there at different times. It
is probable that the Mali empire at its peak extended into
northwestern Ivory Coast, around Odienné. Between the
sixteenth and eighteenth centuries, Manding speakers moved

in from the north as traders and settlers, attracted by gold
and kola nuts which they traded in Mali. They founded kingdoms in Kong (eighteenth century) and Kabadugu (nineteenth
century).

The Agni and Baule are Akan peoples, fragments of the
Ashanti empires in present-day Ghana who migrated in successive waves as far west as the Bandama River.

The Compagnie de Saint-Malo landed five French missionaries at Assinie in 1637. Europeans found the coastal area
inhospitable however; three of these five died within a short
while, and the other two took refuge at the Dutch trading
post of Axim (present-day Ghana). Fifty years later, another
attempt at a settlement was made at Assinie, and a young
prince, Aniaba, was sent to France. He was educated at the
court of Louis XIV, who served as godfather at his baptism.
He then returned with two missionaries and a garrison of two
officers and thirty men. This attempt at permanent settlement
ended in 1704, when a royal captain ordered the colony's removal because of the deplorable conditions there. There was
no formal link with France again for over a century.

French trading posts were established along the coast
early in the eighteenth century; there was some slave trade
activity, although not nearly to the extent found in Benin to
the east. In 1842, Naval Captain Bouët-Willaumez (q.v.),
who commanded the French fleet patrolling for slavers, was
ordered by the Naval Ministry to conclude treaties with coastal
chiefs in the area, to support the naval actions. Such treaties
were signed first at Assinie and Grand-Bassam, and over the
next 25 years at Akapless, Dabou, Grand Lahou, Béréby,
Fresco, Kotrohou, Trépoint, Sassandra, Drewin, Victory, and
Cavally. The treaties gave full sovereignty to France, which
recognized the customary rights of sovereignty and provided
payment of a "custom" in goods, and later in money, with the
right to build forts. Later, posts were built next to the forts
by French trading companies. The first of these was Etablissements Régis Aîné of Marseille, which operated between 1843
and 1858 at Assinie and Grand-Bassam. They were often
attacked and pillaged, especially by the Alladians (Jack-Jacks),
who were angered by this threat to their role of intermediary
between European ships and inland populations. In 1853, a
revolt against the French establishments along the Ebrié lagoon

was violently repressed, after which the French established Fort Ducos at Dabou to monitor the western part of the lagoon.

In 1849-50, a Lieutenant Hecquard set off to reach Segu and Timbuktu from the coast. He traveled up the Potou and Aghien Lagoons, then followed the Mè River north until he was forced to withdraw because of the hostility of the peoples he encountered.

The Ivory Coast almost came under British control in the mid-nineteenth century. Faidherbe considered trading the negotiated concessions to the English for the Gambia in order to consolidate French control of Senegal and the Sudan. Discussions on this subject took place between 1865 and 1867 but died when the English lost interest in the idea.

A French officer-turned-entrepreneur, Arthur Verdier (q.v.), took over the trading post at Grand Bassam when Régis left in 1858. He then established numerous other posts and, in 1860, formed the Compagnie de Kong. Verdier also created a plantation at Elima, on the east bank of the Aby Lagoon; there, in 1881, the first coffee trees were planted in the Ivory Coast, the first mahogany logs were shipped, and the first "school of agriculture" was created.

French intrusion into the Ivory Coast was set back again in 1870. Louis Napoleon's defeat in the Franco-Prussian War set in motion the withdrawal of the French garrisons at the forts of Dabou, Grand Bassam, and Assinie. The fort at Dabou was dismantled, the others rented to Verdier and to an English agent, Schwanzy. The Ivory Coast remained of minor importance in French eyes compared to the Sudan. Verdier (1878) and Treich-Laplene (1886) were named "Residents of France in the Ivory Coast," as representatives of the "Governor of Senegal and dependencies." The single term "Ivory Coast" had only recently been commonly applied to the area, although it was so used by Bouet in 1839. More commonly, separate reference was made to the "Côte des Krou" (or "Côte des Malegens") from Cape Palmas to Sassandra; the "Côte des Lahou," or "de l'Ivoire," or "des Dents," from Sassandra to the mouth of the Bandama; the "Côte des Jack-Jack" or "koua-Koua" from the Bandama to Grand Bassam; and the "Côte de l'Or" east of the Comoé River. Since only the last had any French presence prior to 1893, Verdier's installations were called the "Etablissements Français de la Côte de l'Or."

Verdier sent an assistant, Marcel Treich-Leplene, up the Comoé and Bia Rivers in 1887 to conclude treaties with the Agni Bétié and Indénié kingdoms, and with the trading centers of Bondoukou and Kong. The treaty with Bondoukou was signed only one week before an English mission arrived with the same intention.

At the same time, the area between the coast and the Niger River was explored by Louis Gustave Binger (q.v.), who concluded treaties with various groups in the north. In 1889, Binger and Treich-Laplene met at Kong after their respective treaty expeditions, and returned to Grand Bassam together. Over the period from 1890 to 1894, treaties were signed with village chiefs all along the coast from Grand Lahou to Cavally, thus solidifying the French claim to the western half. France declared the Ivory Coast a French colony in 1893, naming Binger the first governor; two years later, they included it in French West Africa.

The colony's boundary with the neighboring Gold Coast was worked out by Binger and the British Major Lang, beginning with the Tano River (historic point of separation between the commercial areas of Assinie and Axim). In 1903, the frontier farther north was fixed by Delafosse and Watherson. On the west side, an accord was signed in Paris in 1892 with a representative of Liberia establishing the Cavally River as the boundary. Between 1909 and 1914, a Captain Laurent worked out the more northern portion with the Liberians.

The long French military campaign against the Malinké warrior Samori Touré (q.v.) was concluded in the Ivory Coast. There, after establishing his second empire at Dabakala (1893-98) and destroying the commercial city of Kong (1897), he was captured and exiled in 1898.

A hypothetical map of the Ivory Coast colony in 1893 would have shown it extending north only to a line from Man in the west to Bondoukou and Bouna in the east. North of that line the territory was considered to be part of French Sudan. Below the line, as late as 1900, the only areas actually controlled by the French were 1) east of the Comoé, from Grand-Bassam to Bondoukou; 2) in the Bandama region, from Grand-Lahou to Kouadio-Koffi; and 3) along the coast, in a band 70-100 kms. deep. The Baule and other upper-forest peoples were scarcely touched.

Governor Binger and his immediate successors operated under the assumption that trade and commerce would create new economic needs and encourage the population to produce for the market. Somewhat more impatient, Governor Clozel (q.v.) responded to the French Finance Law of 1900 that required colonies to be fiscally self–sufficient. He imposed the "head tax" (q.v.) in 1901 to accelerate entry into the export economy.

A mission of inquiry was sent to the colony in 1907-08, which concluded that "peaceful penetration" had failed. When the Minister of Colonies visited Grand Bassam in 1908, the merchants and European colonists demanded that stronger measures be taken to bring the indigenous population under control. Lt. Governor Angoulvant recorded his view that the Ivory Coast would not achieve its full economic potential until the power of arms brought the reign of the "paix française." As governor, Gabriel Angoulvant completed the military con-quest, or "pacification," of the territory between 1908 and 1915. After 1908, each revolt or resistance effort was brutally suppressed and those involved were severely punished. The most important campaigns were against the Baule in 1902 and 1909, the Dan in 1905-08, the Bete in 1906, the Guro in 1907, and the Dida in 1909-18.

After armed resistance proved futile, local peoples tried more subtle means: to escape control, villages were abandoned in favor of primitive shelters in the forest, and ordinary com-moners were presented to the French as chiefs in order to conceal the identities of the legitimate officeholders.

The Ivory Coast provided 15,000-20,000 troops for the French war effort in World War I; however, it is impossible to know how many of these were volunteers and how many were dragooned: recruiters simply ordered chiefs to provide given numbers. There was considerable, but mostly passive, resistance to military recruiting, including flight into neigh-boring colonies.

A typical colonial economy was established in the Ivory Coast between the two world wars. A keystone in the develop-ment of a transportation infrastructure was the completion of a railroad, begun from Abidjan in 1903, to open up the in-terior for development. Between 1933 and 1947, Upper Volta (now Burkina Faso) was divided between the Ivory Coast and

Sudan, primarily to simplify the movement of Voltaic labor into the coastal area.

The severity of colonial rule was somewhat relaxed during the period of the Popular Front (q.v.) government in France in 1936-37. That administration was soon replaced by one named by the Vichy government, however, and was more authoritarian and racist than any before it, causing intense animosity toward colonial rule during World War II. Since the Vichy-appointed officials and the French colonists made few distinctions among the various African socio-economic categories, they facilitated a sense of unity among wealthy planters, small farmers, the urban évolués, and others.

The politics of independence began after World War II, focusing first on local elections in Abidjan, then on balloting to send representatives to the Constituent Assembly in Paris. Political activity began in the trade unions, the ethnic and other associations in the towns, and in a farmers' association, the Syndicat Agricole Africain (q.v.). The SAA had the best financial base of all these, which helps explain why it soon became predominant. Various groups came together in the Bloc Africain (q.v.) to contest the Abidjan elections, and a less stable coalition narrowly sent Félix Houphouët (q.v.) to the Constituent Assembly. In Paris, Houphouët succeeded in obtaining the abolition of forced labor (q.v.), which gave him undisputed prominence among the Ivoirian electorate. He then came home to participate in the formation of the Democratic Party of the Ivory Coast (PDCI, q.v.), drawing support from the SAA and other groups.

In October 1946, the Ivory Coast and the other territories were joined with France in the French Union. Under this arrangement, former French subjects became citizens (although divided into two classes), and the indigénat--a separate body of law applying to subjects--was abolished. The same month saw the birth of the Rassemblement Démocratique Africain (q.v.), a regional party with affiliated groups (including the PDCI) in each colony.

In Paris, the RDA decided to affiliate with the French Communist Party, which at that time was part of the government. When the PCF went into opposition, however, the RDA was subjected to severe harassment, especially by the colonial administration in the Ivory Coast. In 1950, Houphouët pushed through a disaffiliation over the objections of many other RDA leaders, and soon concluded a warm working relationship with Paris that allowed him to emerge as undisputed leader in the Ivory Coast.

The structural provision for universal suffrage and a single electoral college were provided in the loi-cadre, adopted in 1956. With the achievement of full independence by Ghana in 1957, however, pressure in that direction began building among the French colonies. Under DeGaulle's leadership, the French Union was replaced by the French Community in 1958. It provided for an Executive Council of the heads of government of France and the colonies, headed by the French President, with each territory governed by its own cabinet for local affairs. The demand for independence did not stop long enough for this system to be established, however: In May 1960, the Gaullist government finally offered full independence within the Community. Houphouët, never attracted to independence, was nevertheless forced to accept it along with the rest of the African colonies. On August 7, 1960, the independence of the Ivory Coast was declared.

Another feature of the loi-cadre was its "balkanization" of relations between France and its former colonies. Houphouët saw little gain for the Ivory Coast from a close federation that included such rivals as Guinea and Senegal, and had used his influence in Paris to engineer as much autonomy for individual colonies as possible. The unification impulse from within Africa resulted in the formation by Senegal and Sudan of the Mali Federation. Under heavy pressure from Abidjan, and with at least tacit approval from Paris, none of the other new governments joined in this venture; Dahomey had originally committed to it, but was drawn instead to Houphouët's alternative, the Entente Council (q.v.), formed in 1959 with Upper Volta, Niger, and the Ivory Coast.

Although Houphouët was clearly in control in Abidjan, the sharp turns in ideology and tactics that the PDCI had experienced between 1947 and 1960 had brought a wide variety of perspectives, and inevitable tensions, into ruling circles. Those who had opposed the abandonment of the Communist affiliation in 1950 and those who had been enthusiastic supporters of independence through the late 1950s were mixed with constant loyalists of the President, with expatriate advisors, and with spokesmen of competing ethnic groups. The tensions erupted in the "events of 1963," the gravest political crisis the system has ever faced.

There is no consensus even today as to the exact nature of these events. What is known is that in 1962, Philippe Yacé and other officials warned the President that a challenge to his authority, perhaps a coup, was in the making. Presumably the plotters planned to surround a meeting of the party leaders at the President's compound in Yamoussoukro and arrest them. Instead, at an earlier meeting on January 14, 1963, some of the alleged plotters were themselves identified and arrested. After follow-up actions, those arrested included three ministers, seven members of the Assembly, prefects, subprefects, and other officials. There were secret trials of over 100 individuals, under the direction of J.B. Mockey. Several months later, Yacé reported a more wide-ranging plot, involving Mockey himself, Supreme Court President Ernest Boka, six ministers, and an assortment of other politicians and administrators. The treacheries were described by Yacé at a "loyalty day" rally in Abidjan on August 28, and twenty-seven detainees were given jail terms or death sentences. However, almost all of these were later pardoned and released, and some, including Mockey, were brought back into the government. By the next PDCI Congress in 1965, Houphouët's control was again secure and has not been seriously challenged since.

Following the opening of the Vridi Canal in 1950, the country had begun a period of rapid economic growth that continued through the 1960s and has been called the "Ivoirian Miracle." Expanding agricultural production--principally in cofee, cocoa, hardwoods, pineapples, kola and bananas-- generated the revenues that supported the development of physical and educational infrastructures. By 1960, only the Ghanaian economy was more developed than that of the Ivory Coast in West Africa. The government had begun planning for economic diversification and for expanding the role of the manufacturing sector. Its principal challenge was to continue to attract the foreign capital investment that had fueled the rapid growth.

The Ivory Coast has deliberately maintained close ties with France, encouraging French private investment and technical assistance in the public sector. Economic growth attracted employment seekers from all over West Africa. Agriculture now accounts for only 25 percent of the Gross Domestic

Product, yet the Ivory Coast is Africa's leading exporter of cocoa, coffee, and hardwoods. Oil discoveries in the 1970s moved the country toward petroleum self-sufficiency in the 1980s.

The rational agricultural policies of the Ivory Coast have been explained by the political predominance of agricultural interests. (In other African countries, policy is usually based on the preferences of urban interests.) However, as the Ivoirian urban sector expands and university graduates increasingly make policy, this may change.

On the negative side, the country has experienced a widening gap in income between the wealthiest and the poorest strata. Most of the latter are foreigners, so that the political impact of poverty is minimal, but the expanding gap promises future difficulties. Single-minded growth through private investment has been said to result in a slow accumulation of "social capital": Schools and health facilities have not been developed as rapidly as elsewhere, particularly given the country's relative advantage in wealth.

Also, the growth itself has been slowing. From a high of 10-12 percent annually in the 1960s, it fell to 6-8 percent per year in the world economic slowdown of the 1970s. By 1980 foreign private capital investment had almost stopped, with a corresponding increase in overseas borrowing to maintain investment levels. This was widely blamed on the "conjoncture" of a drop in prices for Ivoirian primary products in 1978 with an increase in imported oil prices and increased real interest rates in international markets.

The 1976-80 development plan marked a change in the strategy of industrialization, from import substitution to the processing of Ivoirian raw materials for export; it was marked by a reduction of advantages favoring substitution industries and the adoption of measures advantaging export industries, especially those in food and wood products.

The Party has not been a locus of decision making; rather, its post-independence congresses have been used to ratify policy lines worked out through a technocratic structure dominated by the President. At times, however, the PDCI has served as a communication device between the political elite and the masses, a role enhanced in 1980 when, for the first time, delegates to the National Assembly and members of municipal councils were chosen in competitive elections. Sporadic political unrest has continued, as during the 1982-83 school year, marked by a series of confrontations between the government and teacher organizations. The high-school and university-level teachers unions were banned at that time.

The central political question almost since independence has been succession to the presidency. Houphouët has kept pretenders off-guard, most recently in having the role of vice-president created but not filled in 1980, then abolished in 1985. Besides a few trusted old lieutenants, the members of his recent cabinets have been newcomers who owe their positions to Houphouët. To those who are not themselves contenders, the question is how the Party and the country will survive the inevitable departure of the only chief executive they have ever known.

THE DICTIONARY*

ABE (ABBE, ABBEY). A people speaking a Lagoon language,
but with Akan social structures. They are reported not
to have been well aware of a common history before recent times. Their region of origin is around the town of
Agboville. Their traditional political framework was not
well developed above the village level. The last major uprising of the Abe against the French took place in 1910.

ABENGOUROU. One of the original six prefectures at independence (now one of 34), near the Ghanaian border in
southeast Ivory Coast.

ABIDJAN. Principal city of the Ivory Coast and prefecture
of the Department of the South. The site, occupied by
the Ebrié villages of Locodjo, Anoumabo, and Cocody, was
chosen in 1903 by the Crosson-Duplessis mission for a railhead on a line connecting the coast with the interior. Six
Europeans and 378 skilled African workers were the first
inhabitants, and railroad construction produced a village
of 1,400 by 1912, when the workers moved farther north.
The population rose to 5,400 by 1921; when the capital
was moved there in 1934, it had a population of 17,000,
increasing to 45,000 by the end of World War II; 127,000
in 1955; 500,000, by the mid 70s; and about 2 million in
1985.
  In 1931 the rail line was extended across the lagoon on
a floating bridge to the island of Petit-Bassam, then by a
dike to the barrier island, and to a new wharf at Port-
Bouët. By 1934, traffic through Port-Bouët exceeded that
through Grand-Bassam. Work began on a canal through
the barrier island at Vridi (q.v.) in 1935, but was suspended during the war.

---

*Numbers in parentheses appearing at the ends of entries
refer to items in the Bibliography.

The geographic layout of the city dates back to a colonial administration plan of 1925 establishing an African
quarter in Treichville and an administrative center on the
Plateau. A park separated the government area from the
plateau's commercial district to the south. A second African quarter, Adjamé, was created about 1930, separated
from the Plateau by military camps. Until 1950, Abidjan
consisted of the Plateau, Treichville, and Adjamé. The
modern residential quarter of Cocody was planned in 1960.
Economic activity expanded with the opening of the Vridi
Canal in 1950, leading to the construction of the port and
industrial sections on the southern part of the island of
Petit-Bassam and on the barrier island from Port-Bouët to
Vridi. The airport was built at Port-Bouët in 1951. A
permanent bridge was constructed between the Plateau and
Treichville in 1957, followed by another in 1967. The Plateau's limited size has resulted in a push skyward, Man-
hattan style. The average height of new construction
there in 1975 was 20 stories.

When Adjamé reached its natural limits at the forest
reserves of Banco and Abobo and the Bay of Banco, new
centers for urban in-migrants grew up at Marcory, Kou-
massi, and Biétry, filling in the rest of Petit-Bassam. By
1970, the continued immigration flow was directed toward
Abobo to the north.

In 1939, Abidjan was declared a commune mixte, second
degree, which meant it was entitled to an elected council
with deliberative powers. The elections were postponed
until after the war, and in 1945 were the first arena in
which the nationalist movement challenged colonial rule.

Abidjan remained the capital of the country until 1983,
when as a major effort toward decentralization, it was announced that the political capital would be transferred to
Yamoussoukro. (65,572, 741, 848, 870, 1009, 1266, 1267,
1283, 1284, 1286, 1290, 1300, 1302, 1305, 1319, 1324, 1325,
1333-1341)

ABOBO-GARE. Low income residential area north of Abidjan
that has attracted large numbers of rural immigrants.

ABOISSO. Town 120 kms. east of Abidjan, north of the Abi
Lagoon, at the northernmost navigable point from the Lagoon on the Bia River. Aboisso was founded by merchants
as the point of exchange between the lagoon and the commercial route to Bondoukou and Kong. In 1895, Treich-

Laplène (q.v.) estimated the population of "Ain-Boisseau" at 400-500. When the route north had been secured by a military post at Zaranou in 1897, trade developed rapidly. The administrative capital of the cercle was moved there from Assinie in 1903, and the Compagnie Française d'Afrique Occidentale (CFAO) opened an office in 1904; the village was razed, and a new geometric town plan laid out. Aboisso grew with the rubber (q.v.) trade until 1913, when the market price of rubber collapsed. With the opening of the railroad north of Abidjan, trade was deflected to the west and Aboisso stagnated. It experienced a temporary revival with the construction of the Ayamé dams in the 1950s. The population was 15,000 in 1975. (947)

ABOUADIE KEOU. War chief who led several Dida sub-groups in an uprising against colonial rule from 1915 to 1919, at first because of assessments of rice destined for the French war effort. He was sentenced to be deported for ten years, but died at Grand-Lahou under mysterious circumstances.

ABRON (BRONG). An Akan group whose homeland is astride the central portion of the Ghana-Ivory Coast border. (They are called Brong in Ghana, where the greater number of them live.) The Abron may have settled in their present area as early as the fifteenth century: Their own tradition has them as the founders of a state at Bondoukou in the fifteenth century under legendary king Adou Bini. They are a matrilineal people with a typical Akan social structure and culture but no centralized political power. (84, 124-126, 582, 654-657, 659, 660, 1029-1033)

ABURE (ABOURE). Lagoon-cluster people of the extreme southeast of the Ivory Coast. Under pressure from the Agni kingdom of Sanwi, they moved from an earlier location and now live between the villages of Moossou and Bonoua, east of Grand Bassam. The Monteil (q.v.) expedition put down an Abure revolt in 1894, growing out of Abure levies on trade on the Comoé River and eastern Ebrié Lagoon. (1034)

ACCORD GENERAL DE COOPERATION ECONOMIQUE FRANCO-IVOIRIEN (GENERAL ACCORD ON FRANCO-IVOIRIAN ECONOMIC COOPERATION). This treaty, covering the years 1961-1966, provided that France would import 100,000 tons of coffee per year until 1966 at 3.20 fr/kg (160 fr CFA).

The specified tonnage was 70 percent of Ivoirian production at the time. The treaty was revised in 1962-63 to 88,000 tons because of Algerian independence. (Algeria's 10,000-ton annual consumption was included in the first treaty.)

ADJAME. An older, lower-income section of Abidjan; after Treichville, the oldest "indigenous" neighborhood. (1286)

ADJUKRU (ADJOUKROU, ADIOUKROU, ADYUKRU). Ethnic group of Kru origins, but having some traits of the Lagoon peoples among whom they live; according to their own tradition, they emigrated from the northwest, unlike nearby groups who claim to have come from the east. Also singular in their region is their traditional age-grade hierarchy, marked by stages of initiation. They inhabit the coastal region along the western part of the Ebrie lagoon near the town of Dabou, where they are heavily involved in palm oil production. They numbered about 30,000 in 1970. (127-129, 333, 875, 971, 1035, 1036, 1171, 1039

ADMINISTRATIVE HISTORY. As in other French colonies, a Governor presided over the administration of the Ivory Coast during the colonial period. The colony was divided into administrative subdivisions called cercles, each presided over by a Commandant de Cercle. These were originally military officers, but they were gradually replaced by civilian graduates of the Ecole Coloniale in Paris. Each cercle was divided into smaller units called subdivisions, presided over by a (European) Chef de Subdivision. The smallest administrative unit was the canton, headed by an African Chef de Canton. Chiefs in larger ethnic groups were sometimes grouped under a single Chef Supérieur.
   With the coming of independence, the nomenclature was changed to parallel that of metropolitan France. Under the Ministry of the Interior, the country was divided into 26 départments, each administered by a Prefect. As of 1978, the departments are subdivided into 163 sub-prefect-- ures, and 28 autonomous and six semi-autonomous communes. The number of sub-prefectures represents an expansion to one per 8,000-10,000 population. Sub-prefects and prefects also have coordinating powers over various agents of ministries, directions, and SODE's.

ADOU BINI. According to Abron tradition, a king who
founded an Abron state at Bondoukou in the fifteenth
century.

AFRICAN AND MAURITIAN COMMON ORGANIZATION (Organisation Commune Africaine et Mauricienne, OCAM). An international organization focusing on economic, social, and
technological development. The membership includes
most Francophone countries of Africa: Mauritius, Rwanda,
Benin, the Central African Republic, Niger, Senegal,
Togo, Burkina Faso, and the Ivory Coast.

AFRICAN BLOC (BLOC AFRICAIN). Ivoirian electoral list
formed to contest a French settler slate in the Abidjan
municipal elections of 1945. The African Bloc managed
to attract the large majority of African voters and, in
the face of an abstention campaign among European voters
overwhelmingly won the election. Afterward, in the ab-
sence of a common program, the loosely knit organization
disbanded. (760)

AFRICAN AND MALAGASY UNION (UNION AFRICAINE ET
MALGACHE, UAM). International organization of eleven
francophone African states formed in September 1961.
Guinea and Mali did not participate. The focus of the
UAM was on developing a common foreign policy, and
especially on maintaining close ties with France. It became a vehicle for the distribution of French foreign aid,
particularly in the formation of Air Afrique. With the
formation of the Organization of African Unity, the UAM
members announced their intention to end the francophone
group. However, the economic and technical sub-groups
it had created--the Union Africaine et Malgache de Coopération Economique, the Union Africaine et Malgache de Défense,
the Union Africaine et Malgache des Postes et Télécommuni-
cations, and Air Afrique continued to exist. Houphouët's
emphasis on the independent development of African states
and non-interference in their international affairs found
voice in the UAM Charter. Structures included an Assembly composed of heads of state and government, with
a general secretariat in Cotonou, Dahomey (Benin). Later
creations were a union of economic cooperation with headquarters at Yaounde, Cameroun, and a defense pact centered
in Ouagadougou, Upper Volta (Burkina Faso).

AFRICAN DEVELOPMENT BANK. Multilateral regional bank
for the promotion of African economic development. The
ADB has been headquartered in Abidjan since its formation
in 1964 by the United Nations Economic Commission for
Africa. All African governments but that of South Africa
are members. The members states initially wanted to keep
the bank under their own control, but their inability to
raise sufficient capital led to the admission of non-African
states. Its capital stock has grown from $250 million to
$1.2 billion, but with less African control.

AGBOVILLE. Town on the Abidjan-Niger rail line 80 kms.
north of Abidjan. Agboville was founded by the French in
1903 to serve as a railway station and shipping point for
coffee and cocoa, which remains its chief economic activity.
(536, 704, 1342, 1343)

AGE GRADE. Form of socio-political organization found in the
Ivory Coast among the Ebrié, Alladian, Abure, Atié, M'Bato,
and Adjukru peoples. In these cases, the male population
is divided into four grades, roughly covering the ages 8-
24, 25-40, 41-56, and over 56. The grades succeed one
another in functions every 16 years, with a complete cycle
every 64 years. (972, 1127)

AHIN, ETIENNE (1934-). Minister of Youth, Popular Education and Sports, 1970-78; Minister of Social Welfare from
1978 to 1980.

AHUI, JOHN. Son of the chief of the Ebrié village of Petit
Bassam, founder of the Harrist Church (q.v.) there, and
leader in the Harrist movement throughout the Ivory Coast.
William W. Harris had passed through the village in 1913-14,
and had baptized large numbers there. Methodist missionaries arrived in the village ten years later declaring it
was Harris' will that his followers become Methodists. The
village was divided over the issue, and in 1928 a three-
member delegation was named to visit Harris in Liberia for
instructions. Harris gave them a written "last will and
testament" and, according to contemporary Harrist belief,
named John Ahui to be his successor. Upon his return to
the Ivory Coast, he and a few disciples traveled throughout
the lagoon and coastal area. The church organization was
institutionalized at a conference in Petit Bassam in 1955,

at which time Ahui's leadership was formally recognized;
he is considered the church's "supreme prophet." (1250)

AIR AFRIQUE. International airline jointly held by a group
of francophone African states including Ivory Coast, financed largely through French investment and government
aid. Air Afrique was formed under the aegis of the African and Malagasy Union (q.v.), and continued in existence
when that organization was discontinued.

AIR IVOIRE. The national airline of the Ivory Coast, established upon independence in 1960. It serves 17 towns and
cities with eight aircraft, and carried 235,000 passengers
in 1980. (445)

AIZI (AHIZI). An ethnic group sometimes identified as Lagoon
cluster (q.v.), and sometimes as Kru cluster, inhabiting
the coastal area along the western portion of the Ebrié
Lagoon. (304, 1037-1039)

AKA, JACQUES. Employee in the colonial court system who
attended the organizing congress of the Socialist Party
(SFIO) of the Ivory Coast in August 1937 and was elected
to its Administrative Commission. He was elected to the
Abidjan Municipal Council on the African Bloc (q.v.) slate
in 1945.

AKAFOU. N'Gban (Baule) chief who led an uprising against
the French in 1902, provoked by requirements to furnish
porters. The N'Gban were defeated and subjected to
severe punishment.

AKAN. A language family often used to group the cultures
in which Akan languages are spoken. This includes the
Ashanti, Fanti, and related peoples in Ghana and the Anyi,
Baule, Akie (Attie), and smaller groups living in the extreme southeast of the Ivory Coast. Together, they make
up about one-fifth of the country's population. The oral
history of the various Ivoirian groups describes a common
origin in the Ashanti kingdom, from which the other groups
broke off and dispersed as a result of conflicts among the
Ashanti and Denkyira. The Akan are one of the major
cultural groupings indigenous to the Ivory Coast, and,
because they were generally the first in contact with

European colonization, they have achieved and have maintained a disproportionate role in the country's political
economy. (95, 101, 619, 622, 1073-1079, 1252)

AKE, SIMEON (1932-   ). Since 1979, Minister of Foreign
    Affairs. Aké began his foreign affairs career in 1959 after
    graduating in law from the University of Dakar in 1957,
    with a degree in public law from the University of Grenoble
    the next year. In 1966 he was named Ivoirian Permanent
    Representative to the United Nations, and served as Presi-
    dent of the Economic and Social Council.

AKOTO-YAO, PAUL (1938-   ). Professor of Natural Science
    at the Ecole Normale Supérieure of Abidjan and a member
    of the Political Bureau of the Democratic Party of the Ivory
    Coast. Akoto-Yao, a former Minister of Education who
    lost that position in 1983 after a series of teachers strikes,
    is considered a possible "technocratic" successor to Houp-
    houët as President. (760, 1027)

ALLADIAN. One of the lagoon peoples of the Ivory Coast,
    with a traditional matrilineal society characterized by a
    powerful chieftaincy, and with gold playing an important
    economic and ceremonial role, as among the Akan groups.
    The Alladian, who occupy the barrier island between the
    lagoon and the Gulf of Guinea, are divided into three sub-
    groups, the Aware, Kovu, and Akuri or Agru. With the
    development of the palm oil trade with Europe in the latter
    part of the nineteenth century, the Alladians (known to
    European traders as the Jack-Jack) became prosperous as
    brokers of palm oil produced by the peoples on the inland
    side of the lagoon. (724) However, some of them continue
    to engage in ocean fishing with large (now imported) nets
    from large outrigger dugouts. They numbered about 10,000
    in 1970. (4, 5, 1047, 1048, 1218)

ALLIALI, CAMILLE (1926-   ). Minister of State, lawyer,
    diplomat, and, since 1966, Justice Minister of the Ivory
    Coast. He attended the Ecole Ponty in Dakar, then studied
    law at the University of Grenoble, practicing later at the
    Paris Bar. He was Vice-President of the Ivory Coast Terri-
    torial Assembly, 1957-59, representative of the Ivory Coast
    in the French Community Senate, 1959-61, and Ivoirian Am-
    bassador to France from 1961 to 1963. He served as
    Deputy Minister of Foreign Affairs from 1963 to 1966. A

Baule, he is also a member of the PDCI Executive Committee
and has been considered a possibility to succeed Houphouët
as President. (760)

AMON N'DOUFFOU (N'DOUFOU, AMATIFOU) (c. 1812-1886).
King of the Anyi Kingdom of Sanwi. He signed a protectorate treaty with France in 1843, in the last year of his
uncle's reign, then became king himself the next year.
This permitted the construction of Fort Joinville at the
entry to the Aby Lagoon at Assinie. He used his alliance
with the French to extend the borders of Sanwi to the
south. N'Douffou was King of Sanwi for 42 years.

AMON TANOH, LAMBERT (1926-). Teacher and union leader. Amon Tanoh studied at a teacher's college in Kati-
bougou, Mali, then taught at a boys' school in Bingerville.
In 1959 he was Secretary General of the Union des Travailleurs de Côte d'Ivoire, the Ivorian branch of the Conakry-
headquartered Union Générale des Travailleurs d'Afrique
Noire (q.v.), which had worked with the PDCI until 1958.
Under government pressure to have local unions disaffiliate
with UGTAN, Amon Tanoh led a breakaway movement, the
Union Nationale des Travailleurs de Côte d'Ivoire (UNTCI).
He later served as a deputy in the Ivoirian National As-
sembly, and as Secretary-General of the PDCI-dominated
Union Générale des Travailleurs de Côte d'Ivoire (q.v.).
In 1963 he was named Minister of Education, a post he held
until 1970. Since then, he has been General Director of
the Ivoirian Center for External Trade. (504)

ANGBA, NICOLAS KOUANDI. Minister of Trade since 1983.

ANGHUI, Hortense Aka. One of the first three women elected
to the National Assembly of the Ivory Coast, she was the
wife of a politician and daughter of Bernard Dadié (q.v.).

ANGOULVANT, GABRIEL. Governor of the Ivory Coast from
1908 to 1916. A political appointee, Angoulvant had little
prior experience in Africa. However, he acted on his
belief that the development of the Ivory Coast could only
follow on the forceful "pacification" of the colony. His
brutal handling of the Baule resistance in 1909 brought him
criticism from merchants, French humanitarians, and the
military command, but political connections apparently prevented his replacement. He presided over the final military

actions against the Baule and other resisting peoples and recorded his impressions in La Pacification de la Cote d'Ivoire. (676, 695, 724)

ANOMA, GLADYS. (1930-). One of the first three women elected to the National Assembly just after independence; daughter-in-law of Joseph Anoma (q.v.). She has a doctorate in tropical botany and is Secretary General of the Association of Ivoirian Women. She has been a member of the Political Bureau of the Democratic Party of the Ivory Coast and Vice-President of the National Assembly since 1975.

ANOMA, JOSEPH. One of the earliest political leaders in the Ivory Coast, delegate from Agboville and Vice-President of the Syndicat Agricole Africain (q.v.) in 1944, and SAA President in 1947 (while Houphouët, in France, was Honorary President). (760)

ANYI (AGNI). Akan ethnic group living mostly east of the Comoé River, along the border with Ghana. Like those of the Baule, the Agni settlements resulted from successive Akan migrations caused by conflict within the Ashanti kingdom; according to their oral tradition, they migrated to their present location under the warrior chief Bridou and settled in the region of Assikasso (now Agnibilékrou). They founded a number of highly centralized and hierarchical kingdoms on the Ashanti model, including Indénié (Ndenye), Sanwi (q.v.) or Krinjabo, Moronou, and Comoénou, and integrated into them a number of neighboring populations, including some Mekyibo, Guro, and Kulango.
    The Anyi were among the earliest Ivoirians in contact with Europeans and among the first to adopt western cultural forms. The last major insurrections against French rule took place in 1894 (Indénié) and 1898 (Assikasso). They are among the most Christianized peoples in the Ivory Coast. (130-132, 241-242, 610, 617, 628, 637, 639-644, 709, 1049-1063, 1212)

AOULOU, KACOU. Teacher in Grand Bassam who attended the organizing congress of the Socialist Party (SFIO) of the Ivory Coast in August 1937 and was elected to the Administrative Commission. He was also secretary for the Grand Bassam section. In 1946, he was Secretary-General of the Progressive Party (q.v.). (673)

APPOLONIEN. See NZIMA.

ASSINIE. Town on the barrier island that was the site of
the earliest recorded European presence in the Ivory Coast,
and point of departure for later French exploration. The
Compagnie de St. Malo landed five missionaries there in
1637, but three of them died within a year from life in
tropical conditions and the last two sought refuge at the
Portuguese post of Axim, in present-day Ghana. In 1687,
a royal French naval ship landed off Assinie and brought
two young men to France. One attracted the attention of
Madame de Maintenon, was educated, baptized with Louis
XIV for his godfather, and commissioned a captain in a
company of musketeers. He returned to Assinie in 1701
to establish a small military post, Fort St. Louis. The
fort was abandoned in 1703. The French returned in 1842
and built Fort Joinville. In the meantime, the Anyi, an
Akan group from the east, had occupied the territory and
integrated the inhabitants into their society. Captain
Bouët-Willaumez concluded the first protectorate treaty at
Assinie in 1843. The administrative offices of the cercle
were moved from Assinie to Aboisso in 1903. The town
experienced severe flooding in 1931, aggravated by the
opening of a canal several kilometers away. In October
1942, Assinie was submerged, and all economic activity
ceased. However, in 1970 a tourist hotel complex was
created there, endowed with 1300 beds, and receives over
15,000 tourists annually. About half the rooms are in a
Club Méditerranée. (631)

ASSOCIATION POUR LA DEFENSE DES INTERETS DES AUTOCH-
TONES DE LA COTE D'IVOIRE (ADIACI). Organization formed
by Akan group leaders in southeastern Ivory Coast in
1934 and approved by the Popular-Front-appointed governor
in 1937. In 1938, it took a position against the recruitment
and retention of Dahomeyans and Togolese in administrative
positions in the Ivory Coast. Composed predominantly of
Anyis, the ADIACI opposed the SAA (q.v.) candidates in
the election to the French Constitutional Assembly in 1945.
(673, 828)

ATCHO, ALBERT. Harrist (q.v.) healer living in the village
of Bregbo, near Bingerville.

ATTIE (also called Akié or Atié). A people living north of
   Abidjan, and west of the Comoé River. They are often
   grouped in the Lagoon cluster, because they speak a language related to other groups in that category. However,
   they are socially similar to the Anyi and Baule and are
   probably the descendants of one of the original waves of
   immigrants from the east. Unlike larger Akan groups, the
   Attie have never been organized into centralized states;
   the most inclusive political unit has been the village. Age
   grades are important in Attié social cohesion. They are
   heavily Christianized, and highly active in coffee and cocoa
   production. (133, 347, 1064-1068)

ATTIEKE. Steamed manioc, a dietary staple of the Ivoirian
   lagoon peoples (q.v.).

ATTOBRA, THEODORE KOFFI (1939-). Since 1976, Minister
   of Water and Forests.

AURA POKU. According to Baule tradition, the founder of
   their society in the Ivory Coast. When Asantehene Osei
   Tutu died in the eighteenth century, his nephews fought
   over the succession. One of them, the brother of Aura
   Poku, was killed, and she led a minority group westward
   from Kumasi to the central area of present-day Ivory Coast,
   where she established the Baule state. In the Baule legend,
   she had to sacrifice her infant son to the Comoé River in
   order for her people to cross it. (625)

AUTORITE POUR L'AMENAGEMENT DE LA VALLEE DU
BANDAMA (AVB). See BANDAMA RIVER DEVELOPMENT
AUTHORITY.

AUTORITE POUR LA REGION DU SUD-OUEST (ARSO). See
SOUTHWEST REGION AUTHORITY.

AVIKAM. Westernmost people of the Lagoon Cluster (q.v.),
   living at the mouth of the Bandama River. Known also
   as Brignan or Gbanda. See also: GRAND LAHOU.

AYE, HYPPOLITE (1932-). Since 1970, a member and vice-
   president of the Economic and Social Council; since 1976,
   a member of the Political Bureau of the Democratic Party
   of the Ivory Coast. Ayé is an Attié; he received his M.D.
   from the University of Toulouse and a diploma from the

National School of Public Health in Rennes (France).
From 1963 to 1966, he was Director of Public and Social
Hygiene at the Directorate of Health. In 1966 he became
Deputy Medical Superintendent for the Department of
Pathology in the University Clinics (Abidjan). From 1970
to 1976, he was Minister of Public Health and Population.

-- B -

BAILLY, DIGNAN. Independent candidate to the French Constituent Assembly in 1945, a journalist who was a longtime
resident of France. His support was largely drawn from
the Bété region around Gagnoa.

BAKWE (BAKOUE, SRIGBE). A sub-group of the Kru ethnic
cluster, thinly spaced in small villages from Soubré to
Sassandra.

BAMBA, NANLO (1916-   ). Career magistrate; from 1966 to
1974, Interior Minister, and, since 1976, Minister of State.
A Tagbana, Bamba was a graduate of the Ponty School in
Dakar. He served from 1936 to 1946 in the Bureau des
Finances in Abidjan, and in the French colonial administra-
tion in Paris (1947-51), in Dahomey, and in the Ivory Coast.
He was named Deputy Prosecutor in Bouaké in 1958, then
examining magistrate in Abidjan. From 1959 to 1961 he was
staff director for Houphouët-Boigny, then Deputy Prosecu-
tor for the State Security Court. In 1958 he was named
Director of the Steering Committee of the PDCI, and was
Director of the National Police from 1960 to 1961. From
1961 to 1963 he was Assistant Staff Director and Deputy
Government Commissioner to the State Security Court and
Deputy Prosecutor at that court. From 1963-66 he was
Minister of Justice and Keeper of the Seals. He was moved
from the Interior Ministry in 1974 to Minister of Water and
Forests, a position he held until 1976.

BAMBARA. An important, predominantly non-Muslim culture
of the Manding, or Mandé, grouping. The Bambara are
centered in Mali, with only a small population extending into
northwest Ivory Coast. Moslems of other Mandé-language
groups tend to refer to non-Moslems generally as "Bambara." (134)

BANANAS. Grown in the southern Ivory Coast on large plantations, for the most part by Europeans, who began planting for export to diversify production after the crisis of
1930. Production stopped almost totally during World War
II, and most plantations were abandoned. They were revived in the 1950s, but production has been no more than
stable because of competition on the strong world market.

BANDAMA RIVER. A river dividing the Ivory Coast roughly
in half, from north to south. It drains about half the area
of the country, and according to this criterion is the most
important Ivoirian river. It is formed by the Marahoué (or
Bandama Rouge) River to the east, and the Nzi River to
the west. They converge in a single stream for 60 miles,
with a mouth in the Tagba Lagoon across from Grand Lahou.
The Bandama enters the ocean through a gap between
barrier islands. It is navigable by small craft for 30-40
miles inland. Since independence, the Bandama has been
dammed at several points to provide hydroelectric power to
the country. See KOSSOU DAM.

BANDAMA VALLEY DEVELOPMENT AUTHORITY (AUTORITE
POUR L'AMENAGEMENT DE LA VALLEE DU BANDAMA, AVB).
A multi-functional regional administration operating in the
drainage area of the Bandama River, with an area of
authority now covering almost one-eighth of the country.
Although growing out of the construction and operation of
the Kossou Dam, the AVB also took on responsibility for
the reconstruction and relocation of facilities necessitated
by the formation of a reservoir of 1700 sq. km. The
Authority eventually took charge of the general economic
and social development of the area, beginning with the relocation of the population displaced by the reservoir. AVB
attempted to convince the dislocated inhabitants to move
to the thinly populated area around the newly developed
port of San Pedro, but only a small proportion of them accepted this arrangement. Seventy-four villages were eventually relocated, with a total population of 75,000. There
were 11,800 "modern" houses (i.e., with permanent walls
and roof) constructed in new villages, with one or more
wells, a school, a market, an administration building and
public square, and a sports field. Food was provided in
full rations the first year and in supplementary rations the
second year by the FAO's World Food Program. (423, 453,
454, 506, 1373)

BANGUI. Palm wine, produced generally from native oil palms (outside plantations) and consumed widely in coastal regions of the Ivory Coast. (947)

BANKING. There are four commercial banks in the Ivory Coast: The Banque Internationale pour l'Afrique Occidentale (BIAO), the Banque Internationale pour le Commerce et l'Industrie en Côte d'Ivoire (BICICI), the Société Générale des Banques en Côte d'Ivoire (SGBCI), and the Société Ivoirienne de Banque (SIB). French nationals hold a controlling interest in all four. (836)

BANNY, JEAN KONAN. See KONAN BANNY, JEAN.

BANQUE CENTRALE DES ETATS DE L'AFRIQUE DE L'OUEST. See CENTRAL BANK OF WEST AFRICAN STATES.

BANQUE DE L'AFRIQUE OCCIDENTALE. The West African Bank, a commercial bank that was the common bank of issue for French West Africa from 1904 until its replacement by the Institut d'Emission de l'Afrique Occidentale Française et du Togo in 1955.

BARRY-BATTESTI, ANGE-FRANCOIS (1932-). Minister of Public Works, Transport, Construction, Postal Service, and Telecommunications. From 1970 to 1983, Minister of Technical and Vocational Training. An Afro-European, Barry-Battesti attended the Universities of Dakar and Grenoble. From 1965 to 1968 he was Director of the Lycée Technique in Abidjan, then became Deputy Director for Technical and Vocational Training Services.

BAULE (BAOULE). An ethnic group traditionally located near the geographical center of the Ivory Coast, between the Comoé and Bandama rivers. The Baule are one of the Akan (q.v.) groups whose common language (Twi) and culture extend over most of Ghana and the southeastern quarter of the Ivory Coast. They number nearly one million, but in contemporary Ivory Coast they play a role in politics and the economy out of proportion to their number. Their oral history describes the Baule as a minority faction in Ashanti political struggles of the eighteenth century. When Asantehene Osei Tutu died, his two nephews are said to have fought over the succession. When one of them was killed, his sister, Aura Poku (q.v.), led the group that

was to become the Baule westward to their present location,
where they defeated and, to a degree, incorporated the inhabitants. Weiskel (724) cautions us to be skeptical of the
emphasis in such myths on "royal origins, massive migration, miraculous escape, and resounding military conquest."
He suggests that the migrants were limited in number and
moved gradually rather than in a dramatic wave, that they
absorbed many of the prior inhabitants as they defeated
them. Furthermore, he attributes less importance to military victory and more to establishment and control of emer-
ging trading patterns in the area as the key to ultimate
Baule dominance.

Baule art is most noted for diverse styles of woodcarving,
especially of statuettes, masks, and door frames, and for
bronzecasting that demonstrates their close relationship to
the Ashantis.

In the nineteenth century the Baule achieved a middle-
man position in trade between the savanna and the coast.
As these north-south trade links developed, the Baule
migration followed them south as far as the confluence of
the Comoe and Nzi rivers. At the same time, they prevented Dyula traders from going farther south, or the Alladians, Nzima, or Avikam from trading farther north than
Tiassalé. During this period, Baule socio-political organization, which had closely resembled that of the Akan
peoples to the east, became less hierarchical: by late in
the last century, the Baule were clearly stateless, led by
no authority beyond the village, and often the extended
family, level. Furthermore, institutionalized rules of
political succession were very weak, so that authority
derived largely from achievements in trade and in forming
cross-family and cross-village alliances. Delafosse characterized the Baule political structure as "anarchy." (Cited
in 724; see 664, 1080, 1083, and 1350)

The Baule strongly resisted colonial rule, having first
believed the French presence to be temporary. They were
brutally suppressed under Governor Angoulvant (q.v.) in
1902 (the N'Gban and Nanafuwe) and 1909 (the Akuwe).

Today the Baule occupy a position of prominence, given
that President Houphouët-Boigny is one of their number.
Although Houphouët has always been a skillful user of
ethnic arithmetic, the Baule have unquestionably achieved
positions of influence in state and society out of proportion
to their number in the country. (70, 86, 92, 98-100, 135-
140, 219, 249, 358, 376, 460, 576, 597, 598-604, 624, 625,
663, 664, 707, 724, 725, 730, 960, 1069-1094)

BAULE "V," THE. Term given to the area between the Nzi
and Bandama Rivers as they come together south of Toumodi. It is an extension of the savanna into the forest
latitude, so that the distance across the forest from the
confluence of the rivers to the ocean is less than 120 kilometers. This was the southernmost area of Baule occupation
in their eighteenth-century expansion.

BECHIO, JEAN-JACQUES. Minister of Civil Service (June
1985).

BEDIE, HENRI KONAN. See KONAN-BEDIE, HENRI.

BELKIRI, ALAIN. Secretary-General of the government of
the Ivory Coast, in Abidjan. According to Awondji (820),
he has been "on loan" to Ivory Coast from France since
before independence.

BENG (BEN, NGAN, GAN, NGEN). Small ethnic group (about
10,000) of the Southern or Peripheral Mandé branch of the
Manding language group. They inhabit the sub-prefecture
of M'Bahiakro, pushed there by Maninka and Akan pressure.
Originally hunter-gatherers and subsistence farmers, they
have entered into the cash economy for the sale of coffee,
rice, and cocoa. They are divided into two kingdoms,
one in the savanna, the other in the forest. Their traditional religion centers on worship of the Earth, of forest
spirits, and less importantly, of ancestors. (1095-1098)

BETE (MAGWE). An ethnic group speaking a Kru language,
concentrated in about 800 villages in the triangle among the
cities of Daloa, Soubre, and Gagnoa. The Bete are thought
to have migrated from the west in the seventeenth century,
displacing Gagu, Dida, and Guro peoples then in the area.
They are patrilineal, patrilocal, and virilocal, yet demon-
strate great variation in other aspects of social structure
and cultural patterns. Still, in the period since independence there has been a heightened self-awareness among
those who call themselves Bete. The Bete did not enter
into regional commercial exchange until the mid-nineteenth
century, then at the initiative of neighboring peoples and
Europeans. Their last armed resistance against colonial
rule was put down in 1906. During the colonial period,
martial and hunting activities were replaced by coffee
and cocoa farming. This in turn brought a substantial

immigration of "Dyulas," Voltaics, and Baules that has
continued to the present. At the same time, many Betes
have moved to the coast, particularly to Abidjan. Thus,
the population of the traditional Bete region has perhaps
equal numbers of Betes and foreigners (about 200,000 of
each). The Bete identity is now influenced more by these
indigenous/outsider and rural/urban contrasts than by pre-
colonial factors. (141-142, 237, 250-251, 621, 1099-1109,
1326)

BEUGRE ORACLE. Oracle from the vicinity of the village of
Beugre in the lower Cavally region of southern Ivory Coast.
He was known in 1891 and in 1909-10 to have counselled
the Baule to resist French advances. The Oracle seems
to have influenced a wide range of ethnic groups, notably
through the area in which the Harrist movement (q.v.)
was to have its greatest impact shortly thereafter. (724)

BINGER, LOUIS-GUSTAVE. French explorer who traveled
from Niger to the city of Kong signing protectorate treaties
as part of the 1885 Congress of Berlin agreement that required occupation of claimed territories. In Kong in 1889
he met Marcel Treich-Laplene, who was working north on
the same mission. Binger was named the first governor
of the autonomous French colony of the Ivory Coast in 1893.
He served in that capacity until 1895. (592)

BINGERVILLE. Colonial capital of the Ivory Coast from 1900
to 1934, when the capital was moved to Abidjan. (726)

BINZEME, KOUAME. Ivoirian lawyer and early politician.
After elementary school he worked for G.E. Vilasco, an
Ivoirian merchant, then went to France for additional edu-
cation. There he completed his secondary schooling and
wrote to the Governor General of French West Africa for
a university scholarship. (The Governor General had been
unaware that there was an Ivoirian student in France.)
Binzeme returned to the Ivory Coast in 1935, where he and
Vilasco founded a newspaper, the Eclaireur de la Côte
d'Ivoire, with a Senegalese, Amadou Seye, as director.
The Eclaireur went out of business the same year, and
Binzeme returned to France to continue his studies. Upon
his return to the Ivory Coast in 1947, he founded a second
paper, Le Progressiste.

In 1945, Binzeme was the candidate of the Comité d'Action Patriotique de la Côte d'Ivoire in the first election to the French Constituent Assembly. His support was largely limited to some Anyi and Nzima. He had been active in the Association of African Students in France, and on his return to the Ivory Coast tried to create a planters' cooperative in the Anyi region. He helped form the Progressive Party in 1946 and ran again in the second Constituent Assembly election that year, but received only 357 votes, compared to Houphouët's 23,271.

BISSOUMA TAPE, ALPHONSE (1932-). From 1966 to 1970, Minister of Youth, Popular Education, and Sports, and a member of the Steering Committee of the PDCI since 1975. He was educated as a chemical engineer, but became better known as the trainer and director of the Ivoirian national soccer team. He was named to the National Assembly in 1960, and was chosen secretary of its Economic and Financial Committee.

BLOC AFRICAIN. See AFRICAN BLOC.

BLOHORN. French soap company that expanded into the Ivory Coast before World War II as a hedge against competition and falling sales. Blohorn later set up its own palm-oil processing plants and plantations near Dabou and in Abidjan. (845)

BOGUINARD, EMILE KEI (1928-). Minister of Civil Service 1976-1983, then named Minister of State.

BOKA, ERNEST. Minister of Education in the pre-independence territorial government and first President of the Ivoirian Supreme Court at Independence. Boka was implicated in the plots against Houphouët in 1963, was arrested, and died while in detention.

BONDOUKOU. The site, according to Abron tradition, of a state founded in the fifteenth century by the legendary king Adou Bini. In the eighteenth century, it grew up as the trading center of the Gyaman kingdom (q.v.), along the Niger-Bobo/Dioulasso-Kong-Bondoukou-Kumasi trade route, and served as the principal point of exchange between Dyula and Ashanti traders. Bondoukou also became a religious and academic center, with numerous Moslem scholars and Koranic schools. At the beginning of the nineteenth century, the English traveler Lonsdale described Bondoukou as smaller than Kong, but better built "because of the influence of the Moors" (Dyulas). It had a population of 3,000 in 1892, according to Binger, who reported major trade there in gold (produced by the Brong kingdoms), ivory, slaves, and cotton cloth spun by the Kulangos. Treich-Laplene and Binger met at Bondoukou in 1888 and signed a protectorate treaty with the Abron king Adjumani. Samory overran Bondoukou in 1897, but the town recovered. Clozel reported in 1907 that the Dyulas were purchasing kola nuts bought in the Gold Coast by the inhabitants of Bondoukou. This practice was ended by the colonial administration through the imposition of heavy French customs at the border in 1905, and the city suffered economically as a result. The population had increased only to 10,000 by 1968. (632, 653, 1125, 1126, 1169)

BONI, ALPHONSE (1909-). President of the Ivoirian Supreme Court since 1963. He was born in Tiassalé, received a legal education in France, served in the public prosecutor's office in Toulouse, and then in the colonial administration. He held legal posts in Togo, Mali, and Senegal, and was named Public Prosecutor in Brazzaville from 1952 to 1958. In 1945 he was chosen as the candidate of the Comité d'Action Patriotique de la Côte d'Ivoire to the Constituent Assembly, but was not well known because of his long-term residence outside the country. He served as Minister of Justice from 1959 to 1963. An Anyi, he has been considered a possible compromise candidate to succeed Houphouët as President. (760)

BONI, DESIRE (1935-). Minister of Public Works, Transportation, Construction and Urbanism. He was named Minister of Public Works and Transportation in 1974 and added the other portfolios in 1977.

BOTO ADAI. A syncretistic religion which appeared just before World War II around Grand Bassam. The founder, Adai, was placed under house arrest during the war, and the movement lost its vitality.

BOU RIVER. A tributary of the Bandama River in northern Ivory Coast.

BOUAKE. A prefecture and the second largest city of the Ivory Coast, located near the center of the country. The name is the French adaptation of Gbuékékro, the Baule village originally on the site when, in 1898, French military forces from the Sudan began construction of a permanent military garrison. From Bouaké they sent expeditions against Samory Touré (q.v.). By the time of Samory's defeat, Bouaké had already become a commercial center with trading paths to Toumodi and Tiassalé to the south, and to M'Bahiakro, Béoumi, Marabadiassa, and Dabakala. Cloth, gold, indigo, tobacco, and iron utensils transited through there. In 1912, the railway was completed from Abidjan to Bouake. The city grew thanks to immigration from the north and from the Gold Coast. Few Baule went there, for they saw it as a "white village." Between the world wars a modern center was established near the railroad station, and tree-shaded avenues were laid out. Population grew from less than 6,000 in 1925 to 22,000 in 1945, and the city became a trading center for food and cloth during the "embargo" imposed on shipping by World War II.

Bouake is one of six regional centers designated for the support of processing industries for local produce in the 1976-80 five-year plan.

The population, about 250,000 in 1980, is predominantly Moslem. (546, 724, 1344-1351)

BOUET-WILLAUMEZ, EDOUARD (1808-1871). French naval captain who signed accords with Anyi King Amatifou and other coastal chiefs and established military posts along the coast in 1842-43. This action re-established the French presence in the Ivory Coast that was then maintained continously into modern times.

BOUNA (GBONA). Capital of a Dagomba-Kulango kingdom founded by Bounkani (q.v.) in the early seventeenth century. Villages in the kingdom were organized into four provinces under the Bouna Massa, or king. The social structure was based on three groups: the aristocratic Dagomba, who sold slaves and taxed farming and commerce; the Kulango (and later Lobi) peasants; and Dyula merchants. This system was eventually overwhelmed by Lobi immigration, and the kingdom was very weak when overrun by Samory in 1897. Bouna never completely recovered. It was the chef-lieu of an administrative district, a subdivision, a sub-prefecture at independence, and then a prefecture. Bouna had a population of 10,000 in 1900, but only 3,500 residents in 1958. (580, 593, 595, 596, 609, 1168, 1174)

BOUNKANI. Founder of the dynasty of Bouna (q.v.). Born of a conquering Dagomba father and a Kulango mother, Bounkani created a loyal military force and used it to conquer a vast territory between the Comoé and Black Volta Rivers. He made the Kulango village of Gbona (Bouna) his capital in the early 1600s. Bounkani died in about 1628. (580)

BOURSE DE VALEURS DE LA COTE D'IVOIRE. The Ivoirian Stock Exchange, created in 1976.

BRA KANON, DENIS (1936-). Minister of Agriculture since 1977 (and, later, of Water and Foresty Resources as well) and Mayor of Daloa since 1980. He was General Director of SATMACI (q.v.) from 1966-77, and Vice-President of the Economic and Social Council from 1971-77. A member of the Political Bureau of the PDCI since 1975, he is a leading spokesman for the Bélé in the government.

BRAZZAVILLE, CONFERENCE OF. Meeting of French colonial administrators, members of parliament, and non-Communist labor leaders convened by the Free French leadership in 1944, at which plans were outlined for economic and political reforms in the French colonies in Africa.

BRONG. See ABRON.

BROU, EMILE. (1937-). Since 1976, Minister in Charge of Relations with the National Assembly.

BRUNOT, RICHARD-EDMOND. Governor of the Ivory Coast in 1924-25. He ran as an independent for the French Constituent Assembly in 1945, as a member of the Socialist Party (SFIO) on a program of nationalization of the economy and the creation of local elected assemblies. His presence on such a platform greatly upset the European settler population.

- C -

CAILLIE, RENE. The great French explorer visited Odienné,
Samatiguila, and Tieme in northwest Ivory Coast in 1827-
28 and noted the importance there of the kola trade.

CAISSE DE STABILISATION ET DE SOUTIEN DES PRIX DES
PRODUITS AGRICOLES (CSSPPA). The Stabilization and
Support Fund for Agricultural Product Prices, established
several years after independence as a continuation of organizations established in the colonial period to support
commodity prices and administer revenues. By a decree
of 1970, it regulates prices on coffee, cocoa, cotton, palm
oil, bananas, copra, and tobacco, making up the difference
between the domestic price and the world market price.
Its intervention is not binding except on coffee, cocoa,
cotton, and oils. Unlike marketing boards in other West
African countries, it does not take physical delivery of
the produce. Rather, it regulates internal marketing and
licenses exporters, who must then sell at a Fund-approved
price; thus, in contrast to the situation elsewhere, micro-
level marketing functions and decisions remain in private
hands. While providing producers with stable incomes,
the CSSPPA also generated large surpluses for the government, thus taxing cash-crop producers; in 1970, it was
estimated that the CSSPPA produced 34 percent of public
savings. However, with the recent slide in commodity
prices, this is no longer true for some of the major crops.
(374, 412, 428, 466, 845)

CASSAVA. A traditional tuber food crop of the Ivory Coast
forest zone.

CATHOLICISM. The Catholic faith first came to the Ivory
Coast in 1687 with the establishment of the French post at
Assinie, but disappeared with the closing of that post. In
1843, Bouët-Willaumez signed an accord with the Agni King
Amatifou and invited missionaries whom he paid in return
for educational work. In 1895, Binger asked the Society
of African Missions in Lyon to establish schools in the Ivory
Coast. In 1905, the French law separating church and
state ended this arrangement, and mission schools had disappeared by 1914. Some of them were reopened after 1929,
but in the face of a generally hostile administration.

The church showed strong early growth along the coast, but lost ground with the advent of Harrism (q.v.). In 1913 there were about 2,400 Catholics.

In 1911, Pope Pius X created a Vicariate Apostolic in the Ivory Coast with a substructure of two prefectures and two vicariates. There were about 30 priests in 1934, when the first African priest was ordained. In 1960, in anticipation of independence, Monsignor Bernard Yago became the first Ivoirian Archbishop of Abidjan, prompting August Denise to congratulate the Church on having "won the race." There are now eight dioceses in the country, all under Ivoirian bishops, with a total Catholic population estimated at 600,000, the majority of which are probably in Abidjan. There are 400 priests, but only about 20 percent of these are Ivoirian. Among European priests, the most common order remains the African Mission Fathers (about 190). The Ivoirian Congregation of Sisters of Our Lady of Peace was founded in 1965; there are about 80 Ivoirian female religious, and about 400 foreigners.

Four hundred Catholic primary schools are attended by about 100,000 pupils (22 percent of the country's total), and there are fifteen secondary and technical schools for 7,000 students (12 percent of the total).

Construction of a new cathedral began in Abidjan in 1983, planned to seat 6,000 worshipers (4,200 sq. meters), and to cost 5 billion francs CFA. (4, 1224-1228)

CAVALLY RIVER.   With its headwaters in the Nimba Mountains of Guinea, the Cavally serves as boundary between the Ivory Coast and Liberia for over half its length. It has no large tributaries. It is navigable by small boats to about 30 miles inland, but the mouth near Cape Palmas is dangerously obstructed by rocks and sandbars. (5)

CENTRAL BANK OF WEST AFRICAN STATES (BANQUE CEN-TRALE DES ETATS DE L'AFRIQUE DE L'OUEST, BCEAO). Established in Paris in 1958, this institution replaced the Institut d'Emission de l'Afrique Occidentale Française et du Togo in 1959 as bank of issue for the CFA franc, the currency common to the Ivory Coast and most francophone West African states. The BCEAO is governed by a Council of Administration, one third of the membership of which is French. (836)

CHIEFTAINCY. The French theoretically supported the concept of direct rule in their colonial administration, that is, without the intermediation of traditional rulers. There were, however, important exceptions: Because of the need to control the Gold Coast border, they reinstated the King of Sanwi in 1920 and recognized other Anyi kings of Indénié, Moronou, Bettié, as well as the king of the Abron. But the institution was modified to the French hierarchical norm, as in the establishment of uniform chiefly ranks, from chef superieur through chef de canton, chef de village, chef de groupe, and chef de quartier. Chef superieures were named for Indénié, Sanwi, the Senufo, the Attié, and the Abé. These were sometimes individuals with traditional claims, but often were individuals of proven loyalty to the administration. The chefs de canton were the effective colonial officials at the lowest administrative level, the only ones with real and definitive territorial administrative power; however, they were seen by the French as nothing more than agents of administration. The chefs de village were often more isolated from colonial power, and were chosen more on the basis of local support. Consequently, they were the least affected by the erosion of legitimacy that followed from ties to the colonial system. (673)

CISSOKO, SOULEYMANE IBRAHIM (1914-). From 1967 to 1976, Minister for Posts and Telecommunications; since 1976 he has been a member of the PDCI Political Bureau, and of the Economic and Social Council. A Bambara and a Muslim, Cissoko was Secretary-General of the Post and Telecommunications Workers' Union from 1947 to 1951. At the same time he was political adviser to an Abidjan branch of the PDCI. In 1962-63 he was head of Itinerant Inspection for Office Control in the Posts and telecommunications administration; in 1963-64 he was Director; and in 1964-66 he was Secretary of State, after which he was named Minister.

CIVIL CODE (CODE CIVIL). A collection of ten laws adopted by the Ivoirian National Assembly on October 7, 1964, which treated, respectively: (1) names, (2) the collection of vital statistics, (3) marriage, (4) divorce and judicial separation, (5) paternity and filiation, (6) adoption, (7) inheritance, (8) testaments and gifts between living persons, (9) implementing provisions, and (10) regulations concerning the obligation to register births, marriages, and deaths.

These are the most important pieces of legislation in what
the government intends eventually to be a comprehensive
civil code on the French model, a rationally organized com-
pendium of civil law. The substance of these laws drew
largely on the French Civil Code, especially as modified
by the laws of 1938 and 1942, but excluding more recent
reforms of French family law. Some of these provisions are
not easily applied in the African context, notably the pros-
cription of polygyny and of the payment of bridewealth,
and the provision of a single, patrilineal form of inheritance.
The effect on women is to give them greater autonomy in
the choice of a husband, but to put them more firmly under
the legal domination of the husband once married. The
Ivory Coast was thus singular on the continent in the extreme to which it went in adopting a foreign body of family
law as its own, with the rationale of promoting national
unity over diverse customary practices. (297, 780, 783,
790, 791, 793-795, 799, 801, 805, 806, 809, 810, 812, 813,
816)

CLIMBIE. A novel by Bernard B. Dadié (q.v.), the most
famous fictional work set in the Ivory Coast, published in
French in 1956 and translated into English in 1971. This
semi-autobiographic work describes the childhood and youth
of a Nzima boy in Grand Bassam, through the Ecole Primaire Supérieure in Bingerville and the Ecole Ponty in
Dakar.

CLOZEL, FRANCOIS-JOSEPH (1860-   ). French governor of
the Ivory Coast, 1902-1908. Clozel completed his military
service in Algeria, then in 1885 entered the colonial service
there. He studied Islamic culture at the Faculté des lettres
in Algiers and in 1891 joined an exploration group to Chad
and the Congo. He met Binger (q.v.) upon his return to
France and came to the Ivory Coast as a young administrator
in 1896. He was assigned to the Anyi-Indenie region,
where he was wounded in an assault of Anyi warriors. Although he was initially opposed to military involvement in
colonial administration, this experience seems to have made
him more open to it. He was promoted to Secretary-General
of the colony in 1899 under a governor (Roberdeau) new
to Africa and was thus virtually in control of administration
over the next three years. Upon his appointment as govern-
or, he emphasized support for the expansion of commerce
as a principal purpose of his administration, and he planned

for port facilities, telegraph lines, and the construction of the Abidjan-Niger railway. During his term the value of the colony's trade more than doubled. (724)

COCOA. "The crop most intimately associated with the political and economic development of the country. From the earliest days, cocoa planters were the most important power base for the current leadership." (864) It was first grown commercially in 1895 near Bingerville. In 1919, the administration required its cultivation in the cercles of Indénié and Agnébi. This requirement was first met with resistance, but high prices changed the local attitude to enthusiasm, heightened in 1927 when taxes on production were eliminated. Cocoa production stood at 2,000 tons in 1922, but had reached 55,000 tons by 1939. After a postwar drop, production reached 62,000 tons annually in 1950 and was at about the same level at independence in 1960. A further boom in production occurred in the 1970s, when production almost doubled every five years, from 180,000 tons in 1970-71, to 262,000 in 1975-76, to 412,000 in 1980-81. Cocoa provided about 30 percent of Ivoirian exports from 1977 to 1979. In 1978, the Ivory Coast surpassed Ghana's production with an output of 297,000 tons (although it seems clear that some of this was smuggled in from Ghana to secure the higher Ivoirian price). The Ivory Coast provided about 27 percent of world production in 1982.

Production is mostly by smallholders: in 1974 cocoa was produced on 225,000 farms with an average size of 3.5 hectares; only one fifth were 10 hectares or larger in size. Assuming a population of seven individuals per farm, one out of every five Ivoirians is directly involved in cocoa farming. Returns from cocoa are five to ten times greater than those from traditional field crops; there is thus a risk that cocoa will drive the latter out of production.

Cocoa trees begin fruiting between three and seven years after planting, and yields begin declining after 25 years. The Ivory Coast is the only major African producer with a tree-stock age pyramid wider at the bottom than the top, as a result of substantial recent planting activity. (314, 315, 318, 428, 495, 570, 722, 864, 1297) See Table 3. See also INTERNATIONAL COCOA ORGANIZATION (ICCO).

COCODY (COCODY-LES-DEUX-PLATEAUX). Upper-income residential quarter of Abidjan, laid out entirely in planned streets. The Hotel Ivoire occupies its southernmost point, on the lagoon.

CODE CIVIL. See CIVIL CODE.

CODE OF INVESTMENTS. The Ivoirian Code des Investissements, which entered into effect in 1959, set the conditions for the private capitalization of the economy. It gave foreign investors the same rights as nationals and in specified fields granted tax reductions or exemptions for five years, exemptions from customs on imported raw materials, and a 50 percent reduction of export taxes on export-oriented products. There are no limitations on the repatriation of profits or capital, nor any regulation of technology transfer. This uniquely liberal approach to foreign investment in the Third World at that time stimulated, along with political stability, rapid industrialization based on foreign investment. (466)

COFFEE. Liberian coffee was introduced into the Ivory Coast by Verdier (q.v.) in 1885. In 1910 a European planter named Beynis succeeded in growing a Gabonese strain, which spread rapidly through the Anyi region. But the "take-off" occured after the introduction of the robusta strain from Java and Belgian Congo in 1915; robusta adapted well to the climate and proved very disease-resistant. Production was 18,000 tons annually in 1939, 95 percent of it produced by African planters; particularly under the influence of Governor Reste in the early 1930s, African growers were encouraged by official propaganda, the example of settler planters, high prices, and various forms of technological support, including the free distribution of plants. Output grew to 54,000 tons in 1950, to 119,000 in 1956, and 147,500 tons in 1960. The regulations of the European Common Market prevented France from subsidizing the coffee price into the 1960s, but poor harvests of robusta in Brazil at a time when the demand for instant coffee was growing in the United States enabled the Ivory Coast production to grow until 1965. By 1978 the country was producing 197,000 tons annually, the maximum allowed under the international coffee agreement. See Table 3. (314-318, 482, 495, 673, 722)

COLA. See KOLA.

COMITE D'ETUDES FRANCO-AFRICAINE (CEFA). An association with a nationalistic tendency, formed in 1945 with
members in Ivory Coast, Senegal, and Guinea. Membership
was diverse, including functionaries, merchants, workers,
and some chiefs; they were, however, generally seen as
the "new elites," generally opposed by most traditional
chiefs as usurpers. The leader was Pierre Engrand, a
former mayor of Dakar. Lamine Guèye in Senegal and
Houphouët in the Ivory Coast were both members. There
were Ivoirian sections in Bobo-Dioulasso, Abidjan, Agboville, and Bouake.
   The CEFA did not advocate separation, but promoted
equal treatment of Africans and their assimilation into the
colonies. It was important in the political awakening of
the Ivory Coast, and was especially important in the north,
where the SAA (q.v.) was less popular. In 1946, the
Governor-General authorized the Ivoirian governor to dis-
solve the organization there for illegal dues assessments.
These actions were rescinded by the intervention of
Houphouët in Paris, but the leaders agreed to a limitation
of their activities. The more radical activities were taken
up by the Groupe d'Etudes Communistes (GEC, q.v.).
The CEFA was eventually absorbed into the RDA (q.v.),
and had ceased activity by 1950.

COMMUNAUTE ECONOMIQUE DE L'AFRIQUE DE L'OUEST. See
WEST AFRICAN ECONOMIC COMMUNITY.

COMMUNAUTE FINANCIERE AFRICAINE (AFRICAN FINANCIAL
COMMUNITY, CFA). The organization of France and her
former African colonies that administers currency policy
in the franc zone. It created a currency parity between
the French franc and the CFA francs of West Africa and
Equatorial Africa at the rate of 1 FF = 50 francs CFA.
Thus, Ivory Coast currency is one that is common to most
of the former French West African colonies and is stabilized
by the tie to the French franc. Trade with France is greatly facilitated by this arrangement. On the other hand,
trade with countries outside the franc zone is made relatively
more complicated, even as concerns trade with other EEC
member countries. The West African CFA franc is issued
by the Central Bank of West African States (Banque Centrale des états de l'Afrique de l'Ouest, BCEAO, q.v.).
(497, 516)

COMOE RIVER. With sources in the Sikasso Plateau of Burkina
Faso, the Comoé has a narrow basin between the much
larger ones of the Bandama to the west and the Black
Volta and Bia to the east. Its major tributaries are the
Léraba from the west and the Iringo and Kongo from the
east. It enters the Ebrié Lagoon near Grand Bassam, and
reaches the Gulf through a gap in the barrier islands.
From the lagoon, it is navigable by small boats about 30
miles inland (to Alépé). The Léraba and Comoé define a
portion of the Burkina Faso-Ivory Coast border. (5)

COMPAGNIE AFRICAINE FRANCAISE. French trading company
incorporated from the Dutheil de la Rochère trading house
in 1910. By 1914 it was the fourth largest trading company
in the Ivory Coast. (728)

COMPAGNIE DE L'INDUSTRIE TEXTILE COTONNIERE (CITEC).
The overseas expansion of the French textile company
Boussac. CITEC marketed finished textiles for Boussac
in the Ivory Coast and produced cotton for metropolitan
industry as well as for its local manufacturer, Etablissements
R. Gonfreville (q.v.). (845)

COMPAGNIE FRANCAISE D'AFRIQUE OCCIDENTALE (CFAO).
A major French trading company, built upon the export
of West African products and the import of manufactured
goods. CFAO acquired the holdings of the (British)
Swanzy, Ltd. in 1898, thus first becoming established in
the Ivory Coast. It was relocated to Abidjan when that
town was created, and used its political influence to have
port facilities developed there in the 1930s. The CFAO
was the first company to have a representative admitted
to the Ivory Coast Council of Administration in 1901. It
is part of a larger conglomerate associated with six banks,
steamship lines, and industry in Marseille and Bordeaux.
(572, 724, 836)

COMPAGNIE FRANCAISE DE KONG. Trading company established in the 1860s as the Maison Verdier by Arthur
Verdier (q.v.) in what was to become the Ivory Coast.
It acquired corporate status in 1894 in order to acquire
the capital necessary (two million francs) to obtain a monopoly concession. The Compagnie de Kong is credited with
having introduced the cultivation of coffee and cocoa into
the Ivory Coast.

COMPAGNIE FRANCAISE DE LA COTE D'IVOIRE (CFCI). One of the most important French trading companies in the Ivory Coast, formed by Unilever's United Africa Company in conjunction with French interests.

COMPAGNIE FRANCAISE DES TEXTILES (CFDT). Company that promoted the growing of Allen cotton in the Ivory Coast, and purchased the product. It was replaced in 1973 by the Compagnie Ivoirienne pour le Développement du Textile (CIDT), which was made responsible for the agricultural development of northwest Ivory Coast. (305)

COMPAGNIE INDUSTRIELLE ET COMMERCIALE DE L'AFRIQUE (CICA). One of the major French trading companies operating in the Ivory Coast.

COMPAGNIE IVOIRIENNE POUR LE DEVELOPPEMENT DU TEXTILE (CIDT). See IVOIRIAN COMPANY FOR TEXTILE DEVELOPMENT.

COMPTOIRS REUNIS DE L'OUEST AFRICAIN (CROA). One of the most important French trading companies in the Ivory Coast.

CONFEDERATION FRANCAISE DES TRAVAILLEURS CHRETIENS (CFTC). The Ivoirian section of this Catholic-oriented French trade union was organized by French activists in April 1947. It encompassed six unions in the public sector and three in the private; its membership never exceeded 2,750.

CONJONCTURE (CONJUNCTURE). Term used during the 1980s to describe the simultaneous rise in petroleum prices and the drop in commodity prices, especially for the Ivory Coast's principal exports, coffee and cocoa. It was the explanation for the dramatic slowdown of Ivoirian economic growth at that time.

CONSEIL DE L'ENTENTE. See ENTENTE COUNCIL.

CONSTITUTION. As adopted in 1960, the Ivoirian constitution proclaims the (French) Declaration of the Rights of Man, and proclaims a "one and indivisible, secular, democratic, and social republic." French is proclaimed the official language. The national slogan is "Union, Discipline, and Work." Executive power is vested in the President of the

Republic, elected for a five-year term by direct universal
suffrage. The President can appoint and dismiss ministers,
can negotiate treaties, and is commander of the armed
forces. The National Assembly exercises legislative power
and is elected in the same manner and for the same term
as the President. It may vote on bills submitted by one
of its members or by the President. The President may
ask for reconsideration of a bill, which must then be supported by two thirds of the membership. A High Court of
Justice may try the President for high treason, or members
of the government for "crimes and misdemeanors committed
in the exercise of their functions, and for conspiracy
against the security of the state." The Supreme Court
consists of four chambers and an Economic and Social Council, on the French model.

The constitutional question of greatest concern in the
Ivory Coast has always been that of presidential succession.
In 1980, the constitution was amended at Houphouët's initiative
to create the post of Vice-President, thus denying succession to the President of the National Assembly. However,
in October 1985, the National Assembly again amended the
Constitution to abolish the post of Vice-President, which
had never been filled. The vice-presidency was replaced
by a provision that, in case the presidency were vacated,
the Chairman of the National Assembly would preside over
the government for an interim period of 45 to 60 days,
during which time he would call a new presidential election.
(737-739)

COOPERANTS. French technical assistants, including teachers,
on assignment in Third-World environments, especially
former French colonies. Numbers are provided by the fact
that co-opérant service can be substituted by young French-
men for military duty. The Ivory Coast has the highest
number of co-opérants in Africa. (864)

CORN (MAIZE, MAIS). An important secondary food crop
throughout the Ivoirian forest and savannah, especially
in conjunction with sorghum, millet, and yams. Apparently
introduced to Africa by the Portuguese from Latin America,
corn adapts well to a tropical climate. (931, 943)

CORRUPTION. The large private sector and the lack of re-
striction on importing materials and exporting earnings in
the Ivory Coast reduce opportunities for official corruption.

There is some official private sharing in contracts, a widespread official practice of benefiting from leasing publicly owned housing and contracting private services with the government, and occasional extortion. Scandals at the highest level (see EMMANUEL DIOULO, MOHAMED DIAWARA) have shaken the country's leadership in recent years. Yet compared to most African states, the Ivory Coast is relatively untroubled by corruption.

COTTON. Cotton has been grown for many years in the Ivory Coast as a secondary product used in traditional weaving and spinning among the Maninka, Senufo, Kulango, Guro, and especially the Baule, whose cloth was highly prized in pre-colonial commerce with the forest zone. Market production expanded rapidly to meet French needs in World War I, from 20 tons in 1912 to 390 in 1914, and 600 tons in 1918. In the 1930s, the administration tried to force production for export, with mediocre results. In the 1960s, the Allen variety was introduced by the Compagnie Française des Textiles, with much better results in the Ivoirian environment. (319-322, 481, 712)

COULIBALY, GBON (PELEFORO GBON SORHO, 1860-1962). Senufo chief of the Tyembaras, who came to power in 1894, succeeding Zouakonion Sorho (q.v.). Gbon had been a hostage from his father to the Kenedugu king at Sikasso, but was sent back to Tyembara with troops to maintain control in that area.

Basically a pacifist and a shrewd diplomat, Gbon protected the interests of Tyembara at all costs. Thus, seeing the greater strength of Samory, Gbon broke with Sikasso to ally himself with Samory in 1894, was spared his wrath, accepted Senufo refugees from other areas, and became spokesman for them all. In 1898 he abandoned Samory to ally himself with the French. Under colonial rule he succeeded in maintaining the respect of both his own people and the French. He persuaded the Senufo ruling class to adopt Islam and, at the proper moment, consecrated Senufo support of the PDCI. Gbon lived through the colonial period into independence, dying at over 100 years of age. (580)

COULIBALY, GON. Vice-President of the National Assembly (June 1985).

COULIBALY, LANZENI.   Keeper of the Seals and Minister of
   Justice (June 1985).

COULIBALY, MAMADOU (1910-1985). President of the Economic
   and Social Council and a senior figure in the Democratic
   Party of the Ivory Coast; Treasurer of the PDCI Political
   Bureau from 1959 to 1980.   He was a Muslim Malinké from
   the north of the Ivory Coast.   Coulibaly attended the
   Ecole Ponty in Dakar and the University of Paris.   He later
   became head of schools in Bingerville.   From 1949 to 1956
   he served on the Social Affairs Committee of the Assembly
   of the French Union, and in 1959-1960 was Ivoirian representative in the French Community Senate.   In 1959 he
   also became a member of the Territorial Assembly of the
   Ivory Coast and the next year entered the independent
   country's National Assembly and was its First Vice-President.
   From 1961-63 he was Ivoirian Ambassador to Tunisia and
   also Manager of Fraternité-Matin.   In 1963-65, he was
   Editor-in-Chief of Fraternite-Hebdo.   He was President of
   the Economic and Social Council from 1963 to his death, and
   had been Director-General of Fraternité-Matin since 1974.
   (760)

COULIBALY, OUEZZIN.   (1909-1958)   Political leader in the
   Ivory Coast and Upper Volta (Burkina Faso).   Born at
   Nouna, near the Malian border of Upper Volta, Coulibaly
   graduated from the Ecole Ponty and taught there from 1935
   to 1942.   He moved to the Ivory Coast, where he was co-
   founder and head of the Teachers' Union and Voltaic leader
   of the RDA, and was elected with Houphouët-Boigny to
   the National Assembly in 1946.   He was defeated in the
   1951 election, but later became an Ivory Coast senator
   and was re-elected to the Assembly in 1956.   He became
   Prime Minister of Upper Volta in 1957, simultaneously holding the National Assembly seat until his death in 1958.
   Coulibaly was among those who urged the PDCI break with
   the French Communist Party in 1950.   His death came three
   weeks before the referendum of the De Gaulle constitution.

COUNCIL OF NOTABLES (CONSEIL DE NOTABLES).   In 1919,
   the colonial administration created the only form of government advisory council in rural areas, at the level of the
   cercle.   The commandants called these councils into session
   only infrequently, to advise on such matters as taxation
   and public works.   According to Labouret, there are no
   examples where the deliberations of a Council of Notables

have ever modified the decisions of an administrator.
(773)

COURTS, COLONIAL. A décret (decree) of 1903 established
a special judicial system for French subjects at the levels
of the village, the province, and the cercle. The first
two levels had very limited jurisdictions, with the right
of appeal of civil and criminal cases going to the tribunal
de cercle. The commandant de cercle presided over the
tribunal de cercle, with two African "notables" as consul-
tants. This court had jurisdiction over all crimes committed
in the cercle. Later, the tribunal de province was replaced
by the tribunal de subdivision. In 1924, another décret
replaced the tribunals at subdivision and cercle levels by
tribunals of first and second degree, and added a tribunal
de homologation at the capital. This system progressively
eliminated the roles of traditional judicial authorities. See
also JUDICIARY. (706)

COWRY. A small seashell of Indian Ocean origin, introduced
into West Africa by European traders and established there
as a currency because it could not be counterfeited. The
value was guaranteed by political authorities or by the
merchants themselves. Cowries were often used for minor
commerce, with major purchases paid in gold. They were
used widely in Bouna, Bondoukou, and Kong, and along
the trading routes (i.e., generally in the savanna), where
they continued in limited use until after World War II.

CREDIT DE LA COTE D'IVOIRE (CCI). A majority government-
owned development finance credit bank established by the
colonial administration in 1955. The original state corporation in the Ivory Coast. (445)

CSSPPA. See CAISSE DE STABILISATION ET DE SOUTIEN
DES PRIX DES PRODUITS AGRICOLES.

CUSTOMS UNION OF WEST AFRICAN STATES (UDEAO,
UNION DOUANIERE DES ETATS DE L'AFRIQUE DE L'OUEST).
Convention replacing the UDAO (West African Customs
Union, q.v.) in 1966. The UDEAO did not establish a
common external tariff and did not have a significant impact on the economic problems of member countries. It
was replaced in 1972 by the West African Economic Community (CEAO), q.v. The members were the Ivory Coast,
Mali, Mauretania, Niger, Senegal, and Upper Volta.

- D -

DABAKALA. Town in the north of present-day Ivory Coast,
the center of Samori's (q.v.) empire from 1893 to 1898.

DABOU. Town about 50 kilometers west of Abidjan on the
Ebrié Lagoon. Its origins are found in the construction
there of Fort Ducos, established to control the western half
of the lagoon. With the French defeat in the Franco-
Prussian War (1870), the troops were withdrawn and the
fort was destroyed. Modern Dabou owes its existence to
a crossroads position between the western lagoon and the
hard-surfaced road to Abidjan and Bouaké (the road to
Abidjan was opened in 1921). The Savonnerie des Lagunes
(Blohorn) opened in Dabou in 1930. The town's future
was put in doubt by the recent opening of a four-lane highway
bypassing it on the Abidjan-Bouaké route.

DADIE, BERNARD B. (1916-). Minister of Cultural Affairs
and Ivoirian author whose major works include the semi-
autobiographic Climbié (q.v.) and several collections of
folk stories, Légendes Africaines and Le Pagne Noir. He
also wrote several plays, beginning during his student
days at the William Ponty School. One of these, Assémien
Déhylé, Roi du Sanwi, was published in 1979. In his introduction to the English edition of Climbié, Ezekiel
Mphalele comments that "Dadié is continuously asserting
the beauty of African life as a constant reminder that
colonialism cheated the black man out of his heritage," and
describes Dadié's passionate belief "that African stories,
legends, proverbs should be retold in their original languages and recorded." Dadie graduated from the Ecole
Ponty. From 1963 to 1977 he was Director General, then
Inspector General of Cultural Affairs; in 1977 he was named
Minister of Cultural Affairs. He was a member of the
Economic and Social Council in 1976-77. (102, 106-111,
113, 201, 207, 210-213, 222, 238, 675)

DADIE, GABRIEL B. Founding member of the Société des
Agriculteurs Africains (q.v.), he was Propaganda Secretary
and a member of the Bureau in 1944, elected Vice-President
in 1947. He was previously a functionary in the postal
department.

DALOA. Prefecture, and third largest city in the Ivory
Coast, with a 1976 population of 60,837. The French administrator Thomarin established a post there in 1905 based
on an agreement with chief Gbéli. After a revolt lasting
from 1906 to 1908, Daloa became chef-lieu of the cercle.
It was made a prefecture in 1963. Daloa is one of six regional centers designated for support of processing industries for local produce in the 1976-80 five-year plan. The
surrounding rural population are primarily Bété.

DAMS. See HYDRO-ELECTRIC POWER.

DAN. An ethnic group occupying the extreme west of the
Ivory Coast, around the towns of Man and Danané, and
extending into Liberia. Self-awareness as a distinct culture
may be as recent as the eighteenth or nineteenth century.
Numbering about 150,000, they are traditional neighbors
of the Guéré and the Wobé, with whom they share a wide
range of cultural patterns, but not the Kru language, and
are thus classified as "Peripheral Mandé." They are inter-
mixed with the Toura, have similar languages, and claim
to be related. They were probably pushed into their
present mountainous and forest location by Manding expansion. They practice high-altitude rice culture and raise
kola nuts, which they have traditionally exchanged for
dried fish from the Niger River through Dyula traders.
Dan armed resistance against colonial rule was put down
under Governor Angoulvant in 1905-08.
  Young men now travel seasonally to the coast, where
they work climbing oil palms, as lumberjacks or loading
logs, or as domestics or errand boys. They are famous
for traditional acrobatic performances in which young children are thrown in the air. The Dan have resisted Islam,
although living on its southern frontier. Dan masks are
known for their realistic style. (259, 960, 1110, 1111,
1220)

D'ARBOUSSIER, GABRIEL (1908-1976). Civil servant and
leader of the Rassemblement Démocratique Africain (RDA,
q.v.). D'Arboussier was born in Djenné, French Sudan
(now Mali). He was the son of French governor Henri
d'Arboussier and an African mother. After obtaining a law
degree from the University of Paris in 1944, he served in
the colonial administration in Brazzaville. He served in
the French Constituent Assembly in 1945-46 as a representative of Gabon and Middle Congo, then stayed on in

Paris as an official of the RDA. In 1947 he was elected
to the Assembly of the French Union from the Ivory Coast
and served at that time as General Secretary of the RDA.
In the late 1950s he was President of the Grand Council
of French West Africa. He split with Houphouët in 1951
on the latter's decision to sever RDA ties with the French
Communist Party.

DEBT, FOREIGN. The 1981 recession led the Ivory Coast
to begin a drastic financial stabilization program under an
Extended Facility Agreement with the International Monetary
Fund. The agreement provided for reduction of the public-
sector debt to 6.3 percent of GDP and to restore a balance of
payments equilibrium by 1983. However, faced with a continu-
ing deficit at that time, the country was forced into a further
retrenchment, and the IMF resheduled the debt in 1984. (374)

DEIMA. Syncretistic sect founded in 1942 by a Godié woman,
Marie Dahonon, known as Marie Lalou. She was a Baptist,
but received a revelation in a forest from a large reptile
with crocodile feet and buffalo horns. The beast taught
her to prepare miraculous ashes (lalou), and she took
sacred water from the pond where it had appeared. In
addition to magic practices, her followers use the cross
and Jesus in their temples. Lalou divinized Houphouët-
Boigny and his mother until he forbade it. She died in 1951.
    The Lalou faith spread among the Godié, Dida, and
Bété, and was introduced among the Baule as Demba. (5)

DELAFOSSE, MAURICE. Colonial administrator and ethno-
grapher. Delafosse arrived in the Ivory Coast at the age
of twenty-three, having already studied Arabic and having
versed himself in the travel accounts of the colony. He
was posted to Baule country and became both fluent in
the Baule language and exceptionally knowledgeable, for
a European, in that people's culture. In 1899, Delafosse
returned to the Ivory Coast from a duty tour in Liberia
to become civilian administrator in Toumodi. He approached
this assignment with enthusiasm, renewing old friendships
with Baule chiefs and resuming his linguistic and ethnographic studies. He was unaware, however, of the degree
of hostility among the Baule to French activities in the
area. Faced with a challenge to his authority from a local
chief, Delafosse ordered that the chief's village be burned
to the ground. In retaliation, two of the chief's men en-

tered Delafosse's compound at night and set it afire, destroying most of his administrative papers and large amounts
of weapons and ammunition. He then began to support a
much greater use of military force to subdue the Baule.
However, Delafosse saw himself primarily as an ethno-
grapher, historian, and linguist whose administrative position was a means to support those activities. (627, 676,
677, 724)

DEMOCRATIC PARTY OF THE IVORY COAST (PARTI DEMO-
CRATIQUE DE COTE D'IVOIRE, PDCI). The single party of
the Ivory Coast since independence. The party was formed
to participate in the June 1946 election for a representative
to the French Constituent Assembly. Its founder and leader of the ticket was Felix Houphouët-Boigny (q.v.), who
in the first election under the PDCI banner obtained 98
percent of the vote in Ivory Coast districts (the Ivory
Coast and Upper Volta were administered jointly at the
time). Houphouët-Boigny has never been seriously challenged for leadership of the party since that time.
    Between 1946 and 1959, the PDCI operated in a system
that was at least nominally multi-party. It competed with
a single opponent in the Constituent Assembly election of
1946, was one of seven political movements in 1951, and
competed against twelve other parties in 1956. It succeeded
in running almost without competition by 1957, and in 1959
all candidates to the territorial Legislative Assembly were
on the PDCI ticket.
    In Paris, the party leadership had decided to affiliate
with the French Communist Party (PCF) in the Constituent
Assembly, but with the move of the Communists to the opposition shortly thereafter, the PDCI was left defenseless
against strong harassment from the colonial administration.
In 1950, Houphouët announced the abandonment of the Communist affiliation, and the next year managed to affiliate
with parties more to the center of the French political
spectrum. By the 1950s, the PDCI had shed its radical
ideology and had adopted a policy orientation focused on
economic growth and development. However, in formal
organization and nomenclature, the early influence of the
PCF can be seen: the local organizational unit is the sous-
section, headed by a secretary-general. At the national
level there was a Central Committee, and there remains a
33-member inner core called the Political Bureau. The
most important structural deviation from the communist

model is that, from the beginning, the PDCI has been designated a mass party, with membership expected of all
citizens. In reality, the structure and operation of the
party has more closely approximated the classic party
machine, with a base of local notables in various ethnic
groups and communities, and an approach to dissent that
is more often co-optive than repressive. A pattern was
set at the Third Party Congress in 1959, when party institutions were increased in size, allowing the addition of
younger members, those not part of the original group of
"militants."

With independence in 1960, the PDCI faced a difficulty
common to most single-party organizations in control: the
need to define a role for the party organization once its
leaders have decision-making authority in the government.
The party has suffered long stages of dormancy, but
unlike other single parties has been periodically revived
as a means of communication between elites and masses.
The communication role was enhanced in the elections of
1980 when, for the first time, delegates to the National
Assembly were chosen in competitive elections. Although
all 649 candidates were party members, there were only
147 seats; furthermore, incumbents won only 26 of those
seats. Municipal Council elections were held a few weeks
later, with a similar infusion of new personnel. At the
same time, an unanticipated effect of competitive elections
was the appearance of serious ethnic tensions and open
solicitation of votes for money.

At the Seventh Congress of the Party in 1980, the
position of secretary general was abolished and replaced
with a nine-member Executive Committee. Five of the
Executive Committee members were young politicians who
recently had become prominent and had earlier been critics
of the government in student movements. In 1985, the
Eighth Congress urged Houphouët-Boigny to seek a sixth
five-year term as President, and called for the abolition
of the vice-presidency. Although the position had never
been filled, Houphouët was angered by the unruly jostling
among leading contenders. The central question remained
how well the PDCI and other Ivoirian institutions would
survive Houphouët's inevitable departure from the scene.
(759-761, 767, 769, 778, 820-828, 846, 847, 864, 865)

DENISE, AUGUST (1906-). Minister of State and early

associate of Felix Houphouët-Boigny; along with Philippe Yacé and Jean-Baptiste Mockey, he was one of Houphouët's top lieutenants in the formative years of the PDCI. Like Houphouët, Denise is a Baule, a médécin africain (African physician) graduate of the Ecole Ponty, and a large landholder who made substantial contributions to the PDCI. Denise held various health and medical positions in the 1930s and was Head of Health Services for the Grand Lahou Cercle from 1943-46. He was a co-founder, along with Houphouët, of the Syndicat Agricole Africain (q.v.) in 1944, and was named at the same time as Houphouët by the SAA as their candidate in the 1946 election to the Constituent Assembly, in the First (Citizens') College. He was general secretary of the PDCI from 1947 to 1959, the highest executive office in the party. He was the PDCI's first candidate for the post of President of the Territorial Assembly, winning the position in 1948, then losing it in 1949 when the party temporarily lost its majority in the Assembly. He has held the office of Minister of State of the Republic since 1959, but by the late 1970s his influence was clearly limited by his advancing age and his poor health. (June, 1985). (760)

DIABY, DJIBRIL. Member of the Bureau of the Syndicat Agricole Africain (q.v.) in 1944 and Secretary-Archivist. He was re-elected to these positions in 1947.

DIALOGUE. Term applied to Houphouët-Boigny's style of rule. Drawing on African tradition, he has co-opted potential opposition by calling them into "dialogue," or palaver. The first such gathering on a large scale was in 1969, when dissent was growing among students and urban occupational groups; further meetings have been called regularly since then, sometimes involving thousands of people at a time, sometimes just a single possible opponent. In 1984, Cohen concluded that "the Dialogue was a watershed in Ivoirian political life because it articulated a set of issues which dominated the next ten years." (846)

DIARASSOUBA (DYARASUBA). Family of Bambara warriors sent by the king of Ségou in the mid-eighteenth century to shore up the Maninka defenses at Odienné, under repeated attack from the Senufo. The Diarassoubas conquered the territory from Odienné to Séguéla and established the state of Nafana, which lasted from the late eighteenth to

the middle of the nineteenth century. The capital was at
Tiyèfou, seven kilometers northeast of Odienné. It was
destroyed in 1848 by Vakaba Touré (q.v.).

DIARRASSOUBA, CHARLES VALY (1938-). Professor of
Economics and Rector at the University of Abidjan since
1974. He was Director of Higher Education and Research
in the Ministry of National Education until 1977.

DIAWARA, MOHAMED TIEKOURA (1928-). Brought into
the Political Bureau of the PDCI in 1966, Diawara was, from
1966 to 1977, Ivory Coast Minister of Planning; from 1974
to 1985, he was Director of the "Club of Dakar." He is
a Diola and a Muslim. Diawara lost his ministry position
following a speech in which Houphouët criticized the economic mismanagement of the country. In 1985, Diawara was
accused of embezzling funds from the West African Economic
Community (CEAO) (q.v.). Most CEAO heads of state,
fearing the extent of the forthcoming scandal, had urged
that Diawara be allowed to make restitution; however, at
the 1984 summit meeting of the CEAO the rotation of the
chairmanship fell to President Thomas Sankara of Burkina
Faso, who asked that Diawara be brought to the CEAO
headquarters in Ouagadougou. Diawara was tried before
a People's Revolutionary Tribunal in Burkina Faso, in which
he defended himself before a panel of ordinary citizens.
He was found guilty, sentenced to fifteen years in prison,
and ordered to restore the missing funds, plus interest
and damages.
   Diawara served in the colonial administration from 1955-
60. From 1961 to 1963 he was Director of Cabinet in the
Finance Ministry, then General Director of Planning. From
1964 to 1966 he was a member of the Economic and Social
Council and Governor of the Ivoirian Bank for Industrial
Development (BIDI). He was named a member of the Political Bureau of the PDCI in 1975. (838, 864)

DIBO, PAUL GUI. Minister of Mining since 1976.

DIDA. A people of the Kru ethnic cluster concentrated in
south-central Ivory Coast, around the towns of Lakota,
Divo, Guitry, and Grand Lahou. They are divided into
sub-groups known as Divo, Yokoboué, Maké, and Lozoua.
The Dida are difficult to distinguish from neighboring
groups on the basis of common institutions or cultural

traits, but are self-identified by an exclusive network of economic and political relations. They were traditionally very decentralized politically, although each village recognizes one lineage as proprietor of the village lands. The eldest male in that lineage supervises settlement by outsiders and adjudicates inter-lineage disputes. They were culturally influenced by the Baule to the north. The Dida militarily resisted colonial rule through the period 1909-1918, and there were in the same period many conversions to Harrism (q.v.) among the Dida and neighboring groups. They did not enter into production for export until after World War II (297). They are now only about one third of the population of their home department of Divo, because of heavy immigration into it. (297, 1107, 1112-1115)

DIKEBIE, PASCAL N'GUESSAN (1936-   ). Minister of Educational Television from 1971 until 1982, when large-scale student and teacher unrest broke out. After a series of teachers' strikes, Dikebié and Education Minister Paul Akoto Yao lost their ministerial posts. (1027)

DIMBOKRO. A sub-prefecture with a population of 16,000. It was named for a small village created by Kouassi Djingbo (Djingbo-Kro). The Baule settled in the region in the eighteenth century. Dimbokro became an administrative post in 1903, and a military post and railway worker camp followed. In 1908, it was named chef-lieu of a cercle. The establishment there of railroad repair shops contributed to the town's economic growth, but an epidemic in 1935 caused the military camp to be moved to Bouaké. The road was completed from Dimbokro to Bongouanou in 1938. A modern textile complex (UTEXI) which employs about 1,500 workers has been established there.

DIOMANDE (KAMARA, CAMARA). Maninka clan which migrated into the Ivory Coast at the beginning of the sixteenth century, gaining control of a vast region from the Konyan Plateau to the Bandama River. They conquered the native Dan and conquered or allied with Maninka clans from earlier migrations. Their reign was supplanted in the eighteenth century by that of the Diarassouba (q.v.).

DIOMANDE, LOUA (1926-   ). Minister of State charged with relations with the National Assembly (from 1971 to 1977).

Diomandé is a Wakoba, and attended the Normal School in Aix-en-Provence, followed by two years of legal studies. He held colonial administrative positions from 1952 to 1959. From 1961 to 1963 he served as Minister in charge of relations with the Entente Council, then, from 1964-70, as Minister of Public Service. In 1970-71 he was Minister of Tourism.

DIOULA. See DYULA.

DIOULO, EMMANUEL. Member of the Steering Committee of the PDCI, and Mayor of Abidjan in 1985. He also occupied the posts of President of SOCOPAO-CI, the Société Interafricaine de Financement, and the Banque Atlantique de Cote d'Ivoire, and served as President of the Administrative Council of the Port of San Pedro. Previously he was President of the Southwest Region Authority (ARSO). Dioulo was once considered a possible successor to the presidency, but his political future was clouded by implication in a financial scandal concerning one of his companies and the National Agricultural Development Bank (BNDA). From exile, Dioulo wrote to President Houphouët that others were as guilty as he, and he threatened to expose their misdeeds. For whatever reason, he was rehabilitated by Houphouët in late 1985, and returned to Ivory Coast in 1986. (822)

DIRECTION DE L'AMENAGEMENT DU TERRITOIRE ET DE L'ACTION REGIONALE (DATAR, THE DEPARTMENT OF DEVELOPMENT OF TERRITORY AND OF REGIONAL ACTION). An organization established by the Planning Ministry in 1973 to develop a series of regional master plans to ensure better distribution of economic activities and investments and more rational use of regional potential. (438)

DJAUMENT, ETIENNE. Leader of the west-Ivcirian UOCOCI, which contested the PDCI in early post-World-War-II elections.

DJIMINI. A people of the Voltaic language family, speaking a language closely related to Senufo and living on the southern fringe of traditional Senufo territory, between the Comoé and Nzi rivers to the east and west and the towns of Kong and Satama-Sokoura to the north and south. They have a history distinct from the Senufo of the Korhogo area: the Djimini region was the site of Samory Toure's last stand against the French. Unlike Gbon Coulibaly (q.v.) of

Korhogo, the Djimini kings resisted the advances of Samory. Informal estimates are that about one third of the Djimini were drafted into Samory's armies, about one third were killed, and one third fled to Baule and Anyi regions to the south. Thus devastated by Samory, the Djimini villages of the region were repopulated after 1900. (1116, 1117)

DO. Liberian prophet who came to the Ivory Coast in 1915, working between Grand Lahou and Grand Bassam. He founded a religious movement (distinct from Harrism), in which he recommended that his followers pray for the reduction or elimination of the head tax (q.v.) and the early departure of the French.

DONO-FOLOGO, Laurent (1939-). Ivoirian Minister of Youth and Sports since 1978, and a member of the Executive Committee of the PDCI. Dona Fologo was formerly Minister of Information (1974-1978) and is a former editor of Fraternité-Matin.

DONWAHI, CHARLES BANZA (1927-). Minister of Agriculture from 1959 to 1963, then three-term deputy to the Ivoirian National Assembly from Soubre-Buyo. He is a nephew of one of the first nationalist leaders. A Bété, he is considered a possible successor to Houphouët as President. (760)

DYARASUBA. See DIARASSOUBA.

DYULA (DIOULA). Designation of members of the Manding ethnic cluster spread over much of the West African savanna. The Dyula are Islamic and are mostly traders; in pre-colonial times they had commercial networks from Senegal to Nigeria and from Timbuktu to the Northern Ivory Coast. With colonization, they expanded into the new towns of the coastal area. Because of their prominence in trade, the Dyula language is the common language of commerce in much of West Africa and is a second language for a large proportion of the Ivoirian population. The word "Dyula" means "itinerant trader" in that language. The term has come to be applied, especially in southern Ivory Coast, to all Moslem merchants from the north, of whatever ethnic or cultural background. "Dyula" is thus a very contextually defined, ambiguous term.

The "True" Dyula, i.e. those for whom this was

primarily a cultural rather than an occupational designation, are from the region of Kong (q.v.), which they developed as a pre-colonial commercial center. (143-153, 214, 215, 254, 452, 589, 613, 614, 616, 618, 636, 649, 1118-1126, 647, 1123, 1169, 1179)

DYULAKRO. The term used in Akan-language areas of the Ivory Coast to designate the quarter of a town in which the northern Dyula (q.v.), and by extension the Moslem, population resides. Such quarters were established at points along Dyula trade routes as early as the fifteenth century.

- E -

EBONY, NOEL. A recent critic of the Ivoirian political economy. Ebony wrote in Demain l'Afrique in 1979 about "social tensions in housing, speculation, prices, unemployment, decline of services and inefficiencies." He attracted sufficient attention to draw responses from the Foreign Minister in the same magazine and from President Houphouët in his National Day address. (864)

EBRIE. A people of the Lagoon cluster, after whom the Ebrié Lagoon is named. They came from farther inland about 1750, pushed to the coast by Anyi expansion. The Ebrié have never been organized into centralized states; their most inclusive political unit has been the village. Age grades are an important aspect of Ebrié social cohesion. They occupy the area in which the city of Abidjan was founded. Although numerically overwhelmed by immigrants, they have managed to preserve their identity and some aspects of their traditional culture, which was oriented toward the water. They are, however, almost entirely Christianized and integrated into the modern economy and society. (306, 347, 1127, 1218)

ECOLE NORMALE WILLIAM PONTY (WILLIAM PONTY SCHOOL). When the Ecole Normale des Instituteurs moved from St. Louis (Senegal) to Gorée in 1913, it took the name Ecole Normale William Ponty. It was reorganized to provide African functionaries in teaching, medicine, pharmacy, and veterinary science. It had great prestige in the African colonies, including the Ivory Coast, and its graduates were the first technical and political generation (including, in the Ivory Coast, Felix Houphouët, Auguste Denise, Mamadou Coulibaly, Mathieu Ekra, and Jean-Baptiste Mockey, qq.v.).

ECONOMIC COMMUNITY OF WEST AFRICAN STATES (ECOWAS). An economic treaty was signed in Lagos, Nigeria, in May 1975 creating this organization of all sixteen West African states. It was the first African international economic organization to include English-, French-, and Portuguese-speaking states. The purpose of ECOWAS is to create an organized zone of exchange and an active policy of economic cooperation at the regional level. Specifically, it plans to eliminate customs duties among member states, abolish trade restrictions, establish a common external tariff, eliminate restrictions on the movement of factors of production, harmonize development policies in agriculture, transport, communications, trade, energy, industry, and financial and monetary policy. According to the treaty, between 1976 and 1978 no increase in import duties could be imposed; between 1978 and 1986 there was to be a gradual elimination of duties among members. A common external tariff was to be achieved by 1991, leading to a common market. Headquartered in Lagos, ECOWAS is governed by the annual meeting of Heads of State and Government. A Council of Ministers and a tribunal have also been created. Provision has been made to compensate member states for losses incurred because of implementation.

As of 1984, application of the provisions was "hypothetical." Nigeria and the Ivory Coast together accounted for 84 percent of the foreign trade of member countries in 1980. A major political obstacle for ECOWAS is the fear in other countries (including the Ivory Coast) that the union will be dominated by Nigeria. (394)

ECONOMY. The Ivoirian Gross Domestic Product (GDP) grew 7.5 percent per year in the first twenty years of independence, to place the country's growth rate among the top fifteen in the world. The total value of the country's Gross National Product (GNP) had reached $7.1 billion by 1983, dropping to $6.5 billion in 1984. Corresponding per capita figures were $798 in 1983 and $671 in 1984. These figures are evidence of a severe economic slowdown. However, in 1985, the Gross Domestic Product per capita in the Ivory Coast was the second highest in Africa, exceeded only by that of South Africa.

This growth was based on rapid growth in the agricultural sector, especially in coffee and cocoa, from which
surpluses for investment were generated, and on the pragmatic combination of domestic and private economic factors.
Although often hailed as an economic miracle, Ivoirian
economic development has been an object of contention
among students of development from varying ideological
backgrounds. Samir Amin has characterized the Ivoirian
process as "growth without development."

Agriculture has a central role in the economy, contributing one third of GDP and 50 percent of exports. It employs about 75 percent of the work force. Food crops and
cash crops each contribute about half of total agricultural
output. Since the 1960s, the government has supported
the development of cash crops with extension services and
market regulation. In the 1970s, the government gave
greater priority to food crops. (267-271, 276, 279, 285,
287, 288, 294, 300, 301, 374, 382, 391-394, 396-399, 402-
404, 406, 408, 409, 412, 414, 417, 418, 420-422, 425, 432,
434, 436, 438, 442-444, 451, 464, 465, 467-469, 471, 473,
475, 477, 479, 486, 488, 491, 492, 497, 498, 500, 864)

EDUCATION. Colonial policy was to give part of the population
a summary education (a knowledge of French and arithmetic)
and to train a native support staff for administrative services. Governor-General Roume in 1911 established a uniform
hierarchy of schools for West Africa: primary-elementary,
professional, and higher primary. Village schools were
staffed by African monitors. Administrators enrolled the
children of chiefs and influential families, and the teacher
then filled in with other children judged to be talented.
The six-year program ended in a Certificat d'Etudes Pri-
maires Elémentaires (CEPE) examination. Less than 10
percent of graduates went on to a higher level, but most
holders of the CEPE left the village for the city. There
were also regional schools in the chef-lieux of most cercles,
for a total of 21 in 1936. Urban schools were only for
Europeans at first, with a level equivalent to schools in
France, although a few Ivoirians with French citizenship
attended. In the 1930s, with no funds allocated for school
construction, groups in Agboville, Dimbokro, Grand Lahou,
and Aboisso put up private subscriptions to build about
fifteen schools.

The école primaire supérieure (higher primary school)

was at Bingerville, from which a few of the best students went on to the Ecole Ponty (q.v.) in Senegal. Other Bingerville graduates became teachers or village monitors.

In 1945 there were only four university graduates in the Ivory Coast, three or four students in French universities, and between 200-300 graduates of the Ecole Ponty. In 1922, only one out of 100 children of school age attended school; by 1948, the ratio had improved to one in 20. Enrollment increased dramatically in the 1950s, from 5 percent of school-age population to over 20 percent. Secondary schools were first created in this period, and scholarships were granted for secondary and postsecondary study in France. There were an estimated 1,000 Ivoirian students in France and another 200 at the University of Dakar.

Education has been a high-priority policy area of the government since independence, and in the last 20 years has primarily been directed to providing skilled manpower. Enrollment of school-age children rose to 49 percent in 1969-70, and to 58 percent in 1978-79. However, in the mid-1960s, the political leadership became aware of serious breakdowns in the educational system, symptomized by high drop-out and repeat rates, and by the inefficient allocation of resources. Major policy reforms were announced by the President in 1967. The need was emphasized the next year when, of 1,000 Ivoirian students who took the baccalauréat (high school) examination, only 147 passed, of whom 50 were French citizens. A National Commission for the Reform of the Educational System (CNRE; the Commission Nationale de Réforme de l'Enseignement) was created in 1972. Over the next ten years, public policy was focused on the introduction of educational television (q.v.) as a technical solution, but that approach was abandoned in 1982. (415, 428, 673, 720, 828, 993-1027, 1277, 1292-1293, 1313)

EDUCATIONAL TELEVISION (ETV). From the late 1960s through the 1970s, the Ivory Coast was involved in a project to enhance the country's success in public education through the use of a centrally-produced televised curriculum. In 1968, the government issued a series of pronouncements on the potential of television in mass education. A Secretariat of State for Educational Television was formed in 1971, and in September of that year the first lessons were broadcast. Adult education programming was added in 1973. A ground station was added in 1976 to receive educational programming from a Franco-German satellite, and in the same year the Secretariat for Primary Instruction and Educational Television was upgraded to a ministry. However, by the late 1970s, important interests had surfaced in opposition to the program, and they were allowed open expression in Fraternité-Matin in 1980. In 1981, the Ministry announced a reduction in the role of television in the curriculum, and 1982 was the last year in which television was used in the primary schools. The ETV program promoted the infusion of resources into the country's educational system, but the technology itself did not live up to the ambitious expectations outlined for it, such as stemming the flow of rural-urban migration. Moreover, by the 1980s most of the foreign aid directed at ETV had expired, and the Ivoirian government would have had to shoulder the entire cost. (994, 1008, 1011, 1026, 1027)

EHUI, BERNARD. Entered the government in 1983 to head the recently-created Ministry of Industry. (June 1985).

EKRA, VANGAH MATHIEU. (1917-   ). One of Houphouët's closest lieutenants and most recently Minister of State charged with the Reform of State Enterprises. Ekra is of Dan origins, his father a planter. He attended the Ecole Ponty, then trained as an administrator and served in various posts in French West Africa, one of which was in Kankan, Guinea. There, in 1946, he set up a branch of the RDA and was elected its Secretary General. He was an early (1947) member of the Groupe d'Etudes Communistes (q.v.). The next year he was admitted to the Executive Committee of the PDCI in Abidjan. In 1949 he was placed under preventive detention for three years by colonial officials for his activities as Secretary-General of the RDA branch in Abidjan. Upon his release, he was made head accountant at the Institut Francais d'Afrique Noire (IFAN). In 1956 he attended the National School of Overseas France in Paris and was attached to the cabinet of the French Overseas Ministry and then to the French High Commissioner in the Ivory Coast.

He was named to the Abidjan municipal council in 1956 and became a member of the National Assembly in 1959. At the same time, he was named the Political Bureau's Secretary for Mass Education. In 1960 he headed the Ivory Coast delegation to the United Nations. From 1961 to 1963 he was Minister of Public Service and Information, and from 1965 to 1970, Minister of Information. Since 1970

he has been responsible for Press Affairs for the
Political Bureau of the PDCI, of which he has been a member since 1965. Ekra was made a Minister of State in 1970,
a title changed to Minister of State for Tourism in 1971, and
to Minister of State for Interior in 1974.
Ekra was given the task of reforming the state sector
of the economy in 1977. Against great political influence,
he succeeded in eliminating a large number of heads of
parastatal corporations and in bringing others under direct
government budgetary control. Ekra is considered one of
the stronger candidates to succeed Houphouët. (760, 864)

ELECTIONS. The 1956 French election was the last fully
competitive electoral contest in the Ivory Coast. Territorial
Assembly elections in 1957 and 1959 were partially competitive, but a single-party unified national slate was the only
entry in the 1959 election, and in all elections until 1980,
when a semi-competitive election within the single party
provided a mechanism for deciding among the growing
number of contenders for political power. (760)

ELECTRICITY. See ENERGY.

ELEPHANT (LOXODONTA AFRICANA). The source of the
country's name, and a widely used symbol, this animal
was once abundant throughout the country. The elephant
was relentlessly hunted and has disappeared except for
limited numbers in the savannah-zone reserves of Bouna
and Marahoué and in the most dense forests of the south,
where there remain perhaps several thousand in all. They
are in danger of disappearing by 1995, as poachers and
continued development threaten them with extinction.
(4, 912)

ENERGY. Dependency on foreign fuels decreased in the
1960s and 1970s because of hydroelectric development and,
in the 1980s, the expansion of domestic petroleum production. The Ivory Coast is not energy self-sufficient, but
fuel oil consumption to generate electricity declined 57.7
percent between 1979 and 1983. Electric power is provided
in the Ivory Coast by Enérgie Electrique de la Côte d'Ivoire
(EECI), organized in 1952. Its capacity has steadily increased with the opening of plants at Ayame I (1959),
Ayame II (1965), Vridi I (1968), Vridi II (1972), Kossou
(1972), and Vridi III and IV (1976); the Taabo Dam was

completed in 1979, bringing capacity to 510 mw, and the Buyo Dam on the Sassandra added another 165 mw. The opening of another at Soubré was delayed but is still in the plans. A severe drought in 1983 effectively reduced output from this largely hydro-electric base to the point where there were serious power outages; however, if the Soubré Dam were ever to be completed it would make self-sufficiency a reasonalbe prospect. Electricity is produced and distributed by Energie Electrique de Cote d'Ivoire, a state utility. There are over 300,000 users of electricity in nearly 1,000 villages. (374, 505, 528)

ENTENTE COUNCIL (Conseil de l'Entente). International organization created in April 1959, consisting of Benin, Niger, Togo, Burkina Faso (formerly Upper Volta) and the Ivory Coast. Following his defeat of the Mali Federation (q.v.) concept, Houphouët sought to replace it with an organization of francophone African states that would allow each to associate directly with France. To check movement toward a more federalist approach, he applied various pressures and offered a range of inducements to other francophone West African governments to entice them into what he called the Entente Council. Niger's Hamani Diori was the easiest to convince, for Niger's arid environment dictated the need for support from France and its wealthier neighbor, the Ivory Coast. Upper Volta was already economically dependent on the Ivory Coast, with 45,000 Voltaic nationals working seasonally on Ivoirian properties and 45 percent of Upper Volta's exports going to the Ivory Coast. Houphouët offered a common customs union, in which duties collected in Abidjan would be shared with Ouagadougou, and shared management of the Abidjan-Ouagadougou rail line. Dahomey was also made to see economic advantage in alliance with the Ivory Coast and France. With French support, the Ivory Coast was able to channel four billion francs CFA into the Entente states' "Solidarity Fund."

The Entente Council is directed by the prime ministers of each member state, who meet annually on a rotation basis in each capital under the chairmanship of that country's prime minister. The Solidarity Fund was established by a contribution of one-tenth of each member state's revenues. (836, 837)

ETABLISSEMENTS PUBLICS. See PUBLIC ESTABLISHMENTS.

EUROPEAN ECONOMIC COMMUNITY (EEC). An organization of most western European countries that has, since its creation by the Treaty of Rome in 1957, worked toward the creation of a common market of member states without internal tariffs but with a common external tariff and with common policies on agriculture, transportation, and monetary and fiscal policy. France and Belgium were still colonial powers when the treaty was negotiated, and they successfully incorporated their colonial policies into it. Thus, the treaty provides that member states shall apply the same rules in their commercial relations with associated countries and territories as they apply among themselves. The principal benefit to African states was a reduction of the tariff on tropical products to 25 percent within four years, and another 50 percent reduction within eight years. An additional advantage for the former colonies was the creation of the Overseas Development Fund, later called the European Development Fund. In the Ivoirian case, the treaty brought the duty on coffee and cocoa down from 16 and 9 percent respectively to 9.6 and 5.4 percent. Of a total French price support contribution of $325 million, 60 percent went to coffee, the Ivory Coast's principal export. Finally, in the first ten years, the Ivory Coast received $39.6 million from the Overseas Development Fund, second only to Senegal in receipts from this source. The relationship of the former colonies to the EEC was renegotiated upon their independence in the Yaounde Convention (q.v.). About one-half of Ivoirian trade is with the EEC. (374, 836, 839)

EVOLUES. In French colonial parlance, "evolved" Africans, those who had adopted certain aspects of French culture, especially language, religion, and lifestyle, as a result of formal education. In the Ivory Coast these included lower-level functionaries, employees of European private companies, and sometimes planters who had attended school. The colonial authorities were ambivalent toward evolues, disturbed by their attraction to "Garveyism" and the difficulty of fitting them into the colonial social structure, but supportive of their acceptance of metropolitan values.

EXPORTS. See Table 3.

- F -

FADIKA, LAMINE (1943-   ). Ivoirian Minister of Maritime
Affairs since 1974. A Malinké, he is considered one of
the youngest possible successors to Houphouët as President.
From 1964-66 he attended the French Naval School. He
was named commander of the Ivoirian Navy from 1970-73
and attended the Advanced School of Naval War (Ecole
Supérieure de Guerre Navale) in Paris in 1973-74. (760)

FAIDHERBE, LOUIS-LEON-CESAR (1818-89). French general,
colonizer, and Governor of Senegal (1854-61, 1863-65).
He wrote extensively on African anthropology and language,
and explored the lagoon and coastal region of the Ivory
Coast, following the course of the Comoé River.

FERKESSEDOUGOU. City established in the nineteenth century by Ferkessé, a Niarafola chief pushed there by the
ruler of Kong. It is the northernmost railway center in
the country. The government has established large sugar
plantations there, and a sugar refinery with a 50,000-ton
capacity. It is one of six regional centers designated in
the 1976-80 plan for the development of processing industries for regional produce. (438)

FONDS D'INVESTISSEMENT POUR LE DEVELOPPEMENT ECONO-
MIQUE ET SOCIAL (FIDES). A development fund established
by the French government in 1946 for the colonial areas.
FIDES offered grants and long-term, low interest loans
through the Caisse Centrale de la France d'Outre-Mer.
Most of the loans were cancelled in the post-independence
period. FIDES was an innovation in that, for the first
time, France used metropolitan funds for colonial development rather than follow the principle that colonies should
be strictly self-supporting. However, the colonial adminis-
trations also contributed to FIDES projects under their
jurisdictions. Between 1947 and 1957, the Ivory Coast received $109 million, which placed it second only to Senegal
in FIDES receipts.

FORCED LABOR. Work without pay as a form of extraction
by the colonial administration. From the earliest days of
European contact, indigenous populations had been pressed
into service to fill labor needs. Until 1912 there was no
uniform policy on the matter, with various local agents

using forced labor as needed for portage and road and
camp construction. The arrêté of 1907 establishing the
indigénat (q.v.) identified refusal to accept a labor assignment as a punishable infraction. All adult males between
the ages of 15 and 50 were required to furnish a given
number of days of labor per year. This was the first universal application of the concept and demonstrated the increased military presence, the need for labor, and the
lack of capital newly characteristic of the colonial situation.
In 1913, a circular set the number of days required in each
cercle.

About 200 French planters controlled one third of Ivoirian
coffee and cocoa production by the late 1930s; however,
they had difficulty attracting laborers given better pay and
working conditions in neighboring Gold Coast (Ghana). To
help the planters, the colonial administration enlarged the
nature of forced labor to include work on plantations.
This was the most detested aspect of colonial rule in the
Ivory Coast, and Houphouët-Boigny campaigned for a seat
in the French Constituent Assembly in 1945 on the promise
that he would see forced labor ended. In Paris, Houphouët
introduced a bill calling for the abolition of forced labor
by non-citizens in all of overseas France. The proposal
attracted little attention in a France just getting reorganized
after World War II, and it passed with neither a floor debate nor a roll-call vote. In Africa, however, its impact
was enormous, and it consolidated Houphouët's political
fortunes. His clever use of political leverage in Paris per-
manently established Houphouët's reputation for effective
leadership. (668)

FOREIGN AID. Since independence, the Ivory Coast has been
a major recipient of financial aid from France, both direct
and indirect. In the first ten years of independence, that
aid totaled about 50 billion francs CFA (approximately $200
million). By 1970, France was supporting 2,476 technical
personnel in the Ivory Coast. (401, 493, 836, 995)

FOREIGN RELATIONS. Since independence, the Ivory Coast
has maintained a consistent foreign policy of close cooperation with France and the West. While moving toward independence, the Ivoirian leadership opposed strong federal
ties among the former West African colonies, as embodied
in the Mali Federation (q.v.). Rather, they supported the
principle developed in the loi-cadre (q.v.) of bilateral ties

between each of the new governments and Paris. The Ivory
Coast also initiated the Entente Council, a subregional
economic organization in which it would be predominant. It
has generally been on good terms with its neighbors, with
the exceptions of Ghana under Kwame Nkrumah (until 1966)
and Guinea before 1978; in recent years the relationship
with more radical governments in Burkina Faso and Ghana
have been less than warm, but correct. Ivoirian influence
in Africa has at times been limited by its pro-western
stance, but particularly by Houphouët's advocacy since the
late 1960s of "dialogue" with South Africa: to the extreme
disapproval of most other leaders, Houphouët met with former
Prime Minister Vorster twice in the 1970s, and has called
for negotiations between black states and South Africa in
the 1980s. (394, 829-841)

FORESTRY. Hardwood timber production has been a key factor
in Ivorian prosperity since independence: the Ivory Coast
is the most important exporter of forest products in Africa,
producing foreign exchange earnings from this source of
about 85 billion CFA francs ($193 million) annually. Pro-
duction increased from 49,000 tons in 1947 to 109,000 in
1950, 212,000 in 1956, and 655,000 in 1960. It reached a
peak in 1976. About three fourths of the wood exported
passes through Abidjan, the rest through San Pedro, with
Italy the most important market.

The industry's future is threatened with depletion of
forest reserves: from 15 million hectares in 1956, they fell
to 11 million in 1966, 5.4 million in 1974, and 4 million in
1978. At the current rate of exploitation, the stock will
be depleted by the year 2000. Two rare woods, iroko and
kondroti, can no longer be exported. Another, assamela,
has almost disappeared. The most common variety now exported is samba. There was massive waste in logging from
the earliest times; because of transportation difficulties,
especially in dry years when the rivers were shallow, logs
were cut and left behind in large quantities. The government goal is a reforestation rate of 10,000 hectares per
year; they received a World Bank loan of 10 billion francs
CFA for this purpose and established, in 1966, a forest development organization, SODEFOR. (495, 520, 914, 915, 930)

FOUTOU. Boiled plaintain or manioc pureé, a common staple
in the forest zone.

FRANC ZONE. A monetary transaction organization composed
of France and thirteen of her former colonies to provide a
freely convertible currency among them. It was first organized after World War II, and reorganized after the
movement to independence. The regional CFA currency
of the former West African states is pegged at equity to
the Equatorial African franc and to the French franc at
the rate of 50 CFA francs = 1 French franc.

FRENCH, THE. The people of the former colonizing power
constitute an important minority population in the Ivory
Coast. There were about 50,000 French citizens there in
the early 1980s, the largest number in any country outside
France (although not the highest per capita), on about the
same level as in Morocco and Algeria. The total has diminished some in the Ivory Coast in recent years. Almost
four fifths of the French in the Ivory Coast have lived
there more than five years. The Ivory Coast has the
greatest number of French technical assistants in Africa,
the largest proportion of French imports and exports of
any African country, the largest number of students in
French universities, and the highest number of large French
firms in any African country. French influence on policy-
making in development-related ministries has made it difficult for non-French investors to compete, in spite of
official interest in diversification. The large French presence has also entailed a heavy balance-of-payments cost
for imported goods and services, as well as in the repatriation of salaries. (1128)

FRESCO. A small port between Grand Lahou and Sassandra,
on the Ngni Lagoon. The historic town site has been abandoned for a safer one on the mainland; the colonial build-
ings, on a narrow barrier island that is constantly threatened by high tides and lagoon floods, are slowly decaying.

- G -

GADEAU, GERMAIN KOFFI (1915-). Grand Chancellor of
the National Order, Gadeau held several ministries between
1961 and 1976. Considered a possible compromise candidate
to succeed Houphouët as President, in spite of his Baule
origins. Koffi Gadeau attended the Ecole Ponty and the
Law Faculty at the University of Dakar. From 1935 to 1955

he served as an accountant in the Treasury, and from 1955 to 1960 was President of the Financial Commission. He began his political activity as a member of the Groupe d'Etudes Communistes and it was he who nominated Houphouët to be a candidate to the French Constituent Assembly in 1946. Upon independence he was named Minister of Internal Affairs and from 1963 to 1968 served as State Comptroller. In 1971 he was appointed Minister of State and in 1975 was named to the Political Bureau of the PDCI. He has a long interest in theater, having founded the Théatre de la Cote d'Ivoire in 1938 and the Center of Culture and Folklore of the Ivory Coast in 1953. (102, 760)

GAGNOA. Prefecture in south-central Ivory Coast and a center of the wood industry. The 1975 population was estimated at 42,000. Gagnoa is often considered a regional center for the Bete people.

GAGU (GAGOU, GBAN). People of south-central Ivory Coast thought to be the oldest resident group in the country. Early anthropological studies described them as shorter than neighboring groups, leading to speculation that they were a mixture of aboriginal pygmoids and later immigrants. Such practices as a continued reliance on gathering as a supplement to agriculture and the recent continued use of bark as a material for clothing and bedding supported this supposition. The evidence of distinction has disappeared rapidly with assimilation into the Guro (q.v.) culture. (The first language of most Gagu is Guro.) They number about 20,000. (4, 5, 580, 1131-1132, 1158)

GARBA, DICOH (1937-). Minister of Animal Production since 1970.

GBAGBO, LAURENT. A university lecturer and critic of the Ivoirian political economy. In 1982 he circulated a suppressed speech he had intended to deliver on democracy and the advantages of a multiparty system. These thoughts were expanded in his monograph La Côte d'Ivoire: Pour une alternative démocratique. (1983). (864)

GERVAIS, JEANNE. (1922-). The first and only woman minister in an Ivoirian government (Women's Affairs, appointed 1976). She was one of the first three women elected to the National Assembly just after independence, as Vice-President of the Ivoirian Women's Association (AFI). She was later President of the AFI. (760)

GNOLEBA, MAURICE SERY (1935-). Minister of State; formerly Minister of Industry and Planning and, from 1974 to 1977, Minister of Trade. A member of the Executive Committee of the PDCI, he is considered one of its Kru-Bete leaders. (760)

GODIE. A people of the Kru ethnic cluster, closely related to the Dida (and sometimes included with them), centered in South-eastern Ivory Coast around the town of Lakota. (166-168, 1114, 1135-1136)

GOLD. Mined in the Ivory Coast and traded at the Niger River for centuries: Arab documents refer to the gold trade in the old empires of Ghana and Mali between the ninth and sixteenth centuries. Akan place names including "sika" (Sikassué, Assikasso) mark sites of traditional mining. Gold export direct to Europe began in the seventeenth century, at first largely through the Nzima people. Gold has great importance in the symbolism of Akan-culture chieftaincies and as a general cultural symbol for wealth and riches. It was mined in the Ivory Coast near Tou-modi, at Kokumbo (q.v.). The first European mining concession was granted in 1895; the competition for concessions ended about 1910, when all the most likely territories had been alloted, with disappointing results. (597, 609, 642, 974, 1042, 1046)

GOLDWEIGHTS. Small objects cast in bronze or brass and used among Akan-speaking peoples to measure the weight of gold dust, a traditional medium of exchange. These goldweights were cast in an extremely wide variety of forms: human, animal, and as utensils and carved boxes. They are now highly prized as art objects. (88, 90-91, 944)

GOLI (GORI). Ethnic group identified by Delafosse (q.v.) as living between the White Bandama and the Fa River, but having been completely integrated into the immigrant Baule-Warébo culture in the pre-colonial period. (4)

GOLY KOUASSI, MICHEL (1932-). Minister of Construction and Town Planning from 1966 to 1970. Goly Kouassi studied architecture in Paris and in 1964 became Secretary of State in the Ministry of Construction and Town Planning.

GONFREVILLE. Cotton textile mill established by Robert Gonfreville, a Frenchman, at Bouaké in 1919. It was the first such mill in French West Africa and grew into the present textile complex of the same name, but was taken over by a large French textile company and foreign banks. Etablissements Gonfreville employs 3,000 workers today. They are known for their modern specialization in table linens. (472)

GOUIN. Small Voltaic ethnic group inhabiting about ten villages in the Ivory Coast north of Ferkéssédougou.

GOUR. See VOLTAIC.

GOURO. See GURO.

GOVERNORS--FRENCH.

Lieutenant Governors:

1893-1895	Louis-Gustave BINGER
1895-1896	Pierre-Hubert-August PASCAL
1896	Eugene BERTIN
1896-1898	Louis MOUTTET
1898-1899	Adrien-Jules-Jean BONHOURE
1899	Pierre-Paul-Marie CAPEST
1899-1902	Henri-Charles-Victor-Amedee ROBERDEAU
1902-1908	Marie-Francois-Joseph CLOZEL
1908-1916	Louis-Gabriel ANGOULVANT
1916-1918	Maurice-Pierre LAPALUD
1918-1924	Raphael-Valentin-Marius ANTONETTI
1924-1925	Richard-Edmond-Maurice-Edouard BRUNOT
1925-1930	Maurice-Pierre LAPALUD
1930	Jules BREVIE
1931-1935	Dieudonne-Francois-Joseph-Marie RESTE
1935-1936	Adolphe DEITTE
1936-1937	Gaston-Charles-Julien MONDON

Governors:

1937-1939	Gaston-Charles-Julien MONDON
1939-1941	Horace-Valentin CROCICCHIA
1941-1942	Hubert-Jules DESCHAMPS
1942-1943	Georges-Pierre REY
1943-1947	Andre-Jean-Gaston LATRILLE

1947-1948	Oswald-Marcellin-Maurice-Marius DURAND
1948	Georges-Louis-Joseph ORSELLI
1948-1951	Laurent-Elisee PECHOUX
1951-1952	Pierre-Francois PELIEU
1952-1954	Camille-Victor BAILLY
1954-1956	Pierre-Joseph-Auguste MESSMER
1956-1957	Pierre-August-Michel-Marie LAMI
1957-1958	Ernest De NATTES

High Commissioners:

| 1959 | Ernest DE NATTES |
| 1959-1960 | Yves-Rene-Henri GUENA |

GRAH, KADJI (1932-). A member of the Political Bureau of the PDCI. Grah is an Alladian; he received his teaching certificate in Paris in 1962 and an engineer's diploma from the National School of Bridges and Roads in Paris in 1964. From 1965 to 1967 he was Regional Director, and from 1967 to 1970, Director-General, for Public Works. He was Minister of Public Works and Transport from 1970 to 1974.

GRAND BASSAM. First colonial capital of the Ivory Coast, from 1895 to 1900. Established in 1842 as a commercial site under the protection of Fort Nemours, the city was devastated by a combined epidemic of plague and yellow fever in August 1899. An estimated two thirds of the European population died, and many others fled. A new, more ventilated site for a capital was chosen at Bingerville, but a wharf was constructed in 1901 that kept Grand Bassam alive economically: For 30 years, goods landed there and were transported to Abidjan via the Ebrié Lagoon. However, with the construction of the port of Abidjan and its railhead (extended to the coast in the early 1930s at Port Bouet), major economic activity gradually ended in Grand Bassam. The wharf was finally closed in 1951, when the Vridi Canal opened at Abidjan.

Recently the Office Nationale de L'Artisanat d'Art has established an artisans' village at Grand Bassam, where representatives of the various ethnic groups of the country explain their work and sell it at marked prices. The Center for Architectural and Urban Research at the University of Abidjan was charged with developing a recently completed plan of restoration of Grand Bassam. (681, 1186)

GRAND LAHOU. Port city on the central Ivoirian coast at

the mouth of the Bandama River, on a narrow barrier island
at the risk of high tides and lagoon flooding. It was first
mentioned by a European in a 1698 narrative and appeared
on a 1729 French map. In 1787 a treaty was signed between
Louis XVI and the chief of the Brignan (Avikam). A
series of treaties was concluded there in 1844-1868 for
France by Fleuriot de Langle, but there was no permanent
European emplacement until commercial houses were built
in 1890, followed by a military post in 1892. Grand Lahou
took on some importance in the European trade of the mid-
nineteenth century, exporting slaves, ivory, and gold from
the interior. This trade was augmented by the export of
rubber from Tiassale, and by 1904 Grand Lahou was described as the most important port in the colony. Subsequently, however, with the replacement of wild rubber by
stock grown on plantations, this trade role was diminished.
As palm oil replaced rubber and luxury exports in importance, Grand Lahou fell into obscurity. Exports ceased
completely in 1941 and did not begin again after the war.
Grand Lahou had a 1910 population of 6,700, down to 3,000
in 1939, and only 4,000 now. It was a colonial chef-lieu
of the Cercle of Lahou and is now a sub-prefecture. (631,
724)

GREAT DEPRESSION (1929-1931). The French Empire suffered
under the Great Depression; its effects were especially
long and deep in Africa. The price of palm oil fell from
252 francs per 100 kg. in 1929 to 156 francs in July 1930,
and to 146 francs in November of that year. The prices
of the six basic commodities of French West Africa fell 70
to 90 percent by 1934. The drop in customs receipts led
authorities to increase the head tax (q.v.), while the drop
in prices for commercial crops reduced farmers' income.
Revenues fell in the Ivory Coast by 92 million francs from
1927 to 1932. One effect was accelerated migration to the
towns: Abidjan had a population of 9,000 in 1926, but
grew to 17,500 in 1936. The drop in cocoa prices (from
487 francs in 1927 to 90 francs in 1935) caused a shift from
cocoa to coffee, which was relatively better priced. (673)

GREBO. An ethnie of the Kru language group, but differing
from other Kru groups in important cultural aspects. They
have traditionally raised plantain bananas, rice, and sugar
cane. From the latter they distill a type of rum which they
call "cane juice," mostly in Liberia where control is more

lax, and from where it is sold into the Ivory Coast.

GROUPE D'ETUDES COMMUNISTES (GEC). A creation of the French Communist Party, which set up "study offices" in Abidjan and other West African cities. The title GEC was adopted in 1945. The GEC in the Ivory Coast was led by French Communists at first, without African members. In 1946 a program was developed around issues of particular interest in the Ivory Coast, where by 1947 there were about 40 members. According to official history, Houphouët was not a member but did attend several meetings. The GEC provided the first political education to early leaders of the PDCI, which helps to explain the apparentement of the PDCI with the Communist Party in the French parliament and the early structure and methods of the PDCI. Two French leaders of the GEC, P. Francheschi and M. Tremouille, were both active in the first days of the PDCI. In 1946-47, the GEC served as an intermediary for the Communist trade union (the CGT) to sponsor training sessions on the formation of unions.

GUERE. People of the Kru ethnic cluster, traditionally residing in west-central Ivory Coast. Closely related to the Wobe (q.v.), with whom they consciously share beliefs and customs, and with whom they are sometimes classified as a single ethnie. Guere social institutions and life style are also very similar to those of the Dan. These two cultures differed most notably in their mask styles: in contrast to the simple, realistic Dan masks, those of the Guere are imaginative and surrealistic. Female initiation societies have been maintained, and age classes of both sexes are still prominent; a singular cultural trait is the presence of women chiefs. Guere society is characterized by weak political authority beyond the lineage or village, with spiritual leadership a separate role. Until recently, the Guere were exclusively subsistence farmers, but they have recently entered into cash cropping, with concomitant rapid social and economic change. Gueres emigrating to other areas have been particularly recruited into police work. (169, 650, 1137-1141)

GURO (GOURO, KOUENI, KWENI). A patrilineal ethnic group estimated to number about 110,000 in 1968, traditionally located between the Bete to the West and the Baule to the East, in the west-central area of the Ivory Coast. They call themselves <u>Kweni</u>, the term "Guro" coming from Baule. They are of Mande origin and language family, and entered the forest region several centuries ago, perhaps under pressure from Maninka migration. Their movement to the east was halted by that of the Baule in the opposite direction. The French put down the last major Guro resistance to colonial rule in 1907.

There has been considerable intermarriage and cultural diffusion with neighboring groups, particularly the Gagu, Wan, and Bete. According to Ariane Deluz, the Baule learned wood sculpture and weaving from the Guro. Guro socio-political structure was decentralized to the village level, with no institutionalized or hereditary chieftaincy. They are also characterized by the presence of exclusive societies. The Guro were without a common consciousness of their identity as such until so identified by the French colonial authorities. They traditionally grew plaintain, manioc, yams, and taro; more recently they have planted rice and have entered into cash cropping of coffee, cocoa, and cotton. Those Guro living in the south of the Ivory Coast also have palm oil plantations and kola trees. These changes have seriously disrupted Guro marriage and family stability. (76, 170, 371, 678, 762, 1142-1158)

GYAMAN. Abron (or Brong) kingdom between the Comoé and Black Volta rivers, on the margin between the savannah and forest, in what is now northeastern Ivory Coast and northwestern Ghana. It was founded about 1690 by Gyamanhene Tan Date and fell under Ashanti domination in 1740. Gyaman regained its independence in 1875, after the defeat of Ashanti by the British, and experienced a period of expansion between 1875 and 1886. Samory invaded in 1895, and shortly thereafter the French occupied the western part (1897) while the British moved into the east. The Abron were a numerical minority in Gyaman but established their dominance, especially over the Kulango, through a combination of diplomacy and force. (582, 618, 654-657, 1033, 1126)

- H -

HAMALLISM. An Islamic reform movement that originated in Mali (then French Sudan) early in the twentieth century. It was introduced into the Ivory Coast by Cheick Hamallah,

who was exiled to Ivory Coast in the 1930s. Hamallism
is characterized by greater acceptance of traditional African
religious practices than are the more orthodox Islamic sects.
(828)

HARMATTAN. Hot, dry air mass moving south into the Ivory
Coast from the Sahara Desert. Where it reaches ground
level, it produces low humidity and rainfall, in other words,
the dry season. This season is defined by the presence
of the harmattan from November to April in northern Ivory
Coast, from November to February at the seventh parallel,
and from December to February along the Coast (where
the harmattan rarely reaches all the way to ground level).

HARRIS, WILLIAM WADE (1850/65-1929). Christian evangelist
and inspiration of the Harrist Church of the Ivory Coast.
Harris was a Liberian, of the Grebo people, born in the
village of Graway near the Ivory Coast border. As a
youth he was baptized a Methodist, although he later left
the Methodist church and became a lay preacher in the
Episcopal church. His work experiences included a period
as a crewman on a British merchant ship traveling the
West African coast, which among other things exposed him
to the separatist churches in Nigeria. Following a period
of work as a bricklayer, Harris became an assistant teacher
at an Episcopal mission. Because of involvement in a local
conflict between the Grebo people and Liberio-Americans,
he lost his teaching job, and, after several additional in-
cidents that marked him as a troublemaker, was imprisoned
for more than a year for treason. While in prison, he experienced a vision in which the Angel Gabriel commanded
him to become a prophet. In 1913, soon after his release,
he headed for the Ivory Coast where he moved from village
to village. He called upon the villagers to forsake their
traditional beliefs and accept Christianity. He was highly
successful in persuading large numbers of people to accept
baptism and to present themselves to Protestant or Catholic
missionaries for instruction and acceptance into a church.
   Harris crossed the Ivory Coast and entered the Gold
Coast, where he also made many converts. Colonial authorities there found his activities disruptive, and after three
months he was asked to leave. He returned to the Ivory
Coast, where he worked until expelled by the French
authorities in December 1914.
   Harris' proselytizing activities had found approval, at

first, with Catholic and French colonial authorities, since
he called on the population to address themselves to the
established missions and to accept established authority.
Later, however, they began to suspect him of encouraging
English-language Protestantism, a combination both groups
found objectionable.

Some of his followers became Catholics, and larger
numbers joined the established Protestant churches:
Harris' campaign is generally accepted as laying the foundation for the contemporary Methodist Church in the Ivory
Coast. Indeed, a Methodist missionary went to visit him
in Liberia and returned with Harris' written instructions
that his followers become Methodists. Many of those who
accepted his beliefs were not satisfied with any existing
church, however, and one village also sent an emissary to
him to seek his advice. That emissary, John Ahui (q.v.),
returned to the Ivory Coast claiming to be Harris' spiritual
heir.

HARRIST CHURCH. A syncretistic religious organization
indigenous to the Ivory Coast. The impetus for its formation was the visit to the territory in 1913-14 of William
Wade Harris (q.v.), who preached the abandonment of
traditional beliefs and the adoption of Christianity. He in-
structed his converts to present themselves to Catholic or
Protestant missionaries for further instruction. Large numbers of them followed this instruction but were unhappy
with the missionaries' unwillingness to accommodate to
various aspects of their culture. In 1928, a delegation was
sent from the village of Petit Bassam to Harris in Liberia,
to complain of their difficulties; they returned with a "last
will and testament" written by Harris and with the message
that one of them, John Ahui (q.v.), had been named by
Harris as his successor in the Ivory Coast. Ahui and a
few disciples traveled throughout the lagoon and coastal
regions of the territory and were accepted by large numbers
of those who had been influenced by Harris. The church
was institutionalized at a conference in Petit Bassam in
1955, and Ahui was recognized as the group's "supreme
prophet." The number of Harrists is reported to have
increased substantially around Grand-Bassam and Alépé
at the time of the formation of the PDCI, with some calling
Harrism "the religion of Houphouët," and seeing it as an
African national religion. There are an estimated 100,000
Harrists in the Ivory Coast, principally among the Ebrie

and neighboring coastal ethnic groups.

Harrists believe that W. W. Harris was sent by God to save the Africans, just as Jesus was sent "to save the whites." However, they consider themselves to be Christians, and the Bible is central to their faith; a Harrist national committee was formed in 1961, designated as representing the "Church of Christ, Harrist Mission." As with many such movements in Africa, Harrist beliefs stress the benefits God brings to believers in this life rather than in the next. Their numbers are concentrated in the most developed region of the country, and they interpret their relative prosperity as a sign of God's favor. Conversely, misfortune is seen to result from sin, usually through the direction of witchcraft practices against others. Thus, witchcraft is condemned, but its persistence is offered as the explanation for misfortune (that is, to the evildoer, not to the potential victim). They interpret the greater wealth and technological advantage of Europeans as resulting from their longer association with Christianity.

Harrist belief allows the practice of polygyny, as long as all wives and children are treated fairly; however, ministers must be monogamous.

Students of the Harrist movement explain its success and perserverance as the result of timing and context: Harris entered the Ivory Coast just after traditional religious practices had been shown ineffective as protection from the colonial system. The new movement provided guidance for success in the new situation, providing functional replacements for traditional institutions but drawing on indigenous beliefs and practices. Although Ivoirian youth who move successfully into a modern urban lifestyle tend to view Harrism as lacking in social status, the church is now accepted by Ivory Coast authorities as a legitimate member of its religiously pluralist society. (1230-1240, 1242-1254)

HEAD TAX. The earliest form of fiscal support for the colonial administration of the Ivory Coast. The (French) finance law of 1900 obligated colonies to be self-supporting. In an arrêté of 1901, Lt. Governor Clozel (q.v.) set a head tax of 2.50 francs per month on each man, woman, and child over the age of ten. Tax roles were prepared each year based on the census, and approved by the Governor, to be collected by local chiefs. At first, the head tax could be paid in cash or kind based on going rates for gold, ivory,

rubber, or other cash-value produce. Later, various categories of exemptions, as for military service, were established. The canton chiefs originally kept 25 percent of
what they collected, but this was reduced in 1904 to 10
percent. At that time, a flexible rate was also established,
based on the wealth of the district, from 1.50 to 4.50
francs. The tax continued to increase until 1919, and in
some areas until 1935, reaching 50 francs in some southern
areas. The head tax was abolished in the reforms of 1946,
but some peasants continued sending a portion of their
harvest to local chiefs even after independence, unaware
that this was no longer required. (662, 667)

HOLAS, BOHUMIL (1909-1979). A prolific author on African
religion and ethnography, Holas came to Abidjan with IFAN.
At independence the local affiliate of IFAN was converted
into the Centre des Sciences Humaines under the Ministry
of Education, with Holas as its director. He directed the
Center's research activities and maintained its National
Ethnographic Museum in Abidjan.

HOUPHOUËT-BOIGNY, FELIX (1905-   ). First and only
president of the Republic of the Ivory Coast and founder
of the Democratic Party of the Ivory Coast (PDCI). Born
in Yamoussoukro (according to some sources, closer to
1900 than the officially stated 1905), then a small village
in the south central area of the country, he is a Baule of
the Akuwe group. Houphouët graduated from the Ecole
Ponty in Dakar in 1925 as a médecin africain (African
physician), one of the first of his ethnic group or from
the Ivory Coast colony to complete the entire course of
education provided under the colonial system. This gave
him status within the educated stratum but did not remove
him from the African political scene as education in France
did some of his compatriots. He served in the colonial
medical service in various posts in the colony until 1940.
In 1933, while stationed in Abengourou, he became interest-
ed in efforts to organize the African cocoa and coffee
growers. During the same tour of duty he married his
first wife; she was of royal Agni descent on her mother's
side, with a Senegalese father. He thus acquired kinship
ties with another major Akan group and with the foreign
African community.
    Through the death of his maternal uncle in 1940, he
fell heir to large amounts of land at Yamoussoukro and was

appointed canton chief of the Akuwe. He took the lead in
organizing the Association of Customary Chiefs (Association
des Chefs Coutumiers), thus extending his influence among
traditional leaders throughout the colony. He widened his
base of support still further when, in 1944, he was elected
first president of the Syndicat Agricole Africain (SAA,
q.v.), an organization of African planters formed in reaction
to racial discrimination by the white-dominated planters'
organization and the price-support policies of the colonial
government.

In August 1945 elections were held for the Abidjan
Municipal Council. European and African citizens, along
with some subjects, were chosen on a common roll among
slates composed of nine subjects and nine citizens each.
Some slates were proposed that included both Europeans
and Africans, while some African contenders put forth
lists dominated by a single ethnic group. Houphouët proposed an innovation that was radical in the context: an exclusively African slate distributed among major ethnic
groups. Most African contenders then withdrew and European voters abstained in protest. The African Block (q.v.)
won an overwhelming victory.

The first election to the French Constituent Assembly
in which Africans participated was held in October 1945
with separate electoral colleges for citizens and non-citizens.
Houphouët was the SAA candidate in the second (non-
citizen) college. He failed to get an absolute majority
in a first round crowded with candidates, and his large
plurality became a bare majority against an Upper Voltan
candidate in the runoff. In Paris, Houphouët fulfilled
a campaign pledge to work against the indigenat (q.v.)
by introducing a bill calling for the abolition of forced
labor by non-citizens in all of overseas France. The proposal attracted little attention in a France just getting
reorganized after World War II, and it passed with neither
a floor debate nor a roll-call vote. In Africa, however,
its impact was enormous, and it consolidated Houphouët's
political fortunes. Forced labor was the most hated aspect of subject status among the colonial populations, and
Houphouët was the person responsible for its removal. He
was re-elected overwhelmingly under a new constitution
in June 1946, running under the banner of the Democratic
Party of the Ivory Coast (Parti Démocratique de Côte
d'Ivoire, q.v.), associated in the Constituent Assembly
with the French Communist Party (PCF).

Houphouët-Boigny was a member of the French National
Assembly for fourteen years, ultimately holding ministerial
office. Because French domestic policy was relatively unim-
portant to him and to other African representatives, they
could use their few votes to good advantage in colonial
policy, their chief interest. Houphouët is reputed to have
developed considerable skill in negotiation and log-rolling
that carried over into his later leadership style. The alliance between the Rassemblement Démocratique Africain
(of which the PDCI was the Ivoirian branch) and the Communist Party, however, was to cause Houphouët and other
associated African leaders great difficulty. Houphouët saw
the alliance as politically expedient when the PCF participated in the French government. When they moved perma-
nently into opposition and took an active role in the stri-
dently ideological politics of 1947-48, the alliance became a
handicap, and Houphouët looked highly suspect to conservative colonial interests. The PDCI entered into a period in
which it was constantly harassed and its activists disen-
franchised and jailed by the colonial administration.
Houphouët was protected from arrest by his parliamentary
status, but his immunity was popularly attributed to his own
special powers and prestige. However, he was becoming less
sanguine about the benefits presumed to flow from continued
involvement with the PCF and in 1950 made the decision to
break with the Communists and accept a reconciliation with
the French government. Thus, while the PDCI organization
was battered and disrupted by colonial persecution, Houphouët's position became more secure. By the early 1950s
he was undisputed head of the party and seemed to the
colonial administration the obvious choice as spokesman for
the Ivoirian population in the move toward independence.

Houphouët rebuilt the party under his firm control, in
the classic style of a political machine, and managed with
great shrewdness to ally the PDCI to leaders of the dominant parties in various government coalitions. At the same
time, his policy focus shifted to the economic growth of
the Ivory Coast, to the exclusion of the larger West African
Federation.

Houphouët was re-elected to the French National Assembly in 1951. In 1956 he was named mayor of Abidjan and
also entered the French government at the ministerial level.
In 1957 he was elected President of the Grand Council of
French West Africa, as well as President of the Ivory Coast
Territorial Assembly. Thus, he held office at four levels:
municipal, territorial, French West Africa, and French.

As a minister in the French government, Houphouët
played a central role in the drafting of the loi-cadre, or
"framework law," which moved the French overseas territories toward internal autonomy.

The grant of independence to the Gold Coast in March
1957 found a cool reception in Abidjan. Houphouët's
vision for the future was largely that of De Gaulle: a
federal community of equal francophone states. He proclaimed that African countries had little to gain from
"nominal independence." When France offered a referendum
on membership in the Communauté Française in 1958 (of-
fering as an alternative independence free of any financial
or administrative support), Houphouët campaigned in favor
of the Community and resigned his French cabinet position
to become Prime Minister of the Ivory Coast. However,
as other francophone colonies pushed for complete independence, particularly in neighboring Guinea, Houphouët
saw the likelihood that continued opposition to independence
would erode his political base. Accordingly, he participated
in the negotiations through which, on August 7, 1960, the
Ivory Coast became an independent republic. In November
of that year the Ivory Coast elected, without opposition,
Felix Houphouët-Boigny as its first president. He was re-
elected in the same fashion in 1965, 1970, 1975, 1980, and
1985.

The first years of independence were marked by spectacular economic growth, but also by several challenges to
the party and its leader. An attempted overthrow in 1963
resulted in 120 to 200 arrests and a series of secret trials
in Yamassoukro. Houphouët consolidated government responsibilities in himself. However, three years later, on the
fifth anniversary of independence, he released three former
ministers and 93 others accused in the plot and reduced
the sentences of ten others, commuting nine death sentences to life imprisonment.

Houphouët has astutely controlled the party and the
country by keeping possible contenders off guard. From
independence through the mid-1970s he delegated limited
powers to three lieutenants: August Denise (q.v.), Jean
Baptiste Mockey (q.v.) and Philippe Yacé (q.v.). He assigned responsibilities and honors in a way that kept as-
pirants in a state of tension, never sure if one or another
was favored. By the late 1970s, however, Mockey had not
shaken the President's suspicions (which originated in the
attempted coup of 1963), and Denise was growing old.

Faced with Yacé's growing influence, Houphouët removed
him as PDCI Secretary-General and President of the National Assembly and created a new nine-member Executive Committee for the PDCI, bringing in a new generation of politicians but promoting no one to second place. The post
of Vice-President was created in 1980, but was never filled
and was abolished again in 1985 at Houphouët's request
because of his annoyance with what he deemed unseemly
competition to be his successor.

Houphouët is respectfully identified as "le Vieux" ("The
Old Man") by most of his compatriots; his style of rule
involves a process known as "dialogue" (q.v.), "a combination of palaver and chiefly audiences under a tree." (695,
768, 828, 829, 842-844, 849, 850, 853, 855-861, 863, 864)

- I -

INCOME DISTRIBUTION. In 1981 it was estimated that there
was a 7-to-1 ratio of average income (including urban residents) between the north and south in the Ivory Coast.
A 1979 estimate showed average agricultural income at 29,000
CFA per annum, compared with an average non-agricultural
income of 165,000 CFA. (466). Nonetheless, Chenery
presents evidence that income inequality is less in the
Ivory Coast than in most African countries. In the
Ivoirian distribution, Europeans are at the top of the
range, then native Ivoirians, then the migrant population;
thus, the range among Ivoirians may be relatively flat.
Government policy is redistributive in that coffee and cocoa
have been taxed to develop agriculture and agricultural industry in the North: cocoa and coffee generate 90 percent
of tax receipts from agriculture, while sugar, cotton, and
rice received 93 percent of government subsidies. (270,
312, 428, 433, 466)

INDENIE. See NDENYE.

INDIGENAT. Term describing the broad disciplinary powers
of French colonial administrators over those individuals
under their jurisdiction who were not French citizens.
They could punish infractions without any form of required
legal process. The indigénat was encoded in two French
décrets (decrees) of 1912 and 1924. An administrative
arrêté instituted the indigénat in the Ivory Coast, enumer-

ating 46 infractions uniquely applicable to indigenous non-
citizens. Sixteen offenses were made punishable by up to
fifteen days in jail or a 100-franc fine. A decree of 1931
authorized French subjects to ask for cases to be heard in
French courts, but this provision was rarely applied. Under the French Popular Front government, there was further liberalization in a decree of 1937 which specified eleven
conditions to be met in order to become a French citizen.
(Less than one percent of the colonial population outside
the four communes of Senegal were citizens by 1937).
Under the Popular Front there was also some softening of
the application of the indigénat. Application became harsh
again, however, under the Vichy government's colonial administration during World War II. Felix Houphouët-Boigny's
political career was successfully launched by his success
in pushing through the French Constituent Assembly
abolition of the indigénat in 1946. See HOUPHOUET-BOIGNY;
FORCED LABOR.

INDUSTRY. Industrial output showed rapid growth in the
1960s and 1970s, with a total turnover of 143 billion francs
CFA in 1970 and 368 billion in 1980. However, industrial
employment rose more slowly, as did the value added by
industry. Thus, Ivoirian industry is highly capital inten-
sive, with a high import content, and is not well-linked to
other sectors. Primary products as a share of total exports
increased slightly between 1975 and 1980, and the share
for manufactured exports fell accordingly. Industrial production is concentrated in the textile and food-processing
industries. (472, 528-545, 561)

INSTITUT D'EMISSION DE L'AFRIQUE OCCIDENTAL FRAN-
CAISE ET DU TOGO (IEAOFT). Bank of currency issue for
French West Africa and Togo from 1955 to 1959, at which
time it was converted to the BCEAO (q.v.).

INTERNATIONAL COCOA ORGANIZATION (ICCO). Organization of cocoa producing and consuming countries, the
signatories of the International Cocoa Agreements. There
have been three such agreements since 1972. The Ivory
Coast signed that of 1975, but refused to sign the latest,
protesting that the floor intervention price was too low.
Countries controlling at least 80 percent of the export
market had to sign the agreement for it to take effect,
which gave the Ivory Coast a veto. It finally went into

effect without the signature of either the largest producer, the Ivory Coast, or the United States (which took the opposite position that the floor intervention price was too high). In 1979-80, the Ivory Coast tried unilaterally to support cocoa prices by withholding 150,000 tons from the market. However, other countries filled in, and the price slump continued. The Ivory Coast was eventually forced to sell at a loss. (428)

INVESTMENT. Soon after independence the Ivoirian government adopted a Code of Investment that encouraged foreign direct investment in real estate, industry, production, and assembly of consumer goods, plantations, mining, and power. Investors were guaranteed tax stability for 25 years and an exemption from duties on the import of raw materials. By 1965 such agreements had been completed with 45 firms having a joint capital of over $100 million. Eighty percent of foreign investment in 1967 was French, while only 3.7 percent was American. Earnings and dividends returned to France rose from $18.3 million in 1963 to $34.2 million in 1968, for an annual average rate of growth of 13 percent. (369, 462, 466, 472, 474, 477, 509, 510, 513, 514, 520, 541, 836)

ISLAM. Islam spread into the Ivory Coast across the savannah of the western Sudan. Of four codified versions of Islamic law, Malekite prevails in the Ivory Coast (and most of Africa). The Maninka rulers of Mali spread Islam through the savannah from the thirteenth to the eighteenth centuries. In the eighteenth century, the Moslem Dioula kingdom of Kong was established in the Ivory Coast. In the nineteenth century, Samory's invasions brought new Islamic elements to the country.

West African Islam is orthodox Sunni but generally retains local traditions and is more tolerant of diversity than elsewhere. It generally follows Sufism, a mystical movement organized into brotherhoods, who follow a great teacher and his spokesmen (marabouts). The brotherhood is a religious order but also offers adherents mutual aid and social discipline. There are four brotherhoods in the Ivory Coast: Qadiriya is dominant, and Tidjaniya is important. Followers of Senoussiya and Ahmadiya are few in number. Qadiriya was founded in the eleventh century in Iraq and came to West Africa in the fifteenth century, centered in Mauretania.

Ahmadiya blossomed in Abidjan in the 1960s and 70s, with over 650 adherents by 1978. It is originally from the Indian sub-continent, entering anglophone West Africa early in the twentieth century. They are the only non-Sunni Moslem brotherhood in West Africa and are distinctive in allowing women to participate in prayers and in their sponsorship of schools and hospitals.

The marabout is a curer and mystic, considered to have powerful fetish power even by non-Moslems. Wahabism, a reform ideology that originated in nineteenth-century Saudi Arabia, is a reaction to maraboutism; it was brought to a school in Bamako, Mali, attended by students from northern Ivory Coast and from Agboville. It was also spread by merchants returning from the hajj. It is especially influential in Bouake among rich Malinké merchants.

In 1955 there were 300 mosques, 970 Koranic schools, and over 320 marabouts in the country. The Encyclopedia of the Ivory Coast estimates there to be 500,000 Moslems. Islam has been making many converts, especially among the Mossi in the cities. (4, 64, 71, 452, 762, 1255-1262)

IVOIRIAN COMPANY FOR TEXTILE DEVELOPMENT (COMPAGNIE IVOIRIENNE POUR LE DEVELOPPEMENT DU TEXTILE, CIDT). The regional development agency for the northern region, focusing principally on supporting the production of cotton. It was organized before independence as the CFDT (Compagnie Française des Textiles, q.v.). (374)

IVOIRIANIZATION. The Ivoirian variant of Africanization, or the replacement of expatriate by indigenous workers, especially at the managerial level. At independence, Houphouët had discouraged what he termed "cut-rate Africanization," arguing that expatriates should be replaced only at the rate at which equally well-trained Ivoirians became available to replace them. The demand for ivorianization increased dramatically in the 1970s: it was estimated in 1978 that 1900 Ivoirians with post-secondary education would seek 700 jobs at that level each year, and that 18,000 secondary-school graduates would compete for 4,600 jobs. The government issued a "charter of Ivorianization" in 1978, requiring firms to submit long-term plans for high-level indigenization. (412, 559)

IVORIAN. See IVOIRIAN.

- J -

JACQUEVILLE. Town on the barrier island halfway between
Abidjan and Grand-Lahou. Known as Half-Jack in the pre-
colonial period, it was a point of European, especially
English, trade with the interior, controlled by the coastal
Alladian (q.v.) people. It is now a sub-prefecture with
a population (1970) of 1,000. (724)

JEUNESSE RDA DE LA COTE D'IVOIRE (JRDACI). Youth
branch of the PDCI founded in 1958 in response to a demand from younger members for their own autonomous
branch of the party. Affected by the consensus in the
Fédération des Etudiants d'Afrique Noire en France
(FEANF) in favor of immediate independence, the JRDACI
sought its own independence in 1959 from the PDCI, while
trying simultaneously to push the parent body in a more
radical direction. In order to bring it under control, the
PDCI leadership removed its privilege of selling membership
cards, so that the JRDACI was forced to depend on the
party for revenue. Control was reestablished by coopting
the JRDACI leaders into party and territorial positions.
However, many JRDACI leaders were implicated in the alleged coup plots of 1963, and the organization was dis-
solved.

JUDICIARY. The Ivoirian court system is modeled on that
of the French. There is a court of first instance (Cour de
Première Instance) in each of the principal towns, with
competence in civil, criminal, commercial, and administrative
cases. There is also a Court of Appeals, and a Supreme
Court in Abidjan. (738, 740, 748, 756, 807, 817)

- K -

KABADUGU (KABADOUGOU). Site of a Malinké trading kingdom established in 1860 at Odienné by Vakaba Toure (q.v.).
The Toure family led a stratum of Islamized warlords in
governing large numbers of non-Moslem captives. (580,
634, 635, 660, 708)

KACOU, ALCIDE (1919-). From 1961 to 1970, Minister for
Public Works and Transport. Kacou was born in Bingerville; he studied at Aix-en-Provence and began

his engineering career in France in steelworks and the railway system. From 1947 to 1950 he was a railway depot chief in the Ivory Coast, and then in Guinea from 1950 to 1952. In 1952 he returned to the Ivory Coast as head of the diesel section in Abidjan. Under the loi-cadre administration in 1957 he became Minister for Technical Education, a post he held into the independence period in 1961. From 1961 to 1963 his title was Minister for Public Works, Transport, Post and Telecommunications; in 1963 the portfolio for Construction was added to these. However, in 1964 the position was reorganized to cover just Public Works and Transport.

KAMARA. See DIOMANDE.

KARITE. See SHEA BUTTER.

KASSI, GEORGES. Treasurer of the Syndicat Agricole Africain (q.v.) in 1944 and 1947.

KATIOLA. A sub-prefecture in the center-north of the country, with a population (1980) of 12,000. The population is predominantly Tagbana (related to the Senufo) who are agricultural, and Mangoro (Malinké) who are traders and craftsmen. It is renowned for its pottery.

KEI BOGUINARD, EMILE. See BOGUINARD, EMILE KEI.

KEITA, BALA. Minister of Scientific Research since 1980 and Minister of National Education since 1983; sometimes mentioned as a possible successor to the presidency.

KOKUMBO. Village in south-central Ivory Coast, at the principal site of Baule gold mining in the nineteenth century. Kokumbo was taken over from the Guro by migrating Baule groups about 1840. Its capture by French troops in 1901 temporarily broke the resistance of the Baule to colonial rule. (576, 599-601, 604, 724)

KOLA. A walnut-sized nut from the Cola Nitida tree that grows only in the shady, humid environment of the forest zone. Chewed, it is a mild stimulant, and is used commercially in the production of cola drinks. It has been grown by the Bete, Guro, and Dan and traded widely by Dyulas as far north as the Niger River. Kola is highly appreciated,

with important social functions, in savannah cultures. It
was primarily traded for salt in pre-colonial Ivory Coast.
(660). In the contemporary Ivory Coast, its harvest
remains an important secondary economic activity, with
most production now in the region just north of
Abidjan (around Adzope, Agboville, and Anyama). Production is rarely specialized; rather, kola is grown on the
margin by coffee and cocoa planters. About 25,000 tons
are exported to the Sahelian countries each year, and about
4,000 tons are consumed locally. (660, 665)

KONAN BANNY (or BANNI), JEAN (1930-   ). Ivoirian Minister of Defense, one of the most powerful members of the
PDCI's Executive Committee. Nephew of President Houphouët and considered to be among the candidates to succeed him. (760)

KONAN BEDIE, HENRI (1934-   ). A longtime associate of
Houphouët, now President of the National Assembly. He
studied law and economics at the University of Poitiers
(France), worked as a civil servant, and was sent to study
at the French Foreign Ministry in 1960. Two months later
he was named Counsellor at the French Embassy in Washington, and upon Ivoirian independence became his country's Chargé d'Affaires, and later, Ambassador to the
United States. He established the Ivoirian Mission to the
United Nations. In 1966 he was brought into the Political
Bureau of the PDCI and named Minister for Economic and
Financial Affairs, a post he held until 1977.
    He has been President of the Ivoirian National Assembly
since 1980. He lost his position as Finance Minister in
1977 following a speech by Houphouët criticizing the economic mismanagement of the country. However, the competitive elections of 1980 restored his political fortunes:
he was re-elected to the National Assembly and appointed to
be its President. Although a Baule, he is considered to be
the most likely successor to Houphouët as President. (760,
864)

KONAN KANGA, ANTOINE. An employee in the Service des
Domaines and the Conservation de la Propriété et des Droits
Fonciers from 1940 to 1950 and a member of the Groupe
d'Etudes Communistes in 1947, Konan Kanga became Finance
Minister from 1959 to 1960, and Mayor of Abidjan in 1961.

KONAN KOFFI, LEON. Minister of the Interior since 1981.

KONE, AMADOU (1953-). Ivoirian author, defender of traditional values against the socially destructive effects of
modernization. His works include four novels, Les Fras-
ques d'Ebinto, Terre Ivoirienne (for children), Traites:
Sous le pouvoir des Blakoros I, and Courses: Sous le
pouvoir des Blakoros II; and two plays, De la chaire au trone
and Le respect des morts. (105, 223-231)

KONE, GASTON OUASSENAN (1940-). Minister of Domestic
Security, and a Brigadier General since 1977. He entered
the government as part of a move to integrate the military
into the civilian leadership of the country. He has been
forceful in his reaction to student strikes. (760)

KONE, LANSINA (1916-). Minister for Labor and Social Welfare in the 1960s. Kone was born in Mahale (northern
Ivory Coast) and served in the French Army from 1937 to
1942. He was elected Assistant Secretary-General of the
PDCI branch in Adjamé in 1947, and in 1949 became Assistant Secretary-General of the African Railway Workers'
Union.

KONG. A trading center founded no later than the thirteenth
century, occupied by the Dyula under the Ouattara dynasty
in the sixteenth century. Based on his visit in 1888, Binger (q.v.) described trade of a wide variety of products:
kolas from the southwest; salt both from the Sahara and
from the Gulf of Guinea; bands of cloth sewn into pagnes
at Kong; red pepper, ginger, and gold. Binger also saw
European imports from across the sahara: Turkish rugs,
cloth from Florence and Algeria, silk, law texts, coral, an-
timony, copper and nickel bracelets, hair ornaments in
metal and horn, medallions, and jewels. Kong was devastated in the early 1890s by drought and the interruption
of trade caused by the capture of Djenne, Mopti, and
Bandiagara in the Sudan by the French. It was finally
captured and destroyed by Samori Touré (q.v.) in 1897.
At that time it had a population estimated by Binger at
15,000. It is now a sub-prefecture with a 1980 population
of 3,000. (587, 589, 592, 606, 607, 613-615, 652, 662,
724, 1123, 1129)

KORHOGO. Prefecture, and largest town in northern Ivory

Coast (population 25,000 in 1970). By tradition, founded
by Nengue, servant of the ruler of Kong, around the
fourteenth century. It was the precolonial capital of the
Tyembara (Senufo) kingdom under Gbon Coulibaly (q.v.),
and had a 1900 population of about 12,500. Korhogo is one
of six regional centers designated in the 1976-1980 five-
year plan for the development of processing industries
for regional produce. (590, 1188)

KOSSOU DAM. The Ivory Coast's largest hydroelectric dam,
on the Bandama River in the center of the country. The
government had originally contracted with Electricité de
France in 1960 to survey the country for hydroelectric
potential. Based on survey recommendations, they decided
on a construction site near the village of Kossou. Planning
was contracted to E.D.F. and to Kaiser Engineers and Con-
tractors, an American firm. The French utility eventually
decided that the project would not be cost effective, and
the French government declined to participate in the financing. Kaiser, however, made their case to an Italian firm
and the U.S. Export-Import Bank for joint financing with
the Ivoirian government, and work began under these aus-
pices in 1969. The project was initially criticized by outsiders as uneconomical, but it came into operation simultaneously with the petroleum price increases of the 1970s.
It created a 1700 sq. km. reservoir, requiring the resettlement of over 75,000 people. See BANDAMA RIVER DEVEL-
OPMENT AUTHORITY. (423, 453, 454, 484, 485, 506)

KOTEBA. A form of musical theater originating in Mali. It
is presented in present-day Ivory Coast by a theater group
founded in 1974 by Souleymane Koly, a Guinean with a
French university education. As director, choreographer,
and dancer, he has created a theater that blends Western
and traditional forms. The emphasis is on movement and
sound, presented either in Dyula or in "parler Moussa"
(q.v.).

KOUTOUKOU. Alcohol distilled from palm wine. Distillation
is illegal, but demand is great, so the activity flourishes
clandestinely. Palm wine cannot be conserved readily, except through distillation, and with koutoukou is in great
demand for holidays and special events of various coastal
peoples. (Berron, 1980)

KRU (KROU). (1) A language cluster encompassing ethnic groups in southwest Ivory Coast and southern Liberia; one of the four main language groups in the country.

(2) An ethnic group inhabiting the coastal area at the frontier between Liberia and the Ivory Coast, known along the West African trade routes as "Krumen" (sometimes classified as Grebo). The origin and date of their immigration to the area is not known, but some scholars suggest that it was as recently as 200 years ago. They served for several generations as seamen on European ships operating on the African coast. Many visited France, England, and Germany in the nineteenth century. The development of the port of San Pedro is now bringing economic modernization to their region, but the Kru have until now lagged behind other groups in their participation in the political and economic institutions of the country. Since 1967, the Kru have joined the Harrist sect (q.v.) in large numbers. (172, 1159-1167)

KULANGO (KOULANGO). A Voltaic group inhabiting northeastern Ivory Coast around Bondoukou and Bouna. They are related to the neighboring Lobi and may number about 50,000. They arrived from the east centuries ago; they were conquered by the Abron in the seventeenth and eighteenth centuries and remained dominated by them until the colonial period. Dyula merchants settled among them from the fifteenth century but did not succeed in converting the Kulango to Islam. Individual villages were traditionally independent, under a civil and a religious chef. (173-176, 594, 660, 713, 903, 1126, 1168-1169, 1178)

KWAYA (KOUAYA). Small ethnic group of the Kru cluster in south-central Ivory Coast.

- L -

LABOR. The immigration of low-paid migrant workers is encouraged by the Ivoirian government to keep agricultural labor costs down as acreage increases. Migrant workers constituted about 30 percent of the population in 1975. (274, 428, 487, 546-565, 688, 725, 870)

LAGOON CLUSTER (LAGUNAIRES). Designation for the extremely complex grouping of peoples along the southeast

coast and lagoons. They have largely shifted from traditional occupations to cash-crop farming. They are not
Akan, but with the Akan they speak a Kwa language.
They are sometimes grouped with the Akan as the Akan-
East Atlantic Complex. Lagoon peoples have attracted many
migrant laborers to their farms, especially Mossi from
Burkina Faso. Baule and Dyula have also moved in, and
have achieved political and economic prominence, to the dis-
comfiture of the "indigenous" people. Cultures commonly
labeled "Lagoon" include the Abé, Abure, Adjukru, Alladian,
Atié, Avikam, Ebrié, Mekyibo, and Nzima (qq.v.). (179,
360, 586, 947, 1170-1172, 1218)

LALOU, MARIE. Founder of the Déima sect (q.v.).

LATRILLE, ANDRE. Governor of the Ivory Coast from 1943
to 1947, Latrille was named to replace the Vichy-designated
Georges-Pierre Rey (q.v.). He was sympathetic to the
need to redress the grievances of the indigenous population, especially as concerned forced labor. Consequently,
he was fiercely opposed by European planters and was removed shortly after the Communist Party was excluded from
the French government.

LEBANESE, THE. There were about 20,000 Lebanese in the
Ivory Coast as of 1970, up from about 100 in 1921. The
Lebanese have continued through the independence period
to play an important role in distribution and retail sales
in the Ivory Coast. Because of their marginal social position in Ivoirian society (they are probably the most dis-
liked non-African group in the country), they took special
pains to support the PDCI in the movement toward independence. (549, 828, 846, 1173)

LOBI. A Voltaic people centered between the Black and
White Voltas, without village organization or chiefs but
based on matrilineages. Toward the end of the eighteenth
century, the Lobi moved northwest and east because of
population pressures and incursions from Mamprussi, Dagomba, and Gonja. A massive emigration lasted over two centuries; this was essentially a nonviolent occupation of new
land, in which the immigrants mixed with the prior occu-
pants. The Lobi, traditionally hunters and warriors, were
welcomed by the kingdom of Bouna but remained isolated
from the neighboring Kulango and Dyula. They were

never really conquered by the Maninka or Samory (q.v.),
nor did French or British columns penetrate far into their
territory. They were nominally "pacified" in 1901, but were
little affected by colonization. The Lobi migration continued
into the colonial period from Upper Volta and Ghana because of the sparse population of the Kulango areas. They
are now much more numerous than the Kulango and are
more numerous in Burkina Faso than in the Ivory Coast.
In the latter country they are a relatively small, scattered
group, and are among the poorest sub-populations in the country, living in the extreme northeast around Bouna. (435,
591, 629, 929, 1174-1178)

LOROUGNON, J. GUEDE (1935-   ). Minister of Scientific
Research from 1971 to 1981. Lorougnon is a Bété. He
received his doctorate in tropical botany from the University
of Paris in 1960. He was an official of the Union Générale
des Etudiants de Côte d'Ivoire (q.v.) and as such was
critical of PDCI policies, but became more cooperative when
he was elected to the National Assembly upon completion
of his studies. From 1964 to 1970 he served as First Vice-
President of the Assembly. In 1970-1971 he served as
Minister of National Education.

- M -

MADI, ALPHONSE DJEDJE. Minister of Public Health and
Population since 1983.

MAHOGANY. Production for export began before the colonial
period: from 1890 to 1907 by indigenous effort, then,
following the economic crisis of 1907, by logging company
monopolies. Mahogany trade was limited by transportation
availability to riverbanks and lagoons. The first production
was on the Tano River, then around Tabou and San Pedro.
Verdier (q.v.) won a monopoly of Ivoirian mahogany production in 1890-91 in spite of opposition from local administrators and other merchants. This concession was the base
from which the Compagnie Française de Kong (q.v.) was
formed, but the company gave up the mahogany concession
for an indemnity of 250,000 frances plus 125,000 francs
per year for fourteen years, with complete rights to an
area of 300,000 hectares.

MALARIA. A disease transmitted by the anopheles mosquito, common throughout Africa, and the most widespread disease in the Ivory Coast. It accounts for 20-30 percent of hospital consultations there. Malaria is responsible for many deaths, especially among children, and makes adults weak and susceptible to other infections because of repeated bouts of fever; at least 80 percent of the Ivoirian population is infected, and up to 90-95 percent of young children. (728)

MALINKE. See MANINKA.

MAN. Prefecture and largest town in the mountainous western region, with a (1970) population of 22,000. Because of its relatively high altitude, Man offers the most temperate climate of the major towns of the Ivory Coast. Nearby is the Dent de Man (Tooth of Man), a rock outcropping especially unique in this country of savannah and coastal plain. One of six regional centers designated in the 1976-80 five-year plan for the development of processing industries for regional produce. (19, 438)

MANDE. See MANDING.

MANDING (MANDINGUE, MANDINGO, MANDE). One of the four major language groupings in the Ivory Coast, encompassing the Maninka, Bambara, and Dyula (qq.v.), cultures. (180-186, 1179)

MANILLE (MANILLA). Form of currency introduced on the West African coast by English traders. A type of bronze, horseshoe-shaped bracelet that was grouped in packets for different values. Manillas were used in the earliest trade at Grand Lahou.

MANINKA (MALINKE). One of the most important subgroups of the Manding language group originating in Mali, and one of the four major cultural clusters in the Ivory Coast. The Maninka are mostly Moslem and have thus been traditionally distinguished from the Bambara who live among them and retain an animist faith. In southern Ivory Coast, Maninka people are often referred to as Dyulas, merely on the basis that they are Moslems from the North and commonly engage in trade (the term "dyula" means itinerant trader in the languages of these peoples.) According to tradition,

they are descendents of the people who formed the Mali
Empire. Inhabiting a wide swath of territory stretching
northwest to the Gambia River, Manding-speaking traders
and settlers moved south into present-day Ivory Coast
during the sixteenth to the eighteenth centuries. There
they found gold and kolanuts to trade in Mali. Theirs is
the predominant culture in northwestern Ivory Coast.
See DYULA. (72, 762, 1180-1183, 612, 634, 635)

MANIOC. A food crop originally imported to Africa from
South America, now a staple in coastal Ivory Coast, where
it is the only food staple that grows well in the sandy soil;
it is also grown elsewhere in the country. The porridge
made from it is called attiéké. Manioc production has increased in recent years because it is inexpensive to grow,
takes little care, and gives a good yield in poor soil.
Manioc flour (gari) is easy to transport and to consume.

MANUFACTURING. Manufacturing has grown at 13 percent
per annum since independence. Its share of GDP was 4
percent in 1960, and 14 percent in 1980. Expansion has
been based on import substitution and the processing of
agricultural raw materials for export. The 1973 tariff reform and quantitative import restrictions have produced
some inefficient import substitution activities, and have resulted in a bias against exporting activities. Manufacturing
has developed in the private sector, mainly as a result of
foreign investment attracted by a liberal and stable investment climate. (374)

MARCHAND, JEAN-BAPTISTE. French army officer who, as
a captain in 1892, was given permission to explore and establish a secure route from the Ivory Coast to the Sudan.
He traveled north on the Bandama in 1893-94, the first
European to traverse the Baule territory. (610, 724)

MASSA. A religious movement among the Senufo (q.v.) founded by a Minianka from the region of San in Mali. Massa
was a self-styled divinity who caused great turmoil in the
Poro-dominated Senufo society, but the resurgence of the
Poro (q.v.) seems to correspond with a contemporary
decline of interest in Massa.

M'BAHIA BLE, KOUADIO (1928-). Former teacher who became Minister of the Armed Forces (later Minister of

National Defense) at age 34. M'Bahia Blé studied at the Ecole William Ponty in Senegal, then served in the French Army. He was assistant principal of a school in Bouake for three years, then was appointed Director of Schools (1953). He was sent to Paris in 1956 to work with Ivoirian students. He thus served as a link between the first two political generations in the Ivory Coast.

In 1957, M'Bahia Blé was elected territorial councillor for Bouake, served in the Constituent Assembly in 1958-59, and then as a member of the Legislative Assembly. From 1959-1963 he was Speaker of the National Assembly. He was named Minister for Youth and Sports in 1963 and within a few months added the Armed Forces Ministry to his responsibility as well. In 1966 he gave up Youth and Sports and served as Minister for the Armed Forces and for the Civil Service until 1980.

MEKYIBO (MEKIBO, EHOTILE, EOTILE, EOUTILE). A Lagoon cluster people living just south of the Anyi of Sanwi, along the Aby Lagoon. They consider themselves the true indigenous population of the present Anyi-Sanwi region, and number between 3,000-5,000.

METHODISM. Established in the Ivory Coast in 1924, when two English Methodist missionaries discovered the Harrist following; having traced Harris back to Liberia in 1927, they claimed he asked his followers to join the Methodist Church. A majority of the Harrists at the time (about 50,000) did. By World War II, Methodists constituted about 4-5 percent of the southern Ivory Coast population. (5)

MILLET. A traditional cereal food crop of the Ivory Coast savannah region, well-suited to the poor soil and low rainfall of the savannah.

MINIANKA. A people living among, and closely associated with, the Senufo (q.v.). (1190, 1192, 1194, 1195)

MOCKEY, JEAN-BAPTISTE (1915-1981). An early stalwart of the PDCI. Mockey studied pharmacy in Dakar and then held several hospital appointments there. He was an early member of the Groupe d'Etudes Communistes (1947) and was a co-founder of the PDCI in 1946. He became administrative secretary of the party and was elected to the Territorial Assembly in 1947. As a result of his political activities, he

was imprisoned by the French in 1949 for two years.
Mockey held the post of party Secretary-General in 1959-
1960; he was the Ivory Coast's first Interior Minister under
the loi-cadre in 1957. He was later the first Ivoirian ambassador to Israel, then held the position of Minister of
Agriculture.

Mockey was implicated in the alleged plot against Houphouët's leadership in 1963, was arrested, and sentenced
to death. Although released in 1967, he was consigned to
political obscurity until 1976. He was named Minister of
Public Health and Population in 1976, redesignated Public
Health, Population and Social Affairs in 1977, and Minister
of State for Public Health and Population in 1978. He thus
seemed well on the road back to influence, but died in an
automobile accident en route to a meeting with the President.

MONA (MWANU). A small ethnic group in west-central Ivory
Coast (near Mankono), related to the Gagu and Guro.

MONDON, GASTON-CHARLES-JULIEN. Governor of the Ivory
Coast from 1936 to 1939. Mondon was named to the post
by the Popular Front government and sought a series of
reforms, notably in forced labor and in the minimum wage.
Faced with stiff opposition from the European population,
he sided with the African planters.

MONROVIA GROUP. Name given to the grouping of African
states that emerged from a conference held in Monrovia,
Liberia, in May 1969. It included the "moderate" francophone states, including Senegal and Ivory Coast, as well
as Ethiopia, Liberia, Nigeria, Sierra Leone, Somalia, Sudan,
Togo and Tunisia. The meeting was called in reaction to
the formation of the Casablanca group of Ghana, Guinea,
Mali, Morocco, and the United Arab Republic. The Casablanca group was committed to a pan-Africanism that would
lessen the European presence in Africa, dating from its
stand against France in the Algerian war. Ghana and
Guinea were thought to be supporting leftist and secession-
ist groups in Senegal and the Ivory Coast. Thus, the
resolutions from Monrovia stressed noninterference by outside parties in the affairs of each state and condemned
"subversive action" by neighboring states; they reflected
the important contribution of Houphouët-Boigny.

MONTEIL, PARFAIT-LOUIS. Commander of the first French

military expedition into Baule territory in 1893-95. He was to defend Kong (q.v.) against Samory's (q.v.) advance, but was prevented from reaching the city by hostile Baule and the forward units of Samory's army. He was ordered to withdraw by a Colonial Ministry reluctant to support a large campaign, and suffered humiliating harassment at the hands of the Baule as he returned south.

MOTORAGRI. State development corporation for motorized agricultural development.

MOUVEMENT DES ETUDIANTS ET DES ELEVES DE COTE D'IVOIRE (MEECI). The successor student organization to the Union Nationale des Etudiants et Elèves de Côte d'Ivoire. The MEECI was the first student organization (in March 1969) to be placed under control of the PDCI. Students protested this and other actions that spring, leading to mass arrests and internment at a military camp before the unrest was quieted.

- N -

NAFANA. Kingdom established by the Diarrasouba (Dyarasuba) clan around 1720 at Odienné, in what is now northwest Ivory Coast. The Diarrasouba were defeated by Vakaba Touré (q.v.) in about 1845 and forced to relocate to the southeast. The Touré rulers continued to war with the Diarrasouba through the nineteenth century until, in 1892 at the battle of Kungbéni, the Nafana kingdom was again defeated. (708)

NAIRAY, GUY. According to Amondji (843), the Director of the Cabinet of President Houphouët "on loan" from the French government, in the Ivory Coast since before independence.

NANGEN SORHO. According to Scnufo-Tyembara oral tradition, the founder of the Tyembara kingdom. Presented in tradition as sent from God, Nangen was probably a real, not just a mythical, person. He distinguished himself as a warrior for Kong, then set out with his followers to establish his kingdom at Korhogo, where he either founded or solidified the Tyembara kingdom. According to tradition, he reigned from 1710 to 1750. (580)

NATIONAL ASSEMBLY (ASSEMBLEE NATIONALE). The uni-
cameral constitutional legislative body of the Ivory Coast,
elected every five years since 1960. The Assembly was
enlarged from 120 to 147 seats in 1980, and in 1985 it was
increased to 175. It is presided over by a Chairman (as
of 1985, Henri Konan Bédié). In 1980 for the first time
members were chosen in competitive elections, with 649
PDCI members as candidates for the 147 seats. Only 26
incumbents won re-election. Although in theory the Assembly can override a presidential veto by a two-thirds
vote, it in fact functions more as a legitimizer and sounding
board for policies developed in the executive hierarchy
than as a true law-making parliament. (757)

NATIONAL UNIVERSITY OF THE IVORY COAST (formerly the
University of Abidjan). The University had an enrollment
in 1981 of 18,732 students. In 1958 there were 960 Ivoirians at French universities, and another 171 at the University of Dakar. There was a self-evident need for expanded
higher education, but it was given added impetus by the
tendency of students abroad to engage in uncontrolled
political activity at odds with government policy. Thus,
a Center of Higher Studies (Centre des Hautes Etudes)
opened in Abidjan that year with an enrollment of over 200
students. In 1961 France agreed to give the financial
and technical aid necessary to transform the Center into
a full-fledged university, open to all Entente states and
granting diplomas and degrees equivalent to those of French
institutions. The Center became the University of Abidjan
in the fall of 1963, with 160 students in schools of Science,
Letters, Medicine, and Law. In 1966, 1967, and 1969 the
respective schools were redesignated Faculties of Science,
Medicine, and Law. Also in 1967, the government created
the University Institute of Technology (Institut Universitaire de Technologie, IUT) with four sections: Commerce
and Administration, Applied Psychology, Medical Technology,
and Electromechanics. There were 2,700 students in 1969,
of which 44 percent were Ivoirian, with other large con-
tingents from Upper Volta (Burkina Faso), Dahomey (Benin), Togo, and Niger. About one fourth of the student
body were French nationals.

University Institutes for Research in Ethnosociology and
Tropical Geography were created in 1966, followed by additional Institutes of Tropical Ecology, Applied Linguistics,
a Center of Audio-visual Teaching and Research, and an

Institute of Art History and African Archeology. These institutions are grouped administratively under the University Center for Research and Development (Centre Universitaire de Recherches et Développement, CURD). (848, 1003)

N'DAW, OUMAR. Minister of Internal Security since 1984.

NDENYE. Pre-colonial Anyi (q.v.) kingdom in eastern Ivory Coast, the wealth of which was built on gold and, later, cocoa. (637, 639-644, 691, 709, 1060)

N'DIA KOFFI, BLAISE (1912-). Minister for Health and Population from 1963 to 1970. A Baule, N'Dia Koffi studied medicine in Dakar. He was director of Treichville Hospital and the Nurses' School of the Ivory Coast from 1957 to 1959 and held other medical posts in Ivory Coast and Upper Volta before entering the government. He was elected to the National Assembly in 1959. He was named Minister of State in 1970, a position redesignated Minister of State for Tourism in 1974. In 1976, he entered the Political Bureau of the PDCI.

NEYO. A small ethnic group (totalling about 5,000) of the Kru cluster living in about twenty villages around Sassandra. They are the original population of that location but compose a small minority of it now. The Neyo are closely related to the Bakwe through proximity and marital alliances, but they speak a language close to Bété and Godié. They were early commercial intermediaries between European ships and inland peoples, in the trade of slaves, rubber and ivory for copper utensils, cloth, marine salt, alcoholic beverages, and weapons and ammunition. (620)

NGAN (BENG, BEN, GAN, NGEN). See BENG.

N'GUESSAN, KOUAME. N'guessan was a member of the Bureau, and Administrative Secretary, of the Syndicat Agricole Africain (q.v.).

N'GUESSAN DIKEBIE, PASCAL (1936-). See DIKEBIE, PASCAL N'GUESSAN.

NIABOUA. A small ethnic group located near the subprefecture of Zoukougbeu. Their language is closely related to Guéré, their social institutions more like those of the Bété. (580)

NZIMA (N'ZIMA). Also known as Appolonians, the Nzima are an ethnic group inhabiting the coastal area on the Ivory Coast-Ghana border. The Nzima became important traders in the late nineteenth century as middlemen between inland peoples and, especially, English ships. The French colonial administration imposed heavy taxes on their trade in 1898 to force them out of competition with French merchants and trading companies. (724) In 1877, the leaders of some Nzima villages asked to be placed under a French "protectorate" because of military attacks by the King of Beyin. Many Nzima merchant families moved from Cape Coast to Assinie and Grand Bassam when the Ivory Coast was proclaimed a French colony in 1893. They began selling lumber and establishing commercial houses until they were edged out of these trades by European companies. Some Nzima were among the first Ivoirians to receive a European education and become French subjects. (724, 1186-87, 1219)

- O -

ODIENNE. Sub-prefecture in the extreme northwest of the Ivory Coast, with a 1980 population of 11,500. Maninkas began migrating south from Mali to the Odienné region in the fifteenth century. Odienné is the traditional center of the Maninka Kabadugu kingdom, established in 1860 by Vakaba Toure. His successor, Va Ahmadou Toure, was an ally of Samory, and was captured with him in 1898. He was released in 1905 and died in Odienné in 1912. A French post was established there in 1898. The population was 2,000 in the year 1900; thus, the city experienced slow growth under colonial rule. Traditionally a transit point in the trade of kola nuts grown in the forest zone and consumed in the savannah region. (605, 660, 1182)

ODIENNE IDEAL. An association formed in 1945 without a large membership, well-elaborated organization, or precise objectives, but providing experience to future political leaders of northern Ivory Coast. The members were from the three northern cercles of Odienné, Korhogo, and Séguéla. When the group broke up in 1947, some members

joined the Independent Party, while others, including
President Yoro Sangaret, joined the PDCI-RDA. (828)

OFFICE DE LA RECHERCHE SCIENTIFIQUE ET TECHNIQUE
OUTRE-MER (ORSTOM). Now renamed the French Research
Institute for Development in Cooperation (Institut Française
de Recherche pour le Développement en Coopération,
IFRDC), this organization is better known under its long-
standing acronym, ORSTOM. Charged with the "promotion
and conduct of scientific and technological research likely
to contribute to the cultural, social, and economic progress
of less-developed countries," ORSTOM has 1,500 research-
ers and technicians in many countries of Africa, the Indian
Ocean, Asia, and Latin America. It has four research
centers in the Ivory Coast: Adiopodoumé (for research in
agronomy); the Center for Oceanographic Research (CRO);
the Center for Human Sciences in Petit Bassam; and the
Center at Bouaké. Its work in agronomy focuses on the
study of the natural environment, the application of technology, and the protection of crops and cropland. Its
Human Sciences staff has been responsible for a large proportion of the anthropological and sociological research on
the Ivory Coast.

OFFICE FOR THE PROMOTION OF IVOIRIAN ENTERPRISE
(Office de Promotion de L'entreprise Ivoirienne, OPEI).
An organization created to group small and middle-sized
Ivoirian firms to facilitate their access to markets and to
make possible their response to demands for bids from state
corporations, which often go to foreign firms or buy needed
materials through importation.

ORGANISATION COMMUNE AFRICAINE ET MAURICIENNE
(African and Mauritian Common Organization, OCAM).
International organization of francophone states, founded
in Nouakchott, Mauritania, in 1965, with its secretariat in
Yaounde, Cameroun. OCAM was originally titled the Organisation Commune Africaine et Malgache. It was the
successor organization to the Union Africaine et Malgache,
formed in 1961. The charter provides for three institutions:
the Conference of Heads of State and Government, the
Council of Ministers, and the Secretariat. Plenary power
is placed on the Conference, which meets once a year.
OCAM has functioned as a primary means for the coordination of policy between France and her former colonies in

Africa. Houphouët has played a definitive role in OCAM since its creation, although isolated on his advocacy of "dialogue" with South Africa. The member states are Benin, Central African Republic, Gabon, Ivory Coast, Mauritius, Niger, Rwanda, Senegal, Togo, and Burkina Faso.

ORUMBO-BOKA. Butte 527 meters high near Toumodi. It was traditionally held sacred by the Baule. Well-preserved prehistoric tools have been found at its base.

OUASSENAN KONE, GASTON. See KONE, GASTON OUASSENAN.

OUATTARA, THOMAS D'AQUIN. Chief of the Ivory Coast General Staff in the 1960s. Ouattara started his military career in the enlisted ranks of the French Army in the mid 1930s. After serving in World War II, he participated in the Indochina campaign, during which time he rose to the rank of Major. He left the French Army in 1961 to become Chief of General Staff, in 1964 was promoted to Lieutenant Colonel, and in 1966 became the first General of the Ivory Coast Army (at the rank of Brigadier General).

OUATTARA, YAYA. Minister for Social Affairs since 1981.

OUDINOT, RUE. The Ministry of Colonies was located on the Rue Oudinot in Paris, and the street name was often used as a pseudonym for the Ministry.

OUOBE. See WOBE.

- P -

PAGNE. Piece of textile material at least one yard wide by several in length, draped over the body toga-style as a common traditional form of dress of forest-zone Ivoirians (especially Akan and Lagoon-cluster peoples). Akan kings wore traditional pagnes woven of kente cloth. The material now is commonly imported, with the "Dutch wax" print a standard. Pagnes are produced in the Ivory Coast by UTEXI (Union Textile Ivoirienne) in Dimbokro, Gonfreville near Bouake, and Uniwax in Abidjan, which made 16 million square meters in 1981-82. Eighty percent of Ivoirian production is sold domestically.

PALM OIL (ELOEIS GUINEENSIS). The first commercial agricultural product harvested explicitly for export in the
Ivory Coast, beginning in the 1840s among the "Jack-Jack"
(Alladian) and Kru peoples. The oil was obtained by
breaking the kernel, a leisure-time occupation of women,
children, and slaves in the early period of the trade, when
it was sold almost exclusively to English buyers. Production rose rapidly at the end of the century, from 1,885
tons exported in 1890 to 4,671 tons in 1892, and palm oil
was the principal export of the colony until 1898. The
palm oil trade stagnated during the period from 1899 to
1912, when rubber was dominant, but became dominant
again between 1913 and 1920. Production fell off over the
next twenty years, especially during the depression, and
then experienced a moderate recovery. Natural oil palm
groves are found throughout the forest zone and in the
wooded savannah, and are especially dense along the seacoast. There are 350,000-400,000 hectares in the country.
(333, 673, 724)
    In recent decades, palm oil production as an agro-
industry has been central to Ivoirian efforts at agricultural
diversification. By 1970 there were 60,000 hectares of palm
tree plantations, and nine refineries in service. In 1983
the country received a grant from the European Development Fund for a fifteen-year replanting program.

PALMINDUSTRIE. The state enterprise that produces about
80 percent of Ivoirian palm oil. (374)

PARASTATALS. See STATE ENTERPRISES.

PARLER MOUSSA (LE FRANCAIS DE MOUSSA). Term for
the variety of French spoken in West Africa by those without formal education. (14)

PARTI DEMOCRATIQUE DE COTE D'IVOIRE (PDCI). See
DEMOCRATIC PARTY OF THE IVORY COAST.

PECHOUX, LAURENT. Governor of the Ivory Coast from
1948 to 1951, responsible for vigorous repression of the
anticolonial movement over that period with the strong
support of the European settler population. He began by
removing French communists from the colonial administration, then worked to create an electoral opposition to the
PDCI. When Houphouët renounced the PDCI's tie with the

French Communist Party, the French government removed
Péchoux and other anti-PDCI administrators, leaving
Houphouët in control in the Ivory Coast.

PETITS BLANCS. "Little whites," term for the lower-class
Europeans performing relatively menial tasks in the Ivorian
economy. Sometimes used by extension to apply to all
Europeans.

PETROLEUM. There was exploration for oil in Sanwi in 1912,
abandoned in favor of the Gold Coast, which seemed more
promising. The discovery of reserves in the area of the
1912 exploration (the Belier field, 15 km. south of Grand
Bassam) was announced by the government in 1977. There
was a larger find at the Espoir field and in 1982 another off
Grand Lahou, following which the petroleum companies
moved to other areas. Production is increasing, with one
third of Ivory Coast consumption of crude oil domestically
produced in 1981. The country is projected to be self-
sufficient in petroleum by 1987. An oil refinery with a
4-million-ton capacity meets domestic requirements and exports to Burkina Faso and Mali. Production is managed
by a state corporation, PETROCI (Société Nationale d'Oper-
ations Petrolières de la Côte d'Ivoire), formed in 1975,
while the refinery is operated by the Société Ivoirienne de
Raffinage, owned jointly by the Ivory Coast, Burkina Faso,
and foreign oil companies. (374, 507, 728)

PEYRISSAC, ETABLISSEMENTS. French trading company incorporated in 1908. Peyrissac operated principally in the
northern savannah of the Ivory Coast and did not get established on the Coast until after the pacification of the
central region.

PINEAPPLES. A product recently introduced to the Ivory
Coast, grown on European-owned plantations in the south
of the country, notably on plantations owned directly by
canning companies. More recently, small-scale Ivorian-
owned plantations have appeared, though they depend on
the canning companies for technical support and purchase
of their crop. (334, 466)

PLANTAIN. Traditionally grown in conjunction with yams,
and now typically with cocoa, plantain is a traditional food
crop in the southeastern Ivory Coast forest zone but is
rarely grown in the southwest even today. (335-338)

POKOU. See AURA POKOU.

POPULAR FRONT (FRONT POPULAIRE). The election of a
government of the Left in France in 1936 had indirect and
direct effects in the colonies. An arrêté of December 1936
increased the minimum wage in the colonies from .5 to 1.25
francs. Then a parliamentary commission visited a number
of Ivoirian and Upper Volta towns, including Dimbokro,
Abengourou, Abidjan, and Grand Bassam. This was followed in April 1937 by a visit from the Minister for Colonies,
Marius Moutet. Not coincidentally, the number of punish-
ments under the indigénat dropped during that year. On
his return to France, Moutet spoke out against forced labor;
the French settler population reacted by sending protests
to rightist papers in Paris, which criticized the government actions. In August an organizational convention of
the Socialist Party (SFIO) of the Ivory Coast was held in
Abidjan, attracting a number of Ivoirians: several interior
cities sent delegations, including Agboville, Grand Bassam,
Abengourou, and Aboisso. Many associations of "évolueés"
(q.v.), including the ADIACI (q.v.), were formed in 1936-
37.

POPULATION GROWTH. There was an annual growth overall
of 5.2 percent in the population of the Ivory Coast from
1960-79. This includes a massive immigration from north
of the country. Even as productivity increased, there was
a decline in agricultural production per capita of 15 percent
over this period. (428, 488, 976-992)

PORO. Initiation society for males common in many ethnic
groups of West Africa, including the Senufo (q.v.) of
northern Ivory Coast (in whose language it is called lô).
Poro initiation rituals require adolescents to spend a period
of time in the forest, usually not far from the village, but
in isolation from it. During this time they are tested and
trained for adult roles and develop close ties with others
in their age set. So obligatory is the rite for entry into
society that even urban Senufo send their children to the
village for the Poro initiation, although some accommodation
has been made to sparing the urban youth from the full
rigors of traditional ceremonies. However, in rural areas
Poro is a powerful means for continued control of society
by the elders, in its four age grades into which the
individual must be initiated.

PORT-BOUET. Site of the Abidjan international airport. A
wharf constructed here in 1931 duplicated that of Grand-
Bassam. Tied to Abidjan and the interior by a rail line,
it became the dominant port of entry until the opening of
the Vridi Canal.

PRESS. There were few serious attempts to launch newspapers
in the colonial period. Newspapers oriented toward African
audiences were viewed with suspicion by the administration
and the European population, and the literate African population was very small. However, the first newspaper published by an African in a francophone state appeared in
Abidjan in 1935, the Eclaireur de la Côte d'Ivoire, and it
survived into the independence period. Notre Voix was
established in 1937 by the Socialist Party (SFIO) of the
Ivory Coast, with a European publisher and editor. In
1939 a white colonial started his own paper, Le Cri du
Planteur. Abidjan-Matin, of the French Breteuil chain,
appeared after World War II, followed shortly by the PDCI
party organ Fraternité. Less than a year after independence, the government established its own news agency, the
Agence Ivoirienne de Presse, and established a national
media monopoly. (51-55, 260, 262-264)

PROGRESSIVE PARTY OF THE IVORY COAST (PARTI PRO-
GRESSISTE DE LA COTE D'IVOIRE, PPCI). Political party
formed in competition with the PDCI for the second Constituent Assembly electoral campaign in June 1946 in opposition
to the rising influence of Houphouët-Boigny and the Syndicat Agricole Africain. The Progressive Party found most
of its support in the region of Abidjan-Grand Bassam-
Aboisso, that is, the area in longest contact with the
French. The party was a transformation of the Committee
of Patriotic Action of the Ivory Coast (Comité d'Action
Patriotique de la Côte d'Ivoire, q.v.), which had supported
the candidacy of Kouamé Binzème to the municipal council
in 1945. The leaders were "intellectuals," those who had
studied in France. The Progressive Party sent delegates
to the Conference of Bamako, at which the RDA was formed,
and was represented on the Ivoirian delegation until May
1947.

PROTESTANTISM. In the colonial period, missionaries needed
administrative permission to evangelize, and Protestants
underwent especially severe scrutiny because they were

usually of English or American extraction. There were
four missions in that period: The Mission Biblique du
Tabernacle for Sassandra and the west; the Mission Wesley-
enne in Assinie, Agneby, the Lagoons, and the Bouaké
region; the Christian and Missionary Alliance, in the Cercle
du Baoulé and the subdivision of Toumodi; and the African
Methodist Episcopal Church, especially suspect to the administration because of its ties to Cape Coast in neighboring
(British) Gold Coast. The AME Church was active in
Attié country, around Adzopé. Before World War II, about
one in ten Ivoirian Christians was Protestant. (See also:
METHODISM) (1224, 1226-1229)

PUBLIC ENTERPRISE (REGIE). A public service, primarily
in transportation and communications in the Ivory Coast,
the budget of which is an annex to the main government
budget. (445)

PUBLIC ESTABLISHMENT (ETABLISSEMENT PUBLIC). A type
of public administrative agency in the Ivory Coast. There
are two categories: 1) Public establishments of administrative character (Etablissements publics à caractère administratif), which undertake educational or research activities
or administer funds for national development; and 2) Public
establishments of industrial and commercial character (Etablissements publics à caractère industriel et commercial,
EPIC), those primarily involved in providing financial and
technical support services to the industrial and commercial
sectors. Public establishments do not have their own
equity and obtain revenues by allocation from the government. (445)

- Q -

QUAQUA COAST. Name given by European traders to the
coast between Cape Lahou and Assini in the seventeenth
and eighteenth centuries. Physical conditions and the lack
of large-scale political organization discouraged Europeans
from establishing permanent trading facilities in this area,
so that most trade with the interior was conducted through
the Gold Coast. (724)

- R -

RAN. See REGIE DES CHEMINS DE FER ABIDJAN-NIGER.

RASSEMBLEMENT DEMOCRATIQUE AFRICAIN (RDA). The
African Democratic Rally, a francophone West African political movement, formed at a congress in Bamako, French
Sudan (now Mali), in October 1946. The Bamako meeting
was convened by African political leaders from various
colonies in response to successful blocking of political reforms by European colonial interests. Because those leaders affiliated with moderate French parties were under
pressure not to attend, the birth of the first inter-colonial
grouping of leaders was heavily influenced by those affiliated with the French Communist Party. Felix Houphouët-
Boigny was elected president of the coordinating committee,
and another Ivoirian, Fily Sissoko, was named secretary-
general. These were indications of the extent to which the
Democratic Party of the Ivory Coast (PDCI) had become influential at the West African level. (The second congress
of the RDA was held in Treichville, Ivory Coast, in 1949.)
The RDA was in effect an umbrella organization composed
of the individual parties in each colony. Thus, the PDCI
was in that period a section of the RDA. The formal link
at the interterritorial level was the congress, and through
a Coordinating Committee (Comite de Coordination) between
congresses. In effect, however, this formal structure was
overshadowed by the personal preeminence of Houphouët-
Boigny both in the PDCI and the RDA. The relatively
well-organized PDCI often gave organizational and financial
support to other sections, which made it first among equals
and suspect to leaders in other colonies with their own
well-developed political movements.
    In 1950, in the face of severe harassment, the RDA
severed its ties with the French Communist Party. The
movement had been greatly weakened in most places, however, and in the 1951 elections to the Constituent Assembly
only three RDA candidates (including Houphouët-Boigny)
won in all of French West Africa. The RDA subsequently
pursued more conservatives policies in Paris, affiliating with
the Union Democratique des Socialistes Republicains (Democratic Union of Republican Socialists), a small but central
French party whose members included Rene Pleven, the
Prime Minister. The affiliation was not a popular decision in
all sections of the party, and the RDA was essentially

inactive at the federal level. In 1955, Houphouët demanded and won the expulsion from the RDA of all sections that did not support the decisions to break with the PCF. This included the parties in Senegal, Cameroun, and Niger, leaving only those in the Ivory Coast, Guinea, and Sudan (Mali). The section in Niger returned to the fold, and new sections were formed in Upper Volta and Dahomey (Benin). Thus, by the 1957 territorial elections, Houphouët headed the strongest political movement in Africa; its candidates won by substantial majorities in four territories and ran strongly in the other two.

As independence neared, the RDA was strained by the disagreement among sections between continued affiliation with France and absolute independence, and later, between a federation of independent African states or complete autonomy. Houphouët generally found himself isolated from other leaders on these issues, and meaningful alliance through the RDA ceased. (680, 820, 828)

REGIE. See PUBLIC ENTERPRISE.

REGIE DES CHEMINS DE FER ABIDJAN-NIGER (RAN). The company managing the railway line from Abidjan to Bobo-Dioulasso and Ouagadougou in Burkina Faso. Railway construction began from Abidjan in 1903 but did not reach the present terminus, Ouagadougou, until 1954. There are now 1,184 km. of rail line, of which 627 is in the Ivory Coast. (715, 717)

RELIGION. About 23 percent of the country is Islamicized, and about 12 percent are at least nominal Christians. See also CATHOLICISM, HARRISTS, ISLAM, METHODISM, PROTESTANTISM. (5)

RESEARCH INSTITUTES. A number of French-sponsored research institutes are established in the Ivory Coast, notably ORSTOM (scientific and technical research), IRHO (vegetable oils), IFCC (coffee and cocoa), IRCT (cotton and textiles), IRCA (rubber), IFAC (tropical fruits), IRAT (tropical agriculture), CTFT (forestry), CRO (oceanography), and IFAN (cultural studies). (19, 478)

RESTAURANT MAQUIS. In Abidjan, a rudimentary open-air restaurant, operating on the margins of legality.

RESTE, DIEUDONNE-FRANCOIS. Governor of the Ivory Coast from 1931 to 1935; Reste was sent to the Ivory Coast to manage recovery from the Depression, and was important in the expansion of the plantation economy. He was nominated by the settler population in the 1945 as their candidate to the French Constituent Assembly (in the First Electoral College, for citizens) and won election. In Paris he took a moderate position on the question of forced labor, which cost him the support of his most conservative backers. In the Second Constituent Assembly election of 1946, he lost to an avowed supporter of forced labor, Lt. Colonel Shock.

RICE. A traditional staple of the Kru peoples, not grown by the Akan. Rice production developed during 1920-1940 because of urban and laborer demand, ease of conservation and transportation, and high nutritive value. It was grown in all regions by 1932, although in the east by Dyulas rather than Akan peoples (673). Because of continued increase in urban demand, the Ivory Coast was importing over 100,000 tons of rice per year by 1971. (286, 339-345, 924, 938, 943)

ROSE, JEAN. Spokesman for French planters in the Ivory Coast in the 1930s and 1940s as President of the Chamber of Commerce and of the Syndicat Agricole de la Côte d'Ivoire. Rose had very conservative views on racial matters and organized against the reforms of the Popular Front. He welcomed the Vichy government's colonial policy and organized politically against the Brazzaville initiatives of 1944. He continued to organize the settlers against the elimination of forced labor and against African political participation, but by the time of the Territorial elections of 1946 the majority of settlers had moved to support more moderate candidates. (673)

RUBBER. Ivory Coast production of rubber became important between 1896-1900, when the collection technique was introduced to the east bank of the Comoé River by an English merchant. The first exploiters were from the Gold Coast (poyofoué) or Sudanese who would pay local authorities for the right to tap trees. During this period the value of wild rubber exported grew from 440,000 Fr. to 4,734,000 Fr. Colonial authorities began pressuring their Ivoirian subjects into rubber production to encourage the trade

caravans from the north to pass through the Ivory Coast
rather than through the Gold Coast; the head tax was
particularly successful in achieving this goal. By 1900,
rubber was more valuable as an export than all other products combined, and by 1907, two thirds of the colony's
commercial activity derived from it. European buyers then
began to look to Malay rubber plantations for their supply;
at the same time, the Ivoirian tapping techniques were
depleting the supply of the wild product. Thus, production
dropped off sharply after 1912. The rubber industry was
responsible for involving the peoples of eastern Ivory
Coast in the cash economy and for inducing changes in
land tenure like those introduced by cocoa production.
Furthermore, because of the fall in price of slaves as a
result of Samory's (q.v.) wars, slaves were introduced into
rubber production; this mode of production supplanted
the household unit base of activity, opening the way for
new types of labor relations. Contemporary rubber production, largely from European-owned plantations around
Dabou, is under the direction of SOCATCI (q.v.). Between 1970 and 1980 production rose from 11,000 to 22,000
tons. (346, 347, 585, 728)

- S -

SADIA, DUON. Minister of Tourism since 1981.

SALLER, RAPHAEL. From 1960 to 1963, the first Finance
Minister of the Ivory Coast. An Antillean, Saller was re-
spected by Houphouët for his experience, business exper-
tise, and contacts. Saller launched the country on its
particular development course, relying on private, largely
foreign, investment. He was succeeded by Konan Bédié
as Minister of Finance and Economic Affairs, and by Mohamed Diawara in Planning. (504)

SAMATIGUILA. Village and Sub-Prefecture north of Odienné,
in the extreme northwest of the Ivory Coast. One of three
villages visited by René Caillé in the Ivory Coast in 1827-
28. It was also the birthplace of Vakaba Touré (q.v.).
The marabouts of the village advised the king of Kabadugu
not to ally with the French when they arrived, thinking
that once installed, the French would stay.
The colonial administration noted the hostility of the

village to their rule. In 1922-23, a large part of the
population demonstrated against the village chief, probably
at the instigation of Muslim leaders. Ibrahima Touré, a
descendant of Vakaba and Va Ahmadou, served as catalyst
for resistance to colonial rule in that period and again in
1934. (673)

SAMORI TOURE. See TOURE, SAMORY.

SAN PEDRO. A recently developed port at the mouth of the
San Pedro River in southwestern Ivory Coast, designed
to serve as a "pole of development" for the country's
western region. San Pedro was conceived in the Southwest
Region Authority (q.v.) plan of 1968, and construction began that year. The first ships unloaded in the port in
1971. Although the planning goal is to have diversified
exports, the principal product passing through San Pedro
is hardwood, which represented 82 percent of total traffic
in 1981. The population in 1980 was 45,000, mostly in the
unplanned quarter of Le Bardo. (489, 1367-1372)

SANOGO, SEKOU. An Ivoirian Maninka elected with Houphouët
to the Grand Council of French West Africa in 1946. Along
with Etienne Djaument, he was a leader of the Cartel Central that challenged the PDCI in the 1952 Territorial Assembly.

SANWI. A traditional Anyi (q.v.) kingdom of about 50,000
population in the extreme southeast of the Ivory Coast,
with its capital in the village of Krinjabo. Sanwi has shown
the strongest cohesion and maintenance of tradition of the
Anyi kingdoms. In 1898, as the commercial activity of
Aboisso, a vassal village to Sanwi, was beginning to rival
that of the capital, King Aka Simadou refused to provide
manpower to maintain his section of the Aboisso-Bondoukou
road. He also tried to forbid European trading houses
from opening offices in Aboisso. The village chief of
Aboisso allowed the openings, and Aka Simadou complained
to the governor but finally was forced to give a concession
to the Company of Kong. Sanwi gave a recent demonstra-
tion of its continued vitality in 1959, when King Amon
Ndoffou III, acting on the counsel of his advisors, declared
Sanwi independent of the Ivory Coast. Basing his action
on an 1843 treaty between his ancestors and Bouët-
Willaumez (q.v.), the emissary of King Louis Phillippe,

Ndoffou sent a delegate to France to request protectorate status and to set up a provisional government. Ivoirian authorities arrested Ndoffou and 412 accomplices and sent them to prison. But in 1961, Houphouët declared a general amnesty: the prisoners were released and exiles were invited to return. (Nkrumah had allowed exiles to set up a "government in exile" in Ghana.) This is often recognized as the most serious attempt at secession ever experienced by the Ivory Coast. (617, 1051, 1056)

SASSANDRA. Sub-prefecture at the mouth of the Sassandra River with a population (1970) of 8,500 on the Atlantic coast. A wharf was built there in 1951, and Sassandra served as the principal port for the southwest region until the opening of San Pedro. The wharf at Sassandra was closed in 1971.

SASSANDRA RIVER. The Sassandra drains the area west of the Bandama basin in the Ivory Coast. Its source is within the country, from the Tiemba River which begins between Odienné and Boundiali, uniting with the Férédougouba or Bagbé River from the Guinea highlands as the Sassandra. Its coastal estuary extends inland ten miles. The mouth is obstructed by sand bars, current, and surf, but small boats can navigate it for about 50 miles inland. It is damned at Buyo, forming the second-largest reservoir in the country. (5)

SATMACI. See TECHNICAL ASSISTANCE COMPANY FOR THE AGRICULTURAL MODERNIZATION OF THE IVORY COAST.

SAWADOGO, ABDOULAYE (1933-). From 1966-1968, Minister Delegate of Agriculture, a post to which he was appointed in 1966 at the age of 33. From 1968 to 1977, Sawadogo was Minister of Agriculture. A Bambara and a Muslim, Sawadogo is an expert in tropical agronomy. He studied at the French National Agriculture School in Montpellier, then completed his diploma in tropical agronomy in Paris. He has been a high official in the Agriculture Ministry since 1961 and was brought into the Political Bureau of the PDCI in 1966. (760)

SEGUELA. Sub-prefecture with a 1980 population of 10,000 in the northwest quadrant of the country. Seguela took on importance as a market where cola nuts from the forest region were bought by Dyula traders in exchange for salt and livestock. Samory Touré devastated the town in 1893 and passed there again in 1897. The population is predominantly Worodugu (related to the Dyula) and Moslem.

SENUFO (SENOUFO). An ethnic group of Bambara origins, estimated to number about 500,000 in 1978, inhabiting the north-central area of the Ivory Coast and neighboring Mali and Burkina Faso, centered in the Ivory Coast on the city of Korhogo (q.v.). The Senufo can be subdivided into about thirty groups, which can be classed into from five to seven clusters according to geographic and historical affinity. They are classified by S. Coulibaly as, from north to south, the Tagbambele, Kassembele, Kiembabele, Nafambele, Kafibele, Fodonon-Kouflo, and Gbonzoro. According to Paulme, the Senufo expanded into the Korhogo region from the north several centuries ago. With the decline of the Mali empire, they expanded north to Sikasso (now Mali) and south to Bouake, but their area of occupation was later reduced by Maninka and Baule incursions: fleeing Maninka domination in the seventeenth century, the Nafare and Tiembara Senufo crossed in large numbers to the left bank of the Bandama. The rise of the kingdom of Kong in the eighteenth century forced them to cross back again. There they mixed with other Senufo already inhabiting the area, such as the Tanga and Fodonon. Under Nangen Sorho (q.v.), they were organized hierarchically on the Maninka model into a powerful state around Korhogo. Here they maintained their independence through much of the nineteenth century under chief Zouakonion. Their model of organization was emulated by other Senufo groups.

In the 1870s, the Islamized Senufo kingdom of Sikasso set out to conquer those to their south. The villages of Guiembé and Niellé were destroyed about 1875; Sinématiali was conquered about 1883, attacked again in 1890, and finally destroyed in 1892, extending the rule of Sikasso south. Then the Zerma, warriors and traders from the Niger valley east of Niamey, attacked the Tagouana and Djimini, defeating the former and signing a truce with the latter. A second Zerma attack brought all the southern Senufo to arms, and the Zerma retreated to the frontier with the Baule (1895), where they founded Marabadiassa. The Zerma rallied to Samory and attacked the Senufo again.

From 1883 to 1898 the Senufo suffered greatly under the attacks and domination of Samory. The exception was

Tiembara, whose chief Gbon Coulibaly shrewdly detached himself from Sikasso to ally with Samory. The contemporary heavy density of population around Tiembara is due to the absorption of Senufo refugees from areas under attack by Samory. (580)

Senufo villages are organized in complete independence of one another. The male secret society plays a major role in Senufo life. Initiation into it is preceded by a cycle of three periods, childhood, adolescence, and adulthood, with a rite of passage between each; the whole cycle takes up almost the first thirty years of life. When initiation is complete, the adult male is no longer obligated to perform agricultural work and becomes one of the elders whom the chief consults on major decisions. Each village identifies a sacred forest, in and from which ritual activities are initiated. Senufo wooden masks and statues are among the most renowned in Africa. The term "Senufo" is a Manding translation of Sénambele, i.e., "those who speak Syénar."

Islamization of the Senufo began before the colonial period and has continued until the present time, but has spread more rapidly among the chiefs than among the general population. (68, 73, 77-79, 82, 85, 87, 94, 189-191, 303, 322, 580, 588, 699, 1188-1204, 1222, 1298, 1358-1361)

SERI GNOLEBA, See GNOLEBA, MAURICE SERY.

SHEA (KARITE) BUTTER. The shea tree (butyrospermum parkii), from which the nut is gathered, grows in northern Ivory Coast. Inside the nut is a fatty substance from which shea butter is made. This product is used for cooking oil, for lamps, and as an ointment and hair-dressing.

SLAVERY. The slave trade was fed in the nineteenth century by Samory's campaigns and internal wars in the Ivory Coast. Samory exchanged prisoners as slaves with the forest peoples for arms, gunpowder, and food. Pacification provoked inter-ethnic warfare in which slaves were taken and were reported sold as late as 1904 at Grand Lahou and Jacqueville, and clandestinely even later. With the disappearance of the slave trade, former slaves were gradually integrated through marriage into the societies in which they lived. (728, 1121)

SOCATCI. The Société des Caoutchoucs de Côte d'Ivoire (Ivory Coast Rubber Company), created by the government to produce natural rubber from plantations, beginning in 1980. At Grand Bereby, SOCATCI is building a rubber processing plant under a grant from the United Kingdom Commonwealth Corporation.

SOCIALIST PARTY (SFIO) OF THE IVORY COAST. The Ivoirian Socialist Party was organized in August 1937 in Abidjan, encouraged by the Popular Front (q.v.) government's liberalization of colonial policy. (673, 828)

SOCIETE COMMERCIALE DE L'AFRIQUE DE L'OUEST (SCOA). A major French trading company established in the Ivory Coast in 1907 by the merger of the Ryff and Roth establishments, in association with the Banque de l'Union Parisienne. It formed the Société Agricole Africaine to develop palm oil and banana plantations in the Ivory Caost. (836)

SOCIETE INDIGENE DE PREVOYANCE (SIP). Established to provide security against seed and food shortages among the African population, SIPs became general purpose agricultural organizations. Membership and a supporting tax were obligatory where an SIP was organized. Local colonial administrators had almost complete discretion of SIP funds, which were frequently used for purposes other than those for which they were formally intended. (669, 773)

SODE. Common abbreviated form of "société de développement," a type of state corporation created as a result of the 1971-75 development plan to increase smallholder participation in the cultivation of various agricultural products. A separate SODE was created for each product. However, according to Chauveau and Richards (287) and Pillet-Schwartz (307), the SODEs have aided large-scale agroindustry more than they have the small farmers who have become dependent on them. Having intervened in and damaged or destroyed the traditional production and marketing systems, the SODEs have not satisfactorily replaced them. (287, 307)

SODEFEL. The "SODE" (q.v.) charged with training producers in modern techniques of fruit and vegetable growing. Operates primarily in the north.

SODEFOR. The "SODE" (q.v.) entrusted with reforestation and wood processing. SODEFOR was created in 1966 and is partially financed by a felling tax.

SODEPALM. A state development corporation (SODE), created in 1963 for the development of oilpalm production in both state-run agro-industrial complexes and small-holder plantations, and to process and market their product. Since 1967, SODEPALM has been charged with expanding production. Processing was later assigned to PALMINDUSTRIE and marketing to PALMIVOIRE. (490)

SODEPRA. The SODE (q.v.) for animal production. Operates primarily in the north.

SODERIZ. The Société pour le Développement de la Riziculture, the "SODE" (q.v.) for rice. SODERIZ operates primarily in the north.

SODESUCRE. The state enterprise (SODE) with entire responsibility for sugar production, controlling six sugar complexes in the north and center of the country. Since 1973, 250 billion CFA francs have been invested in the agro-industrial sugar complexes of Ferkessedougou I and II, Borotou-Koro, Serebou, Zuenoula, and Marabadiasa. Production costs have been running at least twice the amount of the world market price, and the debt on this venture was estimated at over 14 percent of total public debt by 1979. Four additional sugar complexes have been dropped from the plan. Although the decision to use this massive investment in the northernmost part of the country was politically sound, the increased transportation costs have rendered it economically problematic. (374, 505, 534, 535)

SOMPE (SOMBE). Small, uniform pieces of iron that served as traditional units of currency in the colonial circles of the Guro, Haut-Sassandra, and the southern part of the Seguela circle, i.e., in the center-west of the Ivory Coast. Sompé were used in commercial exchange between the forest and savannah peoples, especially in the kola trade.

SONAFI (SOCIETE NATIONALE DE FINANCEMENT, NATIONAL FINANCE CORPORATION). Created to support Ivoirian nationals in acquiring state-owned stock shares. (466)

SORGHUM. A traditional cereal food crop of the northern Ivory Coast savannah region, grown essentially in the same areas as millet, but especially important to the Lobi and Kulango.

SOUBRE DAM. Latest in a series of hydro-electric dams, originally scheduled for operation in the late 1980s; however, construction has been put on hold due to the country's recent financial difficulties. The Soubré Dam would have made the Ivory Coast self-sufficient in energy. Soubré is on the proposed new San Pedro-Man western axis of development. See also ENERGY. (374)

SOUTHWEST REGION AUTHORITY (AUTORITE POUR LA REGION DU SUD-OUEST, ARSO). A multi-functional regional administration created in 1968 to develop the area west of the Sassandra River. Its purposes have been: (1) construction of a deepwater port and city of San Pedro (q.v.), planned to receive a population of 200,000; (2) construction of a north-south axis in the western Ivory Coast, terminating at San Pedro; (3) exploitation of forests for timber and development of iron mining; (4) establishment of industries at San Pedro; (5) creation of agro-industrial complexes based on oil palm, coconuts, and rubber; and (6) resettlement of persons displaced from the Kossou Dam reservoir and the attraction of settlers from elsewhere in the Ivory Coast. (438, 1371)

STATE ENTERPRISES (SOCIETES D'ETAT). The institutional manifestations of the Ivoirian development policy of "state capitalism." Ivoirian state enterprises often have acronym titles beginning SODE (Société de Développement), q.v. They are created by the government, and their equity is fully owned by the state; however, they have extensive budgetary and managerial independence. They have become increasingly important in the Ivorian economy, with an annual investment growth rate of 25 percent between 1965 and 1974. In 1965, public enterprise investment was less than one half the amount in the governmental budget, but was greater than the government budget allocation by 1974. They also grew in number, from five in 1960, to 31 in the late 1960s, to 84 in 1977. They came under criticism in the 1970s, first from the World Bank and then from the President, for inefficiency, excessive independence, and poor financial management. Their directors have been politically powerful individuals, and they have resisted reform rather successfully. However, in 1980 all but nine of the 36 autonomous state corporations were eliminated. The total number of such institutions dropped only from 84 to 72, with some of them maintained but funded under the state budget. (412, 445, 864)

STOCK EXCHANGE. See BOURSE DES VALEURS DE LA COTE D'IVOIRE.

SUBPREFECTURE (SOUS-PREFECTURE). The basic level of administration in the Ivory Coast, based on the French model. See also ADMINISTRATIVE HISTORY.

SUGAR. Because foreign exchange was being expended on the importation of sugar, the government decided to begin a domestic production program in 1983, both to meet domestic demand and to provide an additional product for export. Ivoirian sugar production rose from 4,500 tons in 1974, to 53,700 in 1979, to 168,000 tons in 1981-82, of which 108,000 tons were exported. There is public investment in the six sugar complexes, which had operating costs 2-3 times the world market price for sugar. Thus, sugar was exported at a price substantially below production costs. The government has also created the Société Ivoirienne de Raffinage to refine sugar for markets in Ivory Coast, Mali, and Burkina Faso. See also SODESUCRE. (348-354, 428, 505, 534, 535, 932, 943)

SYLLA, YACOUBA. An Ivoirian merchant, Moslem reformer, and former RDA leader in Gagnoa. Sylla is a follower of Cheick Hamallah, who was exiled in the Ivory Coast in the 1930s, and who while there introduced a version of the Mouride Qadriya emphasizing the religion of labor; this belief system came to be known as Hamallism (q.v.). (828, 1256)

SYNDICAT AGRICOLE AFRICAIN. Organization of Ivoirian planters established in 1944 by Houphouët, August Denise (q.v.), and six others in a break with the European-planter-dominated Syndicat Agricole de la Côte d'Ivoire. The SAA, forerunner of the PDCI (q.v.), was at first dominated by Baule and Agni planters, and by the wealthier among them. However, in order to challenge colonial policy more effectively, the SAA waged a successful recruitment drive among small farmers and reached a membership of 1,600 members by late 1944, expanded to 20,000 in 1947. (828, 836)

SYNDICAT AGRICOLE DE LA COTE D'IVOIRE. See SYNDICAT AGRICOLE AFRICAIN.

SYNDICAT DES AGENTS DU RESEAU ABIDJAN-NIGER. A railroad workers' union formed in 1937 in the Ivory Coast in the wake of the Popular Front (q.v.) reforms.

SYNDICAT DES CHEMINOTS AFRICAINS. A railroad workers' union formed before World War II. In 1947 there were about 5,000 members in cities all along the RAN (Régie des Chemins de Fer Abidjan-Niger, q.v.). When the entire governing bureau was arrested during a 1946 strike, PDCI leaders J. Delafosse and Francheschi met with the governor to secure their release. This was an important event in the process of bringing union leaders into the party. The short and poorly organized strike of 1946 was followed by a more successful one in 1947.

SYNDICAT DES COMMERCANTS ET TRANSPORTEURS AFRI-CAINS. A union created in 1945, with about 250 members by 1947. Most members were Dyula or Senegalese, with important economic resources and a good communications network even in remote rural regions. Several leaders became active in independence politics: Philippe Vierra joined the PDCI, and Fattoh Ellingan the Progressive Party.

SYNDICAT DES FONCTIONNAIRES INDIGENES DE LA COTE D'IVOIRE. A union of government workers formed in 1937 in the wake of the Popular Front (q.v.) reforms, with locals in the principal towns of the colony.

SYNDICAT DU PERSONNEL ENSEIGNANT AFRICAIN. A teachers' union organized after World War II. Its leaders, Djibo Sounkalo, Ayemou Niangoran, Kouassi Kouaido, and B. Sangaret, all were also active in the PDCI.

- T -

TAABO. Site of the second major hydro-electric dam on the Bandama River (95 kms. south of that at Kossou), also constructed by the AVB (Autorité pour l'Aménagement de la Vallée du Bandama, q.v.). Construction began on the Taabo dam in 1975 and was completed in 1979. (1373)

TAPE, BISSOUMA. An official of the Union Générale des Etudiants de Côte d'Ivoire who was an outspoken opponent of the PDCI in the late 1950s but was brought into the fold

by his election to the National Assembly on the PDCI slate
in 1960. Tapé was brought into the PDCI Political Bureau
in 1966.

TARO. Food crop grown in essentially the same areas as plantain, the southeast and south-central forest zone.

TECHNICAL ASSISTANCE COMPANY FOR THE AGRICULTURAL
MODERNIZATION OF IVORY COAST (SATMACI). The state
technical extension service for modernization in coffee and
cocoa production. SATMACI was established in 1958 as
the regional development agency for the Center Zone and
is especially beneficial to the smallholders, who account
for the greatest share of the coffee and cocoa harvest.

TEXTILES. In the pre-colonial period, textiles were generally
produced for local consumption, although some Baule and
Guro cloths were sold to trade caravans. Artisan production was largely replaced by imported cloth during the
colonial period, except during the world wars, when shortages of imports temporarily revived indigenous production.
See GONFREVILLE, PAGNE. (69, 500, 520, 537)

THIAM, AMADOU (1923-). Minister of Information since
1978, and affiliated with Radiodiffusion de Côte d'Ivoire.
Ambassador to Morocco in 1966.

THIERRY LEBBE, ALEXIS (1920-). Senior Minister of State.
From 1977 to 1981, Minister of the Interior; from 1970 to
1977, Minister of Construction and Town Planning; Minister
for Animal Production from 1966-1970. Thierry Lebbe is a
Godié; he worked as a teacher, then entered the French
West African administrative service. In 1958 he was appointed to head the staff of the Minister for Public Affairs.
After training in public affairs in Paris, he held several
administrative posts, including that of prefect; he then
served two years as Secretary of State for the Interior
and for Information before being appointed Minister.

TIASSALE. Town on the Bandama River in south-central Ivory
Coast. A pre-colonial market point where goods were exchanged between the Baule to the north and coastal peoples
to the south. As the export trade in raw rubber grew in
importance, European traders entered Tiassale, and by
1898 it began to look like a "boom town." By 1905 the

French military commander there called it "the most important commercial point in the whole colony." With the ces-
sation of the rubber trade and the completion of the railroad (which bypassed Tiassale), its commercial importance
declined. Now a sub-prefecture on the main highway connecting Abidjan and Bouaké, it had a 1970 population of
3,500. (724)

TIMBER. See FORESTRY.

TONKOUI, MOUNT. One of the highest points in the Ivory
Coast, Mount Tonkoui is located near Man and rises to
1,218 meters.

TOUBA. Sub-prefecture and most important town between
Man and Odienné in extreme western Ivory Coast. In the
pre-colonial period, Touba was an important market for Kola,
bought there by Dyula traders in exchange for salt or
cattle and sheep.

TOUBAB (TOUBABOU). Dyula term used commonly by Africans to designate a European. (719)

TOUMODI. A sub-prefecture of 7,000 population on the main
Abidjan-Yamassoukro-Bouaké highway. Toumodi was a
traditional trading center between the north and Grand
Lahou. The revolt of the Nanafoué Baule in 1900 spread
over the region and continued sporadically until 1915.
Toumodi was chef-lieu of Baule-Sud circle from 1889-1912,
then a sub-division of the Baule-Sud, and of Nzi-Comoé
circles from 1912 to 1960. (576, 868, 1374)

TOURA. See TURA.

TOURE, AMADOU LAMINE. Vice-President of the Syndicat
Agricole Africain in 1944 and 1947, and regional delegate
from Grand Bassam.

TOURE, MOKTAR. Having a claim as a descendent of Vakaba,
Moktar was denied his chieftaincy by the French but won
it in 1946 with the support of the PDCI.

TOURE (TURE), MORIBA. Son of Vakaba Toure (q.v.) and
last independent king of Kabadugu. Moriba came to power
when his brother Va Ahmadou Toure (q.v.) was participating

in Samory Toure's (q.v.) military campaign in 1893. Moriba tried to maintain independence of action between the French and Samory's forces. He called upon the French in 1893 to help him put down a revolt in the province of Naoubou, an action which resulted in the incorporation of his kingdom into the Ivory Coast. Moriba clashed with the French administration over the question of slavery and was himself arrested in 1899. He was removed from his post as chief of Kabadugu and exiled. He returned to Odienné and died in 1901. He had, however, preserved the identity of Kabadugu to the extent that the Ivoirian border with Mali and Guinea are the former limits of Kabadugu. (708)

TOURE (TURE), SAMORY. Maninka leader who gained control of an empire that, between 1880 and 1900, extended over large parts of contemporary Guinea, Mali, Burkina Faso, and the Ivory Coast. Born about 1830 near Sanankoro, Guinea, Samory became a warrior and chief of Bissandougou (Mali). As he began to expand the area of his control, he came in conflict with the French, who (around 1880) were establishing their influence in the Sudan. In 1889, he moved his armies south and east, entering the Ivory Coast. French military pressure forced him to move his headquarters to Dabakala, in northeastern Ivory Coast, in 1893.

The campaigns against him intensified in 1892-93, cutting off his arms supplies through Sierra Leone. He began looking for an arms route through the Ivory Coast, where the Baule were already selling him some arms. From 1894 on, he relied almost exclusively on the Baule for arms. He sent emissaries to the Dyula city of Kong in 1894. However, because Kong allied with the French against him, he attacked and burned it in 1897. He was captured by the French on September 29, 1898, near Guélémou in the Ivory Coast. Samory was sent into exile in Gabon, where he died in 1900. Samory's activities around Kong had a lasting impact, in that the area has remained relatively underpopulated into modern times as a result of the uprooting of populations by his campaigns. (587, 619, 623, 632, 645, 648, 649, 661, 724)

TOURE (TURE), VA AHMADOU (MANGBE MADU). Son of Vakaba Toure (q.v.), founder of the kingdom of Kabadugu, in Odienné, Ivory Coast. Va Ahmadou ruled Kabadugu from 1875 to 1893. A revolt against his rule in 1878-79 was put

down with great difficulty, and shortly thereafter Ahmadou
Toure concluded an alliance with his nephew Samory Toure
(q.v.). Va Ahmadou joined Samory in his military campaigns and was captured with him by the French in 1898.
He was released in 1905 and died in Odienné in 1912. (708)

TOURE (TURE), VAKABA (C. 1800-1858). Founder of the
kingdom of Kabadugu (q.v.), which replaced the Nafana
kingdom of the Diarassouba clan around Odienné in 1848.
Vakaba was born in Samatiguila and worked as a trader
from 1825 to 1840. He then took up a military career in
his uncle's service but established his own business at
Wogona. Because of his wealth and military skill, he was
called to defend his native Samatiguila against a rival claim
about 1842. He built up his own army, defeated the Diarassouba forces, and destroyed Nafana. At his death he
left a powerful and well-organized state to Va Ahmadou
Toure (q.v.). (580, 708)

TOURISM. Lacking spectacular natural sites or the fauna of
East Africa, the Ivory Coast government has hoped to build
a tourism industry based on its first-class facilities and
its ethnic and folkloric diversity. Success has been only
modest, with 109,000 tourist visits in 1975, 220,000 in 1979,
down to 210,000 in 1980. At the end of 1982 there were
over 6,000 hotel rooms in the country, over 4,000 of these
"international class." Tourism accounted for only 2.4 percent of export receipts in 1976, yet was still the fifth most
important product, after coffee, cocoa, wood, and refined
petroleum. A Ministry of Tourism was created in 1975.
(14, 32-34, 419, 567, 568, 747, 792)

TRADE, FOREIGN. In 1978 there was a sharp drop in coffee
and cocoa prices, which produced a 40-percent drop in
the Ivoirian terms of trade. Also contributing to this problem were the price of imported oil and real interest rates
in international financial markets. (359, 361, 365, 366,
372-375, 377-379, 455, 456, 495, 511, 540, 544)

TREICH-LAPLENE, MARCEL. Agent of Arthur Verdier (q.v.),
who on Verdier's behalf explored the Bia and Comoé river
valleys, signing protectorate treaties for France with the
Bétié, Indénié, Bondoukou, and Kong. He met Binger
(q.v.) at Kong in 1889. (674)

TREICHVILLE. The original "African quarter" of Abidjan under colonial rule. It was divided into lots in 1937. Now a relatively well-established residential and commercial area connected to the Plateau district by two bridges. Named for Treich-Laplène, an early French resident in the Ivory Coast.

TTCI. Common designation in the Ivory Coast for a co-opérant, or young Frenchman performing alternative service in a developing country (from the license plate designation for coopérants).

TURA (WENMEBO). A peripheral Mandé group, pushed, beginning in the sixteenth century, by advancing Maninka from around Touba to the higher altitudes of the mountainous area around the town of Man in western Ivory Coast. The Toura are related to, and highly intermingled with, the Dan (q.v.). (1205)

- U -

UBI (OUBI). One of the Kru peoples of southwest Ivory Coast, located near the town of Tai on the Cavally River (Liberian border). They are closely related to, and sometimes identified as part of, the Bakwe. The Ubi have recently become involved in coffee growing. Traditionally, Ubi women have had access to some political rights. (4, 5, 1206, 1312)

UNION AFRICAINE ET MALGACHE. An organization of twelve francophone African states, created in September 1961 as a vehicle for the "Brazzaville group" to counter the more radical stands of the "Casablanca group" of Ghana, Guinea, Mali, Algeria, Morocco, and the United Arab Republic. Its structure consisted of a Conference of Heads of State, without power to make decisions binding upon its members, but rather simply to reflect their foreign policy consensus. It was supplanted in 1965 by the Organisation Commune Africaine et Malgache (OCAM, q.v.).

UNION DES AGNI DE MORONOU. Ethnic association formed in 1944.

UNION DES ORIGINAIRES DES SIX CERCLES DE L'OUEST

(UOCOCI). Ivoirian organization of Kru ethnic groups, created in 1944 under the presidency of Frédéric Gogoua, a planter from Sassandra. There were about 100 people at the first meeting, from Daloa, Gagnoa, Grand Lahou, Man, Sassandra, and Tabou circles. There was a detailed organization and bureau of nine members. The first goals were social and cultural, focused on the educational gap between the eastern and western regions of the colony. As soon as political reforms were announced in 1945, the UOCOCI supported Houphouët in the legislative elections. (828)

UNION FOR THE DEFENSE OF IVORY COAST ECONOMIC INTERESTS (UDECI, UNION POUR LA DEFENSE DES INTERETS ECONOMIQUES). A political coalition through which, in the March 1952 Territorial Assembly elections, the PDCI gained ground it had lost in building up support over the previous three years. (760)

UNION FRATERNELLE DES ORIGINAIRES DE LA COTE D'IVOIRE (FRATERNAL UNION OF IVORY COAST NATIVES,UFOCI). An urban-based, Baule-dominated association that in 1945 nominated the African Bloc (q.v.) to contest the 1945 Abidjan municipal elections (828). This social organization preceded the formation of political parties in the Ivory Coast for the Constituent Assembly election of June 2, 1946. The name suggested the exclusion of non-Ivoirian Africans, toward whom the group did in fact express hostility. (760)

UNION GENERALE DES ETUDIANTS DE LA COTE D'IVOIRE (UGECI). Student organization founded in 1956 in Abidjan, grouping the pre-existing student associations of Abidjan, Dakar, and France. Its constitution provided that the president would be the president of the Association des Etudiants de Côte d'Ivoire en France (AECIF), the oldest of the constituent organizations. The UGECI leadership, affiliated with the Fédération des Etudiants Noirs on France (FEANF), demanded immediate independence. One leader was arrested in the Ivory Coast, and Ivoirians were warned against the group's radical tendencies; the ultimate blow came in 1960, when the government formed a rival organization, the Union Nationale des Etudiants de Côte d'Ivoire (q.v.), endowing it with such benefits that most of the overseas Ivoirian students came over to it. (504)

UNION GENERALE DES TRAVAILLEURS D'AFRIQUE NOIRE (UGTAN). A federation of territorial trade unions formed in Cotonou, Dahomey (now Benin), in 1957 under the leadership of Sékou Touré. The Ivoirian branch, the Union des Travailleurs de Côte d'Ivoire, worked politically with the PDCI until 1958, when it was cross-pressured by political differences between the Ivory Coast and Guinea. In 1959, a breakaway movement from the UTCI formed, under pressure from the government, as the Union Nationale des Travailleurs de Côte d'Ivoire. The UGTAN activists continued to agitate for immediate independence and for trade union rights, and called a strike in October 1959. Leaders were arrested, workers were suspended or dismissed, and the strike collapsed within a week. The most prominent leader, Blaise Yao Ngo (a Guinean), sought refuge in Conakry. From that point on, union activities in the Ivory Coast were under the firm control of the PDCI.

UNION GENERALE DES TRAVAILLEURS DE COTE-D'IVOIRE (UGTCI). The PDCI-dominated federation of trade unions. The leaders of four union groups, separated as a result of political disagreements in the period just before independence, agreed to a merger in June 1961. However, rivalries remained so intense that the UGTCI was not formally constituted until August 1962.

UNION LOCALE DES SYNDICATS CONFEDERES CGT DE LA COTE D'IVOIRE (ULSC). A union federation formed in 1944 in Abidjan as part of the extension of the Confédération Générale de Travail (the French Communist Union) into French West Africa. The steering committee included Camille Kissi Gris of the CGT, Georges Sery of the Syndicat des Ouvriers et Chauffeurs Africains, and Georges Kassy representing the Syndicat des Employées Africains. All had been active in various ethnic, regional, or professional associations since 1937. The ULSC included seven private-sector unions with 5,840 members and three unions in the public sector with 452 members. (580, 673)

UNION MONETAIRE OUEST-AFRICAINE. See WEST AFRICAN MONETARY COMMUNITY.

UNION NATIONALE DES ETUDIANTS ET DES ELEVES DE COTE D'IVOIRE (UNECI). The Ivoirian student organization formed by the government in 1960 to cut support from the rebellious Association des Etudiants de Côte d'Ivoire en France. The UNECI was replaced with the Mouvement des Etudiants et des Elèves de Côte d'Ivoire (MEECI). See also UNION GENERALE DES ETUDIANTS DE LA CÔTE D'IVOIRE.

UNIVERSITY OF ABIDJAN. See NATIONAL UNIVERSITY OF THE IVORY COAST.

USHER ASSOUAN, ARSENE (1930-). A Nzima, Usher Assouan studied law at France's Bordeaux and Poitiers Universities, returning to the Ivory Coast to practice before the Abidjan Court of Appeals. He was administrative assistant to Houphouët, then was Minister of Special Affairs in a French (Guy Mollet) government from 1954-56. He was an early member of the PDCI and was elected Vice-President of the National Assembly in 1960. With independence that year, he became the first permanent representative of the Ivory Coast to the United Nations. He served there for six years, during three of which he represented the Ivory Coast on the Security Council, then was named Foreign Minister and was brought into the Political Bureau of the PDCI. Usher Assouan lost his ministry in the wake of a speech by Houphouët criticizing the economic mismanagement of the country. (864)

- V -

VALLY, GILLES LAUBHOUET. Minister of Rural Development and Civil Defense.

VANIE-BI-TRA, ALBERT (1936-). Minister of Labor and Ivoirianization. A Guro, Vanié-bi-Tra studied law at the University of Dakar and completed his law studies in France. He served as a magistrate from 1958 to 1961 and as judge in Abidjan and Dimbokro from 1961 to 1963. From 1963 to 1971 he was Public Prosecutor, successively at Gagnoa, Daloa, Bouaké, and Abidjan. From 1971 to 1977 he was Minister of Labor and Social Affairs, at which time he assumed his present title.

VERDIER, ARTHUR. A French naval officer turned businessman, Verdier established the Compagnie de Kong (q.v.), a private trading company in the 1860s. Verdier had

represented a Dutch company and was in 1864 the only
European established in the future Ivory Coast. For almost
two decades, Verdier's company preserved the French
presence in face of expanding British activity from the
Gold Coast. He was named Résident de France in 1878 and
four years later retired to France in great wealth, having
delegated company affairs to his agents. His privileges
in the Ivory Coast were removed in 1889.

VICHY (Government). From 1940 to 1943, French West Africa
was under the control of the Vichy government. The Ivory
Coast especially was subjected to racism and the abuse of
power. Separate facilities for Africans and Europeans appeared more frequently, as in railroad train seating.

VOLTAIC (GOUR). A language group that in the Ivory Coast
includes Syénar (the language of the Senufo), Kulango,
and Lobi.

VRIDI CANAL. The Canal that connects the Ebrié Lagoon with
the Atlantic Ocean, making Abidjan a deep-water port capa-
ble of handling ocean-going shipping. The first effort
at a canal was attempted in 1905-07, but the cut quickly
filled with sand during the seasonal drop in the lagoon
water level. Seasonal flooding of Abidjan and Grand Bassam was another reason to open the lagoon to the coast,
and there was a second try at the same location in 1933-34;
it opened by erosion to 100 meters in width, then refilled.
The authorities declared their intention to improve the
Grand Bassam port installations but then decided instead
to begin port construction at Abidjan in 1936. Work began
on the present canal in 1935 but was suspended during
the war. It was completed in 1951. The success of the
Vridi site derives from its position near the "trou sans
fond" (bottomless hole), a natural feature in the ocean
floor that prevents the canal from filling in with sand.

- W -

WAN (OUAN, NGWANU). A sedentary, hoe-agricultural
people who grow coffee and cotton. Numbering about
15,000, their traditional homeland is near the geographic
center of the Ivory Coast in the sub-prefectures of Beoumi
and Mankono. The Wan were not identified as a separate

culture by colonial authorities; rather, they were divided
into two cantons and considered "fringe" groups of the
neighboring Baule and Guro. (1207, 1208)

WEST AFRICAN CUSTOMS UNION (UNION DOUANIERE DE
L'AFRIQUE OCCIDENTALE, UDAO). Created in 1959 among
Benin (then Dahomey), the Ivory Coast, Mali, Mauretania,
Niger, Senegal, and Burkina Faso (then Upper Volta).
Its aims were to maintain the pre-independence customs
union, harmonize import taxation, and to prohibit customs
and fiscal duties among members. Results were disappointing because of a lack of commitment to economic integration
in the 1960s and a lack of permanent institutions to develop
policy. The UDAO was replaced in 1966 by the UDEAO
(Customs Union of West African States, q.v.). (394)

WEST AFRICAN ECONOMIC COMMUNITY (CEAO). A customs
union created among the Ivory Coast, Mali, Mauretania,
Niger, Senegal, and Burkina Faso in 1972. It replaced the
UDEAO (Customs Union of West African States, q.v.),
with the aim of creating a common customs zone, and common import duties and tariffs by 1990. Unlike its predeces-
sor organizations, it has permanent institutions: a Conference of Heads of State, a Council of Ministers, and a
General Secretariat. It has adopted a Regional Cooperation
Tax, a Community Development Fund, and a Solidarity Intervention Fund for Community Development. The Ivory
Coast, as the most advanced member economy, provides
over one half of the contribution to the Community Development Fund and one half of the Solidarity Fund. On the
other hand, it provides a market for Ivoirian manufactures
goods: 54 percent of the manufactured goods exchanged
were of Ivoirian origin in 1978. A major political problem
for the CEAO is a fear in other member countries of domination by the Ivory Coast. On the other hand, only six
percent of Ivory Coast trade is with other CEAO members.
    Beginning in 1982, CEAO officials came upon evidence
of embezzlement that ultimately led to the arrest of Moussa
Ngom, Senegalese former Secretary-General of the organization, Moussa Diakité, Malian former head of the CEAO
Solidarity and Development Fund (FOSIDEC), and Mohamed
Diawara (q.v.), former Minister of Planning of the Ivory
Coast. The three were tried and convicted in Ouagadougou,
Burkina Faso, In 1985. The organization lost 6.5 billion
CFA francs, but its international credibility may have been

enhanced by the successful prosecution of the three officers. (374, 394, 838)

WEST AFRICAN MONETARY COMMUNITY (UNION MONETAIRE
OUEST-AFRICAINE, UMOA). An organization in which the
Ivory Coast, Benin, Niger, Senegal, Togo, and Burkina
Faso centralize their foreign currency reserves, and which
issues the West African CFA franc. As a result of the
economic downturn, the Ivory Coast registered a $118
billion overdraft with the UMOA in 1980. (374)

WOBE (OUOBE). A people of the Kru ethnic cluster, centered
near the town of Man in western Ivory Coast. They are
closely related to the Guere (q.v.), and the two groups
are conscious of common customs, beliefs, and origins.
They number about 53,000 in their home area. (193-200,
650, 960, 1209-1211)

WORLD WAR I. The Ivory Coast contributed 15,000-20,000
troops to the war effort, many of them pressed into service. Their return caused social disruption, in that they
readjusted poorly to rural life and moved in great numbers
to the new cities. To support the war effort, the French
also required sharp increases in production of cotton, rubber, rice, and cocoa, and placed heavy portage demands
on the intermediate populations. The Anyi took advantage
of the proximity of the border: over 12,000 fled to the
Gold Coast and did not return until they were offered amnesty in 1918. (631, 673, 712)

WORLD WAR II. The outbreak of war in 1939 found most
Ivoirians in support of the metropole. In the first place,
they thought France would win; besides, they saw the possibility of improvement of their condition as a result of
war conditions. About 8,000 Ivoirians were mobilized in
1939. The economy was set back dramatically by the war:
the number of ships docking in the Ivory Coast fell from
140 to 89 between 1940 and 1941, and tonnage fell from
748,000 to 289,000. The internal road network fell into
disrepair. (701)

- Y -

YACE, PHILIPPE (1920-   ). One of the original leaders of

the Democratic Party of the Ivory Coast before independence, and the first secretary-general of the Rassemblement
Démocratique Africain. Yacé's political fortunes have risen
and fallen over the years. At times, he has been considered to be the eventual successor to Houphouët, but this
has always provoked a reaction from the President, who
has not tolerated a powerful, ambitious rival. Thus, in
1978 Yacé tried to manipulate the local elections to promote
his own supporters; Houphouët cancelled the elections and,
in 1980, abolished the post of PDCI secretary-general,
which Yacé occupied at the time, and removed him as
president of the National Assembly. Yacé is still considered
to be one of the more likely successors to the presidency.

Yacé is an Alladian (q.v.), but his political support has
been based in the "modern sector," among teachers and
military veterans. His father was a customs official in
Abidjan, and he was a teacher for two years before military
service with the French in World War II. He was awarded
the Croix de Guerre for bravery, and returned home to
teach. He served as secretary-general for district groups
of the PDCI, then was elected to the Territorial Assembly,
where he served for six years. With the creation of the
French Community in 1958, Yacé was elected to the Constituent Assembly of the Ivory Coast and the Community Senate. Upon independence, he became President of the National Assembly; in 1963 he was named president of the High
Court of Justice. In 1965 he was named Secretary-General
of the PDCI, with Houphouët becoming honorary chairman.
He has often served as Houphouët's representative at international meetings. (760, 864)

YAGO, BERNARD (1916). Catholic Archbishop of Abidjan
    since 1960. Yago received a social science diploma and was
    professor at a junior seminary from 1946-48. He has been
    President of the Episcopal Conference of Francophone West
    Africa since 1977 and was named a cardinal in 1983.

YAKUBA (YACOUBA). See DAN.

YAM. Genus Dioscorea, a traditional tuber food crop of the
    Ivory Coast both in the forest zone and among the northern
    Senufo. There are eighteen species in the Ivory Coast;
    some of them grow wild, and some are cultivated. Yams
    are planted to some extent throughout the country, except
    in the southwest; they are not a traditional food among the

peripheral Mandé and are not grown at all by the Kru.
They are especially important to the Agni, Baule, and
other peoples of Akan culture, who mark the beginning of
the yam harvest (between November and February, according to location) with important traditional religious ceremonies. The cultivated yam is of Asiatic origin, although
the indigenous, wild variety is sometimes gathered
during times of famine. (4, 286, 356-358, 868)

YAMOUSSOUKRO. Native village of Houphouët-Boigny, bene-
fitted during his three decades of control by spectacular
growth, receiving over one third of total urban investment
outside Abidjan through the 1960s and 1970s. In 1983 the
National Assembly named Yamoussoukro capital of the Ivory
Coast, for which designation the years of development had
implicitly prepared it. It was already the site of a massive
presidential residence and personal estate, the Maison du
Parti, with a congress hall seating 1,000 and the luxurious
Hotel President. The 1985 population was close to 100,000,
compared to about 500 in 1950. (24, 848)

YAOUNDE CONVENTION. An agreement concluded in 1963
between the European Economic Community (q.v.) and the
eighteen newly independent states that had been African
colonies of EEC member states. The Yaounde Convention
modified Chapter IV of the Treaty of Rome that had established the EEC (q.v.) and defined its relationship to
members' colonies.

YAPOBI, LEON. A commis principal, or senior African functionary, in Abidjan during the 1945-47 elections. He proposed a slate for the municipal elections of 1945 that would
include whites, but the meeting went instead with Houphouët's idea of an African Bloc (q.v.). Yapobi convened
a meeting in the same year at the house of the chef superieur of the Ebrié and Attié in Treichville, at which Houphouët was chosen a candidate for the Constituent Assembly.

YELLOW FEVER. A disease caused by the Amaril virus, transmitted by the Aedes Aegypti (mosquito). Yellow fever was
presumably eliminated in the Ivory Coast through massive
vaccinations in 1960, but there have been more recent out-
breaks in neighboring countries; this suggests the possibility of a return, especially in urban areas. Yellow fever

was responsible for the decimation of the population of Grand Bassam (q.v.) in 1899. (908)

- Z -

ZARANOU. Anyi capital, where Binger (q.v.) spent over three years, and where Treich-Laplene (q.v.) completed a protectorate treaty with the Anyi in 1887.

ZOUAKONION SORHO. By tradition the thirteenth in chiefly line from Nangen as head of the Tyembara Senufo. Zouakonion became chief in the 1840s and defended his region against the Maninka of Odienné. He did, however, lose power to the Senufo kingdom of Kenedugu at Sikasso; he became a vassal of Tiéba and joined forces with him to defeat other Senufo groups, the Tyembara of Niellé, and the Nafambelé. Still loyal to Sikasso, he extended his own authority over the central Senufo region. Zouakonion became very ill and stepped down in favor of his son Peleforo Gbon Sorho, better known by his Manding name Gbon Coulibaly (q.v.). Zouakonion died in 1894 after a reign of 54 years. (580)

BIBLIOGRAPHY

Introduction

Bibliographic entries are especially complete on sources in English, but serious work on many Ivoirian topics requires knowledge of French. The literature in English is particularly extensive in economics, politics, and art, and is most incomplete in sociology, ethnology, most historical topics, and the physical and life sciences. Because the dictionary is primarily oriented toward the English-speaking reader, it does not include the modest literature on the Ivory Coast in languages other than French and English.

In general, works in French not published in standard, relatively accessible sources, are not included here. On the other hand, unpublished dissertations in English are generally included, because they are widely available in the United States in microform through interlibrary loan or from University Microfilms in Ann Arbor, Michigan.

Abbreviations in the Bibliography

ACES	
ACCT	Agence de Coopération Culturelle et Technique
AUA	Annales de l'université d'Abidjan
" " " "	Série A (Law)
" " " "	Série D (Letters)
" " " "	Série F (Ethno-sociology)
" " " "	Série G (Geography)
" " " "	Série H (Linguistics)
" " " "	Série I (History)
" " " "	Série J (Oral Tradition)
" " " "	Série K (Economics)
BIFAN	Bulletin de l'Institut Français d'Afrique Noire
BOFCAN	Bulletin de l'Observation du français contemporain en Afrique noire
BSELM	Bulletin semestriel d'études linguistiques mandé
CEA	Cahiers d'Etudes Africaines
CEDA	Centre d'édition et de Diffusion africaines (Abidjan)
CIRES	Cahiers Ivoiriens de Recherche Economique et Sociale
CIRL	Cahiers ivoiriens de recherches linguistiques
CJAS	Canadian Journal of African Studies
COM	Cahiers d'Outre Mer

IES	Institut d'Ethno-sociologie
IFAN	Institut Français d'Afrique Noire
IJAHS	International Journal of African Historical Studies
JAS	Journal of African Studies
JMAS	Journal of Modern African Studies
MTM	Marchés Tropicaux et Méditerranéens
NEA	Nouvelles Editions Africaines
ORSTOM	Office de la Recherche Scientifique et Technique Outre-Mer
PUF	Presses Universitaires de France
RFEPA	Revue Française d'Etudes Politiques Africaines
RFHOM	Revue Française d'Histoire d'Outre-Mer
RIARHP	Revue de l'Institut Africain de Recherches historiques et politiques
RID	Revue Ivoirienne de Droit
RJPIC	Revue juridique et politique, indépendance et coopération
SAE	Société Africaine d'Edition
SAL	Studies in African Linguistics

GENERAL WORKS

A. TRAVEL

1 Baleine, Philippe de. 1982. Le Petit Train de la Brousse. Paris: Plon.

2 Conte, Arthur. 1981. Côte d'Ivoire, ou, Les Racines de la Sagesse. Paris: Editions Jeune Afrique.

3 Davis, Hassoldt. 1956. Sorcerers' Village. London: Harrap.

B. COLLECTIVE, INTERDISCIPLINARY

4 Encyclopédie Générale de la Côte d'Ivoire. 1978. Abidjan: Les Nouvelles Editions Africains, Editions Franco Impressions. 3 vols.

C. DESCRIPTION

5 American University. 1973. Area Handbook for the Ivory Coast. Washington, D.C.: American University, Foreign Area Studies.

6 Amon d'Aby, F. J. 1951. La Côte d'Ivoire dans la Cité Africaine. Paris: Larose.

7   Bourgoin, Henri and Philippe Guilhaume. 1979. La Côte d'Ivoire:
    Economie et société. Paris: Stock.

8   Carpenter, Allan. 1977. Ivory Coast. Chicago: Children's
    Press.

9   Conférence Olivant de Belgique. 1966. La Côte d'Ivoire:
    Chances et Risques. Brussels.

10 La Côte d'Ivoire. 1981. Afrique industrie infrastructures 11
    (229, April 15): 56-113.

11 Côte d'Ivoire: Vingt Ans. 1980. Abidjan: Editions Fraternité-
    Hebdo.

12 Decraene. P. 1982. Vieille Afrique et jeunes nations. Le
    continent noir au seuil de la troisième décennie de l'indépendance.
    Paris: Presses Universitaires de France.

13 Fregeat, Bernard. 1984. "Présentation de la Côte d'Ivoire."
    Cahiers du communisme 60 (9, September): 80-88.

14 Gaudio, Attilio and Patrick Van Roekeghem. 1984. Etonnante
    Côte d'Ivoire. Paris: Karthala.

15 Holas, Bohumil. 1963. Côte d'Ivoire: Passé, Présent, Perspect-
    ives. Abidjan: Centre des Sciences Humaines.

16 _____. 1962. Ouvrages et Articles 1944-1962. Paris: P.
    Geuthner.

17 Ivory Coast. Ministère de l'Information. Sous-Direction de la
    Documentation Générale et de la Presse. 1968. Aspects des
    Départements et des Sous-Préfectures. Abidjan: Société d'Im-
    primerie Ivoirienne.

18 _____. 1981. Les Deux premières décennies de l'indépendance
    ivoirienne, 1960-1980. Abidjan: Direction de la documentation.

19 Ivory Coast. Presidential Press Service. 1970. Côte d'Ivoire
    1960-1970: Dix Ans de Progrès. Abidjan.

20 Joseph, Gaston. 1917. La Côte d'Ivoire: le pays, les habitants.
    Paris: Larose.

21 Liniger-Goumaz, Max. 1983. "Le 'Fardeau Africain' de la
    France." Genève-Afrique 21 (1): 108-113.

22 Mortimer, Robert A. 1983. "Ivory Coast: Succession and Re-
    cession." Africa Report 28 (1, January-February): 5, 7.

23 Mourgeon, Jacques. 1969. La République de Côte d'Ivoire.

24 Naipaul, V. S. 1984. "The Crocodiles of Yamoussoukro." In
    Finding the Center: Two Narratives (New York: Alfred A.
    Knopf): 73-176.

25 Nédélec, Michel. 1983. Côte d'Ivoire 1892-1982: timbres-poste.
    Abidjan: CEDA.

26 Rosellini, Albert. 1977. The Ivory Coast in Pictures. New
    York: Sterling Publishing Company.

27 Rosen, George H. 1979. "The Ivory Coast: Le folklore, la
    prospérité." Atlantic 244 (December): 14 ff.

28 Rougerie, Gabriel. 1982. La Côte d'Ivoire. Paris: Presses
    Universitaires de France, 5th edition.

29 Spécial Côte d'Ivoire, 1960-1984. 1984. Peuples Noirs - Peuples
    Africains (7 December): 41-42.

30 Vallat, Francis. 1967. "Regards sur la Côte d'Ivoire." Con-
    naissance de l'Afrique (21, March).

31 _____ 1968. "Regards sur la Côte d'Ivoire." Connaissance de
    l'Afrique (25, February).

D. GUIDES

32 Bussang, Françoise and Gilles Leblanc. 1979. En Côte d'Ivoire.
    Paris: Hachette.

33 Ivory Coast. Office Nationale du Tourisme. 1980. Côte d'Ivoire,
    Ses Villes: Abidjan et son agglomération. Abidjan.

34 Remy, Mylène. 1981. The Ivory Coast Today (3rd edition).
    Paris: Editions Jeunes Afriques.

E. MAPS AND ATLASES

35 Ivory Coast. Ministère du Plan. 1971-79. Atlas de Côte d'Ivoire.
    Abidjan.

36 Pneu Michelin. 1982. Ivory Coast/Côte d'Ivoire.

37 SODEMI. 1964. Carte géologique de la République de Côte
    d'Ivoire (1/100,000). Abidjan: Direction des Mines et de la
    Géologie.

38 Vennetier, Pierre, ed. 1983. Atlas de la Côte d'Ivoire (2d edition). Editions Jeune Afrique.

F. STATISTICAL ABSTRACTS

39 Ahonzo, Etienne. 1984. Population de la Côte d'Ivoire. Abidjan: Direction de la Statistique.

40 La Côte d'Ivoire en Chiffres. (issued annually). Dakar: SAE.

G. BIBLIOGRAPHIES

41 Ivory Coast. Bibliothèque Nationale. 1969. Bibliographie de la Côte d'Ivoire.

42 _____. Ministère de l'Education Nationale. 1969- Bibliographie de la Côte d'Ivoire (quarterly). Abidjan: Bibliothèque Nationale.

43 _____. Analyses documentaires sur la Côte-d'Ivoire: Bibliographie sélective en sciences humaines. Programme d'éducation télévisuelle 1968-1980 7.

44 Janvier, Geneviève. 1972, 1973, 1975. Bibliographie de la Côte d'Ivoire. Vol. 1: Sciences de la Vie. Vol. 2: Sciences de l'Homme. Vol. 3 (with Guy Peron): Sciences physiques et de la terre. Annales de l'université d'Abidjan, out of series.

45 Loucou, Jean-Noël. 1982. Bibliographie de l'Histoire de Côte d'Ivoire (1960-1980). Abidjan: University of Abidjan, Department of History.

46 Roose, M. 1974. Liste bibliographique des travaux: Sciences Humaines 1954-1973. Abidjan: ORSTOM.

47 _____. 1976. Liste bibliographique des travaux de l'ORSTOM en Côte d'Ivoire: Sciences Humaines. Abidjan: ORSTOM.

48 _____ and Philippe Bonnefond. 1973. Bibliographie des travaux concernant la Côte d'Ivoire. Abidjan: ORSTOM.

49 Schwartz, Alfred. 1964. Etude de sciences humaines en Côte d'Ivoire: Essai de bibliographie. Paris: ORSTOM.

50 Sugar, Howard. 1984. "Bibliography for the political economy of Ivory Coast." In I. William Zartman and Christopher L. Delgado, eds. The Political Economy of the Ivory Coast (New York: Praeger) pp. 219-243.

H. PERIODICALS

51 Eburnéa. (1967-present). Abidjan.

52 Fraternité-Hebdo (1969-present, formerly Fraternité) Abidjan.

53 Fraternité-Matin. (1964-present) Abidjan.

54 Ivoire Dimanche. 1971-present. Weekly.

55 Réalités Ivoiriennes. Paris.

CULTURE

A. ARCHEOLOGY

56 Bayles des Hermens, R. de. 1973. "Découvertes isolées d'outils
    préhistoriques en Côte d'Ivoire et en Haute Volta." Notes
    Africaines 137: 6-8.

57 Bayles des Hermens, R. de, et al. 1983. "Recherches pré-
    historiques dans le Nord-Ouest de la Côte d'Ivoire: Mission
    1983." L'Anthropologie 87 (2): 241-247.

58 Chenorkian, R. 1984. "Etude typologique de la céramique de la
    couche 1 de l'amas coquillier de Songo Dagbe (Lagune Ebrié),
    Côte d'Ivoire." AUA:I 12: 19-42.

59 _____. 1983. "Ivory Coast Prehistory: Recent Developments."
    The African Archeological Review (1): 127-142.

60 Leclerc, P. and P. Reynard. "Amas de coquillages de Basse
    Côte d'Ivoire." AUA:I 3: 161-175.

61 Mauny, R. 1972. "Contribution à la connaissance de l'archéolo-
    gie préhistorique et proto-historique ivoiriennes." AUA, I
    1: 11-32.

62 Rivallain, J. 1984. "Apports des sondages archéologiques et
    des résultats d'enquêtes orales à la connaissance du milieu marin
    et humain du littoral du pays Alladian." AUA, I 12: 43-71.

63 _____. 1983. "Sites littoraux du pays alladian: Premières
    enquêtes et premiers sondages." AUA, I 11: 25-60.

B. ARCHITECTURE (see also RELIGION)

64 Ferguson, Phyllis. 1968. Aspects of Muslim Architecture in

the Dyula Region of the Western Sudan. Legon: Institute of African Studies.

65 Urbanisme. 1969. Abidjan, Côte d'Ivoire. Paris: nos. 111-112.

C. ARTS

66 Anquetil, Jacques. 1977. Côte d'Ivoire: L'artisanat créateur. Paris: Agence de coopération culturelle et technique.

67. Artistes Contemporains de Côte d'Ivoire: Youssouf Bath, N'Guessan Kra. (Exposition) 1984. Paris: Association Francaise d'Action Artistique.

68 Bochet, G. 1965. "Les masques senoufo: de la forme à la signification." BIFAN, 27 B, 3-4: 636-677.

69 Boser-Sarivaxévaxnis, Renée. 1972. Les Tissus de l'Afrique Occidentale. Basel: Pharos Verl Hansrudolf Schwabe AG.

70 Boyer, Alain-Michel. "1983. Miroirs de l'Invisible: La Statuaire Baoule." Art d'Afrique Noire 45 (Spring): 21-34.

71 Bravmann, René A. 1974. Islam and Tribal Art in West Africa. London: Cambridge University Press.

72 _____. 1975. "Masking Tradition and Figurative Art among the Islamized Mande." In Daniel F. McCall and Edna G. Bay, eds. African Images: Essays in African Iconology (New York: Africana Publishing Company), pp. 144-169.

73 Convers, M. 1975. "Masques en étain sénoufo." Arts d'Afrique 16 (Winter): 24-36.

74 Domowitz, Susan and Renzo Mandirola. 1984. "Grave monuments in Ivory Coast." African Arts 17 (4) 46-52.

75 Etienne-Nugue, Jocelyne and Elisabeth Laget. 1985. Artisanats Traditionels en Afrique Noire: Côte d'Ivoire. Paris: Harmattan.

76 Fischer, Eberhard and Lorenz Homberger. 1986. Masks in Guro Culture, Ivory Coast. New York: Center for African Art.

77 Glaze, Anita J. 1981. Art and Death in a Senufo Village. Bloomington: Indiana University Press.

78 _____. 1978. "Senufo Ornament and Decorative Arts." African-Arts 12 (1, Nov.): 63-71, 107.

79 Goldwater, R. 1964. Senufo Sculpture from West Africa. New York: The Museum of Primitive Art.

80 Gnonsoa, Angèle. 1983. Masques de l'Ouest Ivoirien. Abidjan: CEDA.

81 Holas, Bohumil. 1969. Animaux dans l'art ivoirien (Second Edition). Paris: P. Geuthner.

82 _____. 1978. L'Art Sacré Senoufo: Ses Différentes Expressions dans la Vie Sociale. Abidjan: NEA.

83 _____. 1953. "Motif à face double dans les arts plastiques éburnéens." Acta Tropica 10 (2): 97-112.

84 Itzikovitz, M. 1975. "A propos d'un bronze abron." Arts d'Afrique 16 (Winter): 8-11.

85 Jamin, Jean. 1979. "Le double monstrueux: Les masques-hyène des Senoufo." Cahiers d'Etudes Africaines 19 (73-76) 125-142.

86 Konan, Kakou. 1978. "La sculpture et la signification de l'art baoulé." AUA:F 7: 33-36.

87 Laget, Elisabeth. 1984. Bestiaire et génies: Dessins sur tissus des Sénoufo. Paris: Quintette.

88 Leyten, Harrie M. 1979. Goldweights from Ghana and the Ivory Coast: Tales in Bronze. Amsterdam: Khepri van Rijn.

89 Lima, Willy Alante. 1984. Trah Bi Winin, l'Ivoirien. Présence Africaine 129 (1st trim.): 122-125.

90 Niangoran-Bouah, Georges. 1984. The Akan World of Gold Weights. Abidjan: NEA.

91 Niangoran Bouah, Georges. 1963. "Poids à Peser l'Or." Présence Africaine 46: 202-220.

92 Ravenhill, Philip C. 1980. "Baule Statuary Art: Meaning and Modernization." In Special Issue on Baule Aesthetics, Working Papers in the Traditional Arts, No. 5. Philadelphia: Institute for the Study of Social Issues (ISHI).

93 Richter, Dolores. 1980a. Art, economics and change: the Kulebele of Northern Ivory Coast. La Jolla, CA: Psych/Graphic.

94 _____. 1979. "Senufo mask classificaiton." African Arts 12 (3): 66-73.

95 Soppelsa, Robert Thomas. 1982. "Terracotta Traditions of the Akan of Southeastern Ivory Coast." Ph.D. dissertation, Ohio State University.

96 Verger-Fèvre, Marie-Noel. 1985. "Etude des masques faciaux
de l'ouest de la Cote d'Ivoire conservés dans les collections
publiques françaises. " Pt. 1 Arts d'Afrique Noire 53: 17-29.

97 _____. 1982. "Masques faciaux de l'ouest de la Côte d'Ivoire."
Africa-Tervuren 28 (3): 54-63.

98 Vogel, Susan Mullin. 1977. "Baule Art as the Expression of
a World View." Ph.D. dissertation, New York University.

99 _____. 1980. "Beauty in the Eyes of the Baule: Aesthetics
and Cultural Values." In Special Issue on Baule Aesthetics,
Working Papers in the Traditional Arts, No. 5. Philadelphia:
Institute for the Study of Social Issues (ISHI).

100 _____. 1973. "People of Wood: Baule Figure Sculpture."
The Art Journal 33: 23-36.

101 Warren, D. M. and J. Kweku Andrews. 1977. "An Ethno-
scientific Approach to Akan Art and Aesthetics." Working Papers
in the Traditional Arts, No. 3. Philadelphia: Institute for the
Study of Human Issues.

D. DRAMA

102 F. J. Amon d'Aby, Bernard Dadié, and G. Coffi Gadeau. 1965.
Le Théatre Populaire en République de Cote d'Ivoire. Abidjan:
Cercle Culturelle et Folklorique de la Cote d'Ivoire.

103 Bohui, D.-J. 1983. "Reflexion sur une mise en scène: 'La
termitière' de B. Ladi, ou Comment le geste et la parole se
nouent en suture." AUA:D 16: 229-238.

104 Jefferson, Louise M. 1982. "A clash of codes: L'oeil by Bernard
Zadi Zaourou." French Review. Champaign, IL 55 (6, May):
824-834.

105 Koné, Amadou. 1975. De la chaire au trône. Paris: Radio
France Internationale.

106 Kotchy-N'Guessan, Barthélémy. 1984. La Critique Sociale dans
l'Oeuvre Théatrale de Bernard Dadié. Paris: Harmattan.

107 _____. 1976. "Sémiologie du temps et de l'espace (dans le
théatre de Bernard B. Dadié)." AUA:D 9: 427-434.

108 _____. 1979. "Le temps et l'espace dans le théatre de Dadié
(suite et fin)." AUA:D 12: 269-282.

109 Koudou, Aiko. 1981. "Iles de tempête (Bernard B. Dadié):
schéma idéologique." AUA:D 14: 185-193.

110 Kunze, C. 1983. "African folk culture in the struggle for national emancipation: Bernard Dadié's adaptation of fairy tales." In G. Brehme and T. Beuttner, eds., African Studies (Berlin: Akademie-Verlag), pp. 13-22.

111 Smith, Robert P., Jr. 1982. "History and Tragedy in Bernard Dadié's Béatrice du Congo." French Review 55 (6, May): 818-823.

112 Sonfo, A. 1979. "Le théâtre de Zâgoua Nokan." AUA:F 8: 31-63.

113 Warner, Gary. 1983. "Technique dramatique et affirmation culturelle dans le théâtre de Barnard Dadié." Ethiopiques Dakar 1 (1): 53-70.

114 Waters, Harold A. 1985. "Nokan's Abraha Pokou." Journal of African Studies 12 (2): 111-132.

115 Zadi Zaorou, Bernard. 1979. Les sofas, suivi de l'oeil Paris: L'Harmattan.

E. LANGUAGES AND LINGUISTICS

116 Delafosse, Maurice. 1904. Vocabulaire comparatif de soixante langues ou dialectes parlés en Côte d'Ivoire. Paris: Leroux.

117 Fadiga, K. and D. Koffi. 1981. "Blocage politique et tendance à la récupération culturelle." AUA:D 14: 43-54.

118 Grandet, E. 1975. "Eléments d'enquête linguistique sur les monnaies de Côte d'Ivoire." AUA:H 8(1): 91-98.

119 Gregoire, H.-C. 1977. "Bilinguisme et multilinguisme en Côte d'Ivoire." CIRL (1, April): 87-124.

120 Kokora, P. D. 1983. "Rapport introductif du bilan sur la recherche." CIRL 13: 17-26.

121 Naymark, J. and R. Sctrick. 1977. "Préliminaires théoriques à une recherche de psycho-linguistique en Côte d'Ivoire." AUA:H 10: 83-111.

122 Tierou, Alphonse. 1977. Le nom africain ou langage des traditions. Paris: Maisonneuve et Larose.

Abidji

123 Aka, Moise Adjebe, et al. 1984. Syllabaire Abidji. Abidjan: NEA.

Abron

124 Dolphyne, F. A. 1976. Delafosse's Abron wordlist in the light
of a Brong dialect survey. Mitt. der Basler Afrika Bibliographien 14: 35-46; and in H. M. J. Trutenau, ed. Languages
of the Akan area: Papers in western Kwa linguistics and on the
linguistic geography of the area of ancient Begho. (Basel):
35-46.

125 Tufuor, Lawrence. 1984. L'Abron: "Langue sans consonnes
nasales." AUA:H 13: 161-196.

126 _____. 1984. "Contacts de langues en pays abron (Côte
d'Ivoire)." Bulletin de l'Observation du Français contemporain
en Afrique noire 5: 11-53.

Adjukru

127 Herault, Georges. 1981. "L'information ségmentale nécessaire
à l'élaboration des règles tonales de l'Adioukrou." Studies in
African Linguistics, suppl. 8 (Dec.): 51-54.

128 _____. 1976. "Quelques conjugaisons verbales en Adioukrou
(exemples d'applications des règles tonales)." In H. M. J.
Trutenau, ed. Languages of the Akan area: papers in western
Kwa linguistics and on the linguistic geography of the area of
ancient Begho (Basel: Mitt. der Basler Afrika Bibliographien);
pp. 47-61.

129 Stewart, John M. 1983. "Downstep and floating low tones
in Adioukrou." Journal of African Languages and Linguistics
5 (1): 57-78.

Anyi

130 Leben, William R. 1982. "Tone in the verbal system of Anyi."
In Current Approaches to African Linguistics, vol. 1: 177-184.

131 Retord, Georges. 1972. "L'Agni, variété dialectale sanvi:
Phonologie, analyses tomographiques, documents." AUA:H 5:
fasc. 1.

132 _____. 1980. Etude radiocinématographique des articulations
de l'Agni-Sanvi. Paris: Diffusion Champion.

Attié

133 Hood, E., et al. 1984. Syllabaire Attié (dialecte Daindin).
Abidjan: NEA.

Bambara

134 Braconnier, Cassian, et al. 1984. "Vocables d'Odienné non attestés en bambara." Mandenkan 7 (Spring): 85-104.

Baule

135 Coninckx, C. 1978. "A propos de l'expression gestuelle de la numération: le cas du baoulé et du bété." AUA:H 11 (1): 97-103.

136 Effimbra, Georges. 1959. Manuel de baoulé. Paris: Nathan.

137 Timyan, Judith. 1977. "A Discourse-based Grammar of Baule: The Kode Dialect." Ph.D. dissertation, CUNY.

138 _____. 1981. "A Semantic Analysis of Quantification: Evidence from Baule." Studies in African Linguistics, suppl. 8 (Dec.): 131-133.

139 _____. 1975. "Les tons du Baoulé: comparaison de deux dialectes." AUA:H 8 (1): 262-281.

140 Timyan, Judith, with Georges Retord. 1978. N wan yo... Cours de baoulé (with cassettes). Abidjan: University of Abidjan.

Bété

141 Charette, M. 1983. "La Construction associative en bété de Gbadi." In Current Approaches to African Linguistics, vol. 2. J. Kay et al., eds. (Dordrecht and Cinnaminson: Foris), 99-125.

142 Sportiche, Dominique. 1983. "Bété reciprocals and clitic binding." In Current Approaches to African Linguistics, J. Kaye et al., eds vol. 2. (Dordrecht and Cinnaminson: Foris).

Dyula

143 Braconnier, Cassian. 1983. "L'inaccompli neutre en dioula d'Odienné: Construction nominale ou verbale?" Mandenkan: Bulletin semestriel d'études linguistiques mandé. 6 (Autumn): 3-8.

144 _____. 1983. Phonologie du dioula d'Odienné. Paris: Agence de la coopération culturelle et technique.

145 _____. 1983. Le Système tonal du dioula d'Odienné (2 vols.). Paris: Agence de Coopération Culturelle et Technique.

146 _____. and Sanoussi Diaby. Dioula d'Odienné (parler de Samatiquila): Matérial lexical. Abidjan: Institut de linguistique appliquée.

147 _____. 1983. Les tons d'Odienné: Guide pratique. Paris: ACCT.

148 Charette, M. 1983. Le Phénomène du rehaussement tonal en jula. Mandenkan: Bulletin semestriel d'études linguistiques mandé 6 (Autumn): 9-20.

149 Derive, M. J. 1976. "Dioula véhiculaire, dioula de Kong et dioula d'Odienné." AUA:H 9 (1): 55-83.

150 Dumestre, G. 1970. Eléments de Grammaire Dioula. Abidjan: University of Abidjan, Institut de lingistique appliquée.

151 Gingiss, Peter. 1973. "The Meaning of Dyula as it Applies to Language." Focus on International Affairs (University of Houston) 5 (1): 20-24.

152 Partmann, Gayle H. 1975. "Quelques remarques sur le dioula véhiculaire en Côte d'Ivoire." AUA:H 9 (1): 241-259.

153 Sangare, Aby. 1983. "Note sur les prédicatifs et le système tonal du parler de Kong." Mandenkan 6 (Autumn): 91-97.

Ega

154 Bole-Richard, Rémy. 1983. "La classification nominale en Ega." Journal of West African Languages 13 (1): 51-62.

Fon

155 Capo, H. 1978. "A propos des corrélations de palatalisation et de labialisation en fon." AUA:H 11: 5-19.

French

156 Alalade, F. O. 1977/78. "The role of French in symbolizing and exacerbating social differences in the Ivory Coast." Current Bibliography of African Affairs 10 (2): 163-176.

157 Duponchel, L. 1975. "Le dictionnaire du français de Côte d'Ivoire." Annales de l'université d'Abidjan H 8 (1): 35-53.

158 Hattiger, J. L. 1984. "La série verbale en français populaire d'Abidjan." AUA: H 13: 69-88.

159 Hattiger, J. L. and Y. Simard. 1983. "Deux exemples de transformation du français contemporain: Le français populaire d'Abidjan et le français populaire de Montréal." Bulletin de l'Observatoire du français contemporain en Afrique noire 4: 59-74.

160 Kokora, D. P. 1983. "Situation sociolinguistique en Côte d'Ivoire et emprise du français: Les variétés de celui-ci et les attitudes langagières qu'elles suscitent chez les locuteurs." Cahiers ivoiriens de recherches linguistiques 13: 128-147.

161 Kwofie, E. N. 1976. The grammar of spoken French in the Ivory Coast: A study in second language acquisition. Grossen-Linden: Hoffmann.

162 Turcotte, Denis. 1980. "La planification linguistique en Côte d'Ivoire: faire du français le véhiculaire national par excellence." Canadian Journal of African Studies 13 (3): 423-439.

Gba, Gban

163 LeSaout, Joseph. 1971. "Alternance consonantique et vocalique en gba, guro et nwa." AUA:H vol. 4, fasc. 1: 73-87.

164 _____. 1976. Etude descriptive du Gban (Côte d'Ivoire): Phonétique et phonologie. Paris: Société d'études linguistiques et anthropologiques de France.

Gblokwe

165 Vogler, Pierre. 1984. "Note sur le verbe et sa tonalité gblokwe (Côte d'Ivoire)." Afrique et langage 21 (1st semester): 35-47.

Godié

166 Gratrix, Carol. 1975. "Morphotonologie du Godié." AUA:H 8 (1): 99-114.

167 Marchese, L. 1975. "Morphonologie du verbe godié." AUA:H 8 (1): 215-239.

168 _____. 1977. "Subordinate clauses as topics in Godie." Studies in African Linguistics 8 (suppl. 7, Dec.): 157-164.

Guéré

169 Paradis, Carole. 1983. "La régle d'élision syllabique et les séquences vocaliques en Guéré." In J. Kay et al, Current Approaches to African Linguistics (Dordrecht and Cinnaminson: Foris): 181-193.

Guro

170 LeSaout, Joseph. 1971. "Alternance consonantique et vocalique en gba, guro et nwa." AUA: H 4, fasc. 1: 73-87.

Koyo

171 Kokora, D. P. 1979. "Another Look at the 'Q'-Morpheme: Evidence from Koy." AUA H 12: 157-177.

Kru

172 Thalmann, P. 1978. "Tonèmes et règles tonales du krou tépo." AUA:H 11 (1): 133-148.

Kulango

173 Bianco, A. 1979. "Phonologie du Koulango de la région de Bondoukou." AUA: H, 5-123.

174 Leenhouts, I. and I. Person. 1975. "L'accent en Loron." AUA:H 8 (1): 191-203.

175 _____. 1977. Esquisse phonologique du Loron. AUA:H 10: 53-82.

176 Tufuor, Lawrence. 1984. "Petit lexique Koulango-Français." CIRL 15: 83-161.

Kur

177 Grah, Claire. 1984. "La classification nominale dans les parlers kur: l'exemple du nivoli." Afrique et Langage 21: 19-34.

Kwa

178 Herault, Georges. 1983. Atlas des langues kwa de Côte d'Ivoire. Paris: Agence de coopération culturelle et technique.

Lagoon

179 Dumestre, G. 1971. Atlas Linguistique de Côte d'Ivoire: Les langues de la Région Lagunaire. Abidjan: University of Abidjan, Institut de linguistique appliquée.

Manding

180 Bamba, Moussa. 1983. Textes Mahou. Paris: Agence de la Coopération Culturelle et Technique.

181 Bird, Charles S. 1970. "The Development of Mandekan (Manding): A Study of the Role of Extra-linguistic Factors in Linguistic Change." In David Dalby, ed. Language and History in Africa (London: Frank Cass), pp. 146-159.

182 Braconnier, Cassian, John Maire and Kalilou Tera. 1983. Etude sur le mandinque de Côte d'Ivoire. Paris: ACCT.

183 Creissels, Denis. 1984. "Le système des marques prédicatives du korokan (parler manding de la région de Tiéningboué, Côte d'Ivoire)." Mandenkan 7: 15-25.

184 Delafosse, Maurice. 1929-1955. La Langue mandingue et ses dialectes, 2 vols. Paris: Paul Geuthner.

185 Derive, M. J. 1985. "Etude comparée des parlers manding de Côte d'Ivoire." Mandenkan 10: 63-73.

186 Halaoui, Nazam. 1984. "L'expression du manding dans le français d'un roman africain." Bulletin de l'Observation du franis contemporaine en Afrique noire 5: 179-191.

Muan

187 Bolli, M. and E. Flik. 1978. "La phonologie du muan." AUA:H 11 (1): 59-96.

Niaboua

188 Bentinck, J. 1975. "Le Niaboua, langue sans consonnes nasales?" AUA:H 8 (1): 5-14.

Senufo

189 Boutin, Pierre. 1982. "Relations de détermination en fodonon (parler sénoufo de la région de Dikodougou, Côte d'Ivoire)." Afrique et Langage 18: 5-36.

190 Laughren, Mary. 1976. "Serial verba." Bulletin IFAN 38
(B, 4, Oct.): 872-89.

191 Mills, E. et al. 1984. Syllabaire Senoufo-Senari (Cebaara).
Abidjan: NEA.

Southern Mandé

192 Halaoui, Nazam, Kalilou Tera and Monique Trabi. 1983. Atlas
des langues mandé-sud de Côte d'Ivoire. Paris: Agence de la
coopération culturelle et technique.

Wobe

193 Bearth, T. and Christa Link. 1980. "The tone puzzle of
Wobe." Studies in African Linguistics 11 (2, August): 147-207.

194 _____. 1978. "Les tons du wobé: étude fonctionnelle."
AUA:H 11 (1): 21-57.

195 Egner, I. and V. Hofer. 1978. "Information marquée dans
la proposition wobé." AUA:H 11 (1): 105-119.

196 Hofer, Verena and T. Bearth. 1975. "Système vocalique et
sandhi vocalique en Wobé." AUA:H 8 (1): 135-138.

197 Link, C. 1975. "L'interprétation de la consonne médiane dans
la structure syllabique CCV en Wobé." AUA:I 4: 5-33.

198 Paradis, Carole. 1984. "Le comportement tonal des constructions
associatives en Wobé." Journal of African Languages and Linguistics 6 (2): 147-171.

199 Singler, John Victor. 1984. "On the underlying representation
of contour tones in Wobe." Studies in African Linguistics 15
(1): 59-75.

200 Weesbe cian a nyu -je o pode: Guide du maître pour le syllabaire wobe. 1982. Man (Ivory Coast): Société internationale
de linguistique.

F. FOLKLORE AND LITERATURE

201 Ade, Oso S. 1983. "L'ecrivain africain et ses publications:
Le cas de Bernard Dadié." Peuples noirs--Peuples Africains 6
(32, April): 63-99.

202 Amon d'Aby, F. J. 1984. Murmure du roi: recueil de dix
contes. Abidjan: NEA.

203 Anouma, Joseph. 1977. Les matins blafards. Paris: P. J. Oswald.

204 Bailly, Sery Z. 1981. "Darkness, revolution and light: the symbolism of Charles Nokan's works." AUA:D 14: 81-92.

205 Boni, S. Tanella. 1984. Labyrinthe: Poèmes. Akpagnon: Le Mée-sur-Seine.

206 Bonneau, R. 1977. "Les Inutiles: roman de Sidiky Dembele." Afrique littéraire et artistique 44: 17-23.

207 Conteh-Morgan, John. 1985. "History or Literature; A critical study of Bernard Dadié's Béatrice du Congo." Canadian Journal of African Studies 19 (2): 387-397.

208 Chatenet, Jean. 1970. Petits Blancs, Vous serez tous mangés. Paris: Editions du Seuil.

209 Contes de Côte d'Ivoire. 1983. Paris: CLE International; Abidjan: NEA.

210 Dadié, Bernard Binlin. 1983. Assemien Dehyle, roi du Sanwi. Abidjan: CEDA.

211 _____. 1956. Climbié. Paris: Seghers.

212 _____. 1966. Légendes et poèmes. Paris: Seghers.

213 _____. 1979. Opinions d'un nègre (aphorismes) 1934-1946. Dakar: NEA.

214 Derive, Jean. 1984. "Une paillardise rituelle: Les chants des captifs dioula." Cahiers de littérature orale 15:105-134.

215 _____ and M. J. Derive, eds. 1980. Ntalen jula / Contes dioula. Abidjan: CEDA.

216 _____. 1984. Proverbes populaires de Côte d'Ivoire. Abidjan: CEDA.

217 Dodo, Jean D. 1978. Sacrés dieux d'Afrique: roman. Abidjan: NEA.

218 _____. 1977. Wazzi: la "mousso" du forestier: roman. Abidjan: NEA.

219 Duviard, Dominique. 1979. "Nana Gnamien Yi Ago: Conte entomologique du pays baoulé." AUA:F 8: 65-75.

220 "Entretien du G.R.T.O. (Groupe de Recherche sur la Tradition

Orale) avec Dibéro sur l'esthétique." In Colloque sur Littérature et Esthétique Négro-Africaines. Abidjan: NEA.

221 Huannou, A. "La technique du récit et le style dans Les Soleils des Indépendances." Afrique littéraire et artistique 38: 31-38.

222 Jay, Salim. 1984. "Côte d'Ivoire: 'Les jambes du fils de Dieu' par Bernard Dadié; 'Les soleils des indépendances' par Ahmadou Kourouma; 'La Carte d'identité' par Jean-Marie Adiaffi." L'Afrique Littéraire 73-74 (3-4 trims.): 48-58.

223 Koné, Amadou. 1982. Courses, Sous le pouvoir des Blakoros II. Abidjan: NEA.

224 _____. 1979. La force de vouloir. Abidjan: CEDA. (juvenile lit.)

225 _____. 1975. Les fresques d'Ebinto. Paris: La Pensée Universelle (reedited by CEDA and Hatier, 1979).

226 _____. 1976. Jusqu'au seuil de l'irréel. Abidjan: NEA.

227 _____. 1980. Liens. Abidjan: CEDA.

228 _____. 1980. Le Respect de Morts and De la chaire au trône. Paris: Hatier.

229 _____. 1979. Terre Ivoirienne. Abidjan: CEDA. (juvenile lit.)

230 _____. 1980. Traites, Sous le pouvoir des Blakoros I. Abidjan: NEA.

231 _____, Gérard D. Lezou, and Joseph Mlanhoro. 1983. Anthologie de la littérature ivoirienne. Abidjan: CEDA.

232 Lezou, Gérard Dago. 1977. La Création Romanesque devant les Transformations Actuelles en Côte d'Ivoire. Abidjan: NEA.

233 _____. 1979. "Perspectives de la littérature négro-africaine: l'exemple de Charles Nokan." In Colloque sur Littérature et Esthétique Négro-Africaines (Abidjan: NEA) pp. 313-326.

234 _____. 1974. "Temps et espaces romanesques en Côte d'Ivoire." AUA:D 7: 273-97.

235 Loncke, Jocelyne. 1978. "Quelques traits de style dans les oeuvres de Zégoua Nokan." AUA:F 7: 103-109.

236 Ly, Amadou. 1981. "Quelques réflexions sur la forme des Soleils des indépendances de Kourouma." Annales de la Faculté des Lettres et Sciences Humaines (Dakar) 11: 117-134.

237 Maigne, V. 1976. "Les grands genres poètiques en pays bété sud." AUA:D 9: 467-482.

238 Mayes, J. A. 1977. "Bernard Dadié and the aesthetics of the chronique: an affirmation of cultural identity." Présence africaine 101/102: 102-118.

239 Michelman, Fredric. 1982. "Independence and Disillusion in Les soleils des indépendances: A New Approach." In David F. Dorsey et al., eds. Design and intent in African literature (Washington, D.C.: Three Continents Press), pp. 91-95.

240 Mondah, Joseph et al. 1983. Contes de Côte d'Ivoire. Paris: CLE International.

241 N'guessan, Marius Ano. (no date). Contes agni de l'Indénié. Abidjan: Imprimerie Nationale.

242 _____. 1976. "Le conte agni de l'Indénié." AUA:D 9: 501-507.

243 Okafor, Raymond N. 1979. "Politics and literature in the Ivory Coast." Kiabara (Port Harcourt) 2 (Rains): 164-190.

244 Oussou-Essui, Denis. 1979. Les saisons sèches. Paris: L'Harmattan.

245 Paulme, Denise. 1976. "Deux thèmes d'origine de la mort en Afrique occidentale." In Paulme, ed. La mère dévorante: essai sur la morphologie des contes africains (Paris): 122-137.

246 Schikora, Rosemary G. 1982. "Narrative Voice in Kourouma's Les soleils des indépendances." French Review 55 (6, May): 811-817.

247 Sutherland, Esi. 1981. "The role of literature and its creator in society: a review of selected works by Zegoua Nokan." Ufahamu 10 (3, Spring): 69-78.

248 Tadjo, Véronique. 1984. Latérite. Paris: ACES.

249 Timyan, Judith. 1981. Mes mensonges du soir: Contes baoulé de Côte d'Ivoire. Paris: Conseil international de la langue française.

250 Wondji, Christophe. 1979. "Le bàgnon chez les Bété." In Colloque sur Littérature et Esthétique Négro-Africaines (Abidjan: NEA): 87-92.

251 Zogbo, G., ed. 1980. Bheteh-nini: Contes Bété. Abidjan: CEDA.

G. MUSIC AND DANCE

252 Augier, P. 1983. "Enseignement et identité culturelle: l'incidence des programmes occidentaux sur l'attitude des étudiants."
African Music 6 (3): 42-52.

253 Dédy, Séri. 1982. "Opinions des publics face à la musique
ivoirienne." AUA:F 10: 101-119.

254 Dérive, Marie Jose. 1978. "Chants de chasseurs dioulas."
AUA:J 2: 143-171.

255 Ehouman, Simone. 1979. "Introduction à l'étude des formes
expressives de l'Attoungblan." In Colloque sur Littérature et
Esthetique Négro-Africaines.

256 Nourrit, Chantal and William Pruitt. 1983. "Musique tradition-
elle de l'Afrique Noire, discographie: 6, La Côte d'Ivoire."
Paris: Radio-France Internationale, Centre de Documentation
Africaine.

257 Seri, Dedy. 1984. "Musique traditionelle et développement
national en Côte d'Ivcire." Tiers-Monde 25 (97, March): 109-
124.

258 Valbert, Christian. 1979. "L'avenir des danses traditionnelles
en Côte d'Ivoire." Arts d'Afrique Noire 29 (Spring): 7-22.

259 Zemp, H. 1972. Musique Dan: La Musique dans la pensée et
la vie sociale d'une société africaine. Paris: Mouton.

H. INFORMATION AND MEDIA

260 Glasman, Monique. 1984. "L'information dans un pays en
développement: La Côte d'Ivoire." Projet 182 (February) 147-
158.

261 Lenglet, Frans. 1980. "The Ivory Coast: Who Benefits from
Education/Information in Rural Television?" In Emile G. McAnany,
ed. Communications in the Rural Third World (New York:
Praeger), pp. 49-70.

262 "La Liberté de la presse en Côte d'Ivoire." 1984. Peuples
noirs--Peuples Africains 7 (41-42, December): 104-140.

263 Skurnik, W. A. E. 1981. "A New Look at Foreign News Cover-
age: External Dependence or National Interests?" African
Studies Review 24 (March): 99-112.

264 Tao, I. 1974. "Presse et Publique en Côte d'Ivoire IV,"
Interstage (97, July) pp. 15-24.

265   Touré, A. 1981. "La petite histoire de Nalewe Kpingbin Tie-
      coroba: Une émission de la radiodiffusion nationale ivoirienne."
      Politique Africaine 1 (3, Sept.): 44-54.

I. CINEMA

266   Bachy, Victor. 1983. Le Cinéma en Côte d'Ivoire (3d ed.).
      Paris: L'Harmattan.

                    ECONOMICS

267   "Ivory Coast. 1970." In Surveys of African Economies, vol.
      3. (Washington, International Monetary Fund): 220-308.

268   "Ivory Coast. 1958." Inventaire Economique de la Côte d'Ivoire
      (1947-1956).

269   Lory, Georges. 1981. Introduction à l'économie ivoirienne
      Abidjan: Société Africaine d'édition.

270   Stolper, Wolfgang F. 1980. Income Distribution and Economic
      Policies: The Case of Two African Countries. Tubingen, FRG:
      Mohr.

271   United Nations. 1986. "The Background, General Assembly
      Special Session on the Critical Economic Situation in Africa,
      27-31 May 1986." New York: United Nations Department of
      Public Information.

A. AGRICULTURE

272   Benoit-Cattin, Michel. "Croissance du surplus et évolution de
      la productivité: le cas de l'agriculture traditionalle de la Côte
      d'Ivoire." CIRES 18 (September): 59-75.

273   Bigot, Y. 1983. "La culture attelée et ses limites dans l'évo-
      lution de savanes de Côte d'Ivoire." Machinisme agricole tropi-
      cale 84 (Oct.-Dec.): 44-52.

274   _____. 1980. "La force de travail comme critère d'échantil-
      lonage: application à l'étude du système de production agricole
      dans la région de Nielle (Nord-Côte d'Ivoire)." CIRES 24/25
      (March-June): 143-162.

275   _____. 1976. "La mécanisation des cultures en région de
      savane de Côte d'Ivoire." CIRES 10 (June): 27-42.

276 Boni, Dian. 1985. L'économie de plantation en Côte d'Ivoire forestière. Abidjan: NEA.

277 Bonnefond, Philippe. 1975. Le développement de la motorisation agricole en Côte d'Ivoire: Résumé des principales données. Abidjan: ORSTOM.

278 _____. 1973. Les exploitations motorisées de la région d'Odienné: campagne agricole 1971-72. Abidjan: ORSTOM.

279 _____. 1980. Statistiques Ivoiriennes: Secteur Agricole. Abidjan: ORSTOM.

280 _____. 1971. Temps de travaux manuels et rentabilité financière en agriculture semi-motorisée (moyenne Côte d'Ivoire). Abidjan: ORSTOM.

281 _____. 1972. Les tractoristes d'Odienné. Abidjan: ORSTOM.

282 Camara, Camille. 1984. "Les cultures vivrières en République de Côte d'Ivoire." Annales de géographie 93 (518, August): 432-453.

283 Centre Ivoirien de Recherche Economique et Sociale. 1978. "Mécanisation et développement agricole en Côte d'Ivoire, ou les Conditions Nécessaires à la réussite de la mécanisation des exploitations agricoles." CIRES.

284 Chaleard, Jean-Louis. 1984. "L'occupation du sol et dynamique spatiale des grandes plantations modernes dans le département d'Agboville (Côte d'Ivoire). "In C. Blanc-Pamard et al, eds., Le développement rural en question (Paris: ORSTOM): 323-352.

285 Chataigner, Jean. 1975. "Inventaire des recherches d'économie rurale en Côte d'Ivoire." CIRES 7/8 (Oct.-Dec.): 117-128.

286 Chauveau, J.-P.; Dozon, J P; Richard, J. 1981. "Histoires de Riz, Histoires d'Igname: Le Cas de la Moyenne Côte d'Ivoire." Africa (Great Britain) 51 (2): 621-658.

287 Chauveau, J.-P. and Jacques Richard. 1977. "Une périphérie recentrée: A propos d'un système local d'économie de plantation en Côte d'Ivoire." Paris: ORSTOM, and CEA 17 (68): 485-523.

288 Condé, S. 1981. "Agriculture d'exportation et agriculture vivrière dans le développement économique de la Côte d'Ivoire." AUA:K 4: 5-17.

289 Coulibaly, S. 1977a. "Les champs en évantail en Côte d'Ivoire." COM 118 (April-June): 131-152.

290 de la Vaissière, Pierre. 1980. "Systèmes agraires en zone forestière de Côte d'Ivoire." CIRES 24/25 (Mar.-June): 121-141.

291 _____. 1976. "Typologie des exploitations agricoles en zone forestière de Côte d'Ivoire: Premiers résultats." CIRES 7/8 (Oct.-Dec.): 117-128.

292 Diambra-Hauhouot, Asseypo. 1974. "Le ravitaillement d'Abidjan en produits vivrier de base non importés." AUA:G (6): 7-45.

293 Drevet, J. F. 1979. Evolution récente de l'agriculture villageoise en zone forestière. AUA:G 8: 77-109.

294 Dumont, René. 1962. Afrique Noire: Développement Agricole: Reconversion de l'économie agricole: Guinée, Côte d'Ivoire, Mali. Paris: PUF.

295 Founou-Tchuigoua, Bernard. 1979. "Quels changements dans l'agriculture ivoirienne?" Africa Development 4 (1, Jan.-Mar.): 71-78.

296 Gastellu, Jean-Marc and S. Affou Yapi. 1981. "Ou situer les grands planteurs villageois?" CIRES 30 (Sept.): 31-49.

297 Hecht, Robert M. 1985. "Immigration, Land Transfer and Tenure Changes in Divo, Ivory Coast, 1940-80." Africa 55 (3): 318-336.

298 Ivory Coast. Ministère de l'Agriculture. 1982. Réflexions pour un programme national d'installation de jeunes agriculteurs modernes. Abidjan.

299 Kellermann, Jean. 1960. "Rapport d'une mission d'étude des principaux problèmes d'hydraulique agricole et pastorale en Côte d'Ivore." Paris: Imprimerie Technigraphie.

300 Kouadio, B. 1975. "L'importance économique des produits vivriers de base en Côte d'Ivoire." CIRES 7/8 (Oct.-Dec.): 9-27.

301 Lawani, L. 1978. "La formation des prix du producteur au consommateur." CIRES 19 (Dec.): 81-89.

302 Le Buanec, B. and B. Jacob. 1981. "Seventeen years of mechanical cultivation on a watershed in the center of the Ivory Coast: Soil and Yield Evolution." Agronomie Tropicale 36 (3, July-Sept.): 203-211.

303 LeRoy, X. 1983. L'introduction des cultures de rapport dans l'agriculture vivrière sénoufo: Le cas de Karakpo. Paris: ORSTOM.

304 N'dri, O. 1977. "L'homme et la terre à Tiagba." AUA:G 7:
     85-130.

305 Peltre-Wurtz, Jacqueline. 1984. "La Charrue, le travail et
     l'arbre." Cahiers ORSTOM, Série Sciences Humaines 20 (3-4):
     633-644.

306 Pillet-Schwartz, Anne-Marie. 1982. Aghien: Un terroir Ebrié,
     quinze ans de "techno-structure" en Côte d'Ivoire. Paris:
     ORSTOM.

307 _____. 1978. "Les Grandes Entreprises de culture et la
     promotion des paysans en Côte d'Ivoire." Etudes Rurales (70,
     April-June): 65-79.

308 Prady, B. 1985. Immigration et économie de plantation dans
     la région de Vavoua (Centre-Ouest ivoirien). (microfiche)
     Paris: ORSTOM.

309 Ruf, François. 1980. "Perspectives de développement agricole
     dans les zones en voie de saturation foncière du Centre-Ouest."
     Abidjan: Université Nationale de Côte d'Ivoire, CIRES.

310 _____. 1984. "Quelle intensification en économie de plantation
     ivoirienne? L'histoire, systèmes de production et politique
     agricole." Agronomie Tropicale 39 (4, October-December):
     367-382; 40 (1, Jan.-Mar.): 44-53.

311 Sawadogo, Abdoulaye. 1977. L'Agriculture en Côte d'Ivoire.
     Paris: PUF.

312 Silue, Moussa. 1979. "Recherche sur les causes de la dispersion
     des revenus monétaires agricoles en Côte d'Ivoire: résultats
     provisoires." CIRES 20/21 (Mar.-June): 113-138.

313 Weekes-Vagliani, Winifred. 1985. Rôle des Acteurs et des In-
     stitutions dans le Processus Alimentaire: Le Cas de la Côte
     d'Ivoire. Paris: Organization for Economic Cooperation and
     Development (OECD).

Cocoa, Coffee

314 Affou Yapi, Simplice. 1983. "Les propriétaires absentéistes
     face au développement de la production cacaoyère et caféière."
     Abidjan: ORSTOM.

315 Boni, Dian. 1978. Aspects géographiques de binome café cacao
     dans l'économie ivoirienne. Abidjan: NEA.

316 Foucher, Jean-François. 1983. "Planteurs de café et saturation

foncière dans le sud-est ivoirien: Productivité du travail, statuts sociaux, équilibres vivriers." <u>CIRES</u>: 33-34 (June-September): 1-57.

317 Tricart, J. 1957. "Le café en Côte d'Ivoire." <u>COM</u> 10 (39): 209-233.

318 Zelensky, V. 1955. "Le Cadastre des plantations caféières et cacaoyères en Côte d'Ivoire." <u>Agronomie Tropicale</u> 9 (5): 551-581.

Cotton

319 Barry, M. B. et al. 1977. "Culture cotonnière et structures de production agricole dans le nord-ouest de la Côte d'Ivoire." <u>CIRES</u> 15/16 (Sept.-Dec.): 29-49.

320 Campbell, Bonnie. 1984. "Inside the Miracle: Cotton in the Ivory Coast." In Jonathan Barker, ed. <u>The Politics of Agriculture in Tropical Africa</u> (Beverly Hills, CA: Sage), pp. 143-171.

321 Monnier, Yves. 1971. "Le complexe agro-industriel de Côte d'Ivoire: Notion de schéma standard de croissance industrielle--le coton." <u>AUA</u>:G vol. 3.

322 Peltre-Wurtz, Jacqueline. 1976. "Actions de développement et structures agraires traditionelles: L'intégration de la culture du coton au système agricole senoufo (région de la Bagoué)." Abidjan: ORSTOM.

Fishing

323 Surgy, Albert de. 1964. <u>Les pêcheurs de Côte d'Ivoire.</u> 2 vols. (Paris: CNRS.)

Livestock

324 Barry, M. B. 1975. "Economie de l'élévage transhumant dans le nord Côte d'Ivoire." <u>CIRES</u> 7/8 (Oct.-Dec.): 69-86.

325 _____. 1978. "Qui sont les éléveurs de Côte d'Ivoire?" <u>CIRES</u> 19 (December): 23-28.

326 Centre Ivoirien de recherche économique et sociale. 1978. "Quelques aspects économiques de l'élévage bovin en Côte d'Ivoire: Production et commercialisation." Abidjan: University of Abidjan, Centre reprographique de l'enseignement superieur.

327 Chataigner, Jean. 1978. "Les relations homme, troupeau,
     espace dans le nord de la Côte d'Ivoire." CIRES 19 (Dec.):
     9-22.

328 _____. 1978. "Les systèmes de production de l'élevage
     bovin et leur évolution en Côte d'Ivoire." CIRES 19 (Dec.):
     29-48.

329 Douhet, Marc. 1980. L'apiculture en Côte d'Ivoire: Régions
     Nord et centre. Maisons-Alfort (France): Institut d'élévage
     et de médécine vétérinaire des pays tropicaux.

330 Estur, G. 1978. "Le role de la culture attelée dans la pro-
     duction bovine." CIRES 19 (Dec.): 49-54.

331 Fresson, Sylviane et al. 1982. Evaluation du projet d'élévage
     bovin dans le nord de la Côte d'Ivoire. Paris: Ministère de
     Coopération et du Développement.

332 Hennebert, P. 1978. "L'approvisionnement de la Côte d'Ivoire
     en viande bovine: évolution de 1970-1976." CIRES 19 (Dec.):
     57-68.

                              Oil Palm

333 Cauvin, C. 1973. "De la palmeraie naturelle à la plantation
     sélectionnée. Toupa: un village en pays Adjukru. AUA:G 5:
     7-146.

                             Pineapple

334 Culture de l'ananas d'exportation en Côte d'Ivoire: Manuel du
     planteur. 1984. Abidjan: NEA.

                             Plantain

335 Centre Ivoirien de recherche Economique et Sociale. 1980. "La
     Production et la commercialisation de la banane plantain en Côte
     d'Ivoire: Premiers éléments d'un dossier technico-économique."
     Abidjan: University of Abidjan: CIRES.

336 Chataigner, Jean, with Kouadio Trano. 1980. "L'économie de
     la banane plantain en Côte d'Ivoire." CIRES 27 (December):
     31-102.

337 Massirou, Taofick. 1979. "Recherche sur l'existence d'un
     surplus de la banane plantain de Côte d'Ivoire." CIRES 20/21
     (March-June): 139-194.

338 Tano, Kouadio. 1980. "La banane plantain dans la région de Ouragahio." CIRES 27 (Dec.): 103-181.

Rice

339 Davis, C. G. and B. Adama. 1979. "L'évolution de la production et la consommation du riz en Côte d'Ivoire 1950-1972." CIRES (20/21, Mar-Jun): 63-112.

340 Dozon, Jean-Pierre. 1974. Autochtones et allochtones face à la riziculture irriguée dans la région de Gagnoa. Abidjan: ORSTOM.

341 _____. 1975. "La problématique rizicole dans la région de Gagnoa." Abidjan: ORSTOM.

342 Forest, F. and J. M. Kalms. 1984. "Influence du régime d'alimentation en eau sur la production du riz pluvial: simulation du bilan hydrique." Agronomie tropicale 39 (1): 42-50.

343 Kalms, J. M. and J. Imbernon. 1983. "Modalités d'alimentation en eau du riz pluvial: Bilan de recherches méthodologiques effectuées à Bouaké en Côte d'Ivoire." Agronomie Tropicale 38 (3, July-September): 198-205.

344 Lang, Harald. 1979. The economics of rainfed rice cultivation in West Africa: The case of the Ivory Coast. Saarbrucken, FRG: Verlag Breitenbach.

345 Vandevenne, R. and M. Arnaud. 1980. "Le rendement en riz blanchi entier de quelques variétés de riz, en fonction des conditions écologiques du culture." Agronimie tropicale 35 (4, Oct.-Dec.): 381-394.

Rubber

346 Monnier, Yves. 1974. "Le complexe agro-industriel de l'hévéa." AUA:G, 4: 191-268.

347 Pillet-Schwartz, Anne-Marie. 1980. "Une tentative de vulgarisation avortée: L'hévéaculture villageoise en Côte d'Ivoire. CEA 20 (70-78): 63-82.

Sugar

348 Aubertin, Catherine. 1983. Le programme sucrier ivoirien: une industrialisation volontariste. Paris: ORSTOM.

349 Benoist, J.-P. 1979. Le Village Piège: Urbanisation et agro-industrie sucrière en Côte d'Ivoire. Paris: PUF.

350 Bertrand, R. et al. 1980. "Conception des études pédologiques nécessaires pour la création d'un complèxe agro-industriel sucrier: Exposé et critique d'un cas concret en Côte d'Ivoire." L'agronomie tropicale 35 (1, Jan.-Mar.): 8-24.

351 Claus, R. 1982a. "La fertilisation minérale de la canne à sucre en Côte d'Ivoire: Etude, résultats et recommandations." Agronomie Tropicale 37 (2, April-June): 115-130.

352 _____. 1980. "Contribution au désherbage chimique de la canne à sucre pluviale dans le Nord de la Côte d'Ivoire." L'agronomie tropicale 35 (1, Jan.-Mar.): 86-91.

353 _____. 1982. "Potentiel, normes et perspective de la canne à sucre pluviale dans le Nord de la Côte d'Ivoire." Agronomie tropicale 37 (4): 340-353.

354 Hauhouot, Asseypo. 1979. "Une première approche géographique de l'intégration régionale des complèxes sucriers de Côte d'Ivoire: l'exemple de Ferké I et de Borotou la Boa." AUA:G 8: 5-32.

Tobacco

355 Filleron, J. Ch. 1982. "Le complèxe agro-industriel de Côte d'Ivoire: Le Tabac." AUA:G 4.

Yams

356 Boni, K. 1977. "La commercialisation de l'igname dans la région de Korhogo." CIRES 14 (June): 9-30.

357 Rodriguez, H. 1983. "Intérêt d'une variété d'igname portoricaine en Côte d'Ivoire: la Florido." Agronomie tropicale 38 (2): 154-157.

358 Visser, Leontine E. 1977. "L'igname, bonne à manger et bonne à penser: Quelques aspects de l'agriculture ahouan (Côte d'Ivoire)." CEA 17 (68) 525-544.

B. COMMERCE

359 Atsain, Achi. 1981. "La structure du commerce extérieur de la Côte d'Ivoire: Approche par un modèle à équations simultanées." CIRES 28/29 (March-June): 49-88.

360 Berron, H. 1973. "Les principaux marchés de gros des produits de la pêche de la lagune Abi." AUA:G (5) 267-284.

361 Côte d'Ivoire. 1982 (3d. ed.). Paris: Centre français du commerce extérieur.

362 Diawara, M. T. 1977. "Ivory Coast." In P. A. Neck, ed. Small enterprise development (Geneva: International Labour Office): 155-160.

363 Gohibi, Bernard. 1978. Les assurances maritimes en Côte d'Ivoire. Abidjan: Ministère de la Marine.

364 Grupp, R. E. 1983. "Transposition en Afrique noire de méthodes commerciales modernes: l'entreprise succursaliste 'Chaine Avion' en Côte d'Ivoire." In Entreprises et entrepreneurs en Afrique, XIXe et XXe siècles, vol. 2 (Paris: L'Harmattan): 353-367.

365 Ivory Coast. 1982. La Réglementation du Commerce Extérieure (2d ed.). Abidjan: CEDA.

366 _____. Ministère du Commerce. 1979. How to do business in Ivory Coast: Everything you have to know to be successful in business in Ivory Coast. Paris: SAE.

367 Kouadio-Koffi, Didier. 1960. La création d'entreprises privées par les nationaux en Côte d'Ivoire depuis 1960. Abidjan: CEDA.

368 Lewis, Barbara C. 1976. "The Limitations of Group Action among Entrepreneurs: The Market Women of Abidjan, Ivory Coast." In Nancy J. Hafkin and Edna G. Bay, eds. Women in Africa: Studies in Social and Economic Change (Stanford, CA: Stanford University Press) pp. 135-156.

369 Lister, Douglas W. 1976. "European Economic Presence in Francophone Africa: The Ivory Coast." In C. Gregory Knight and James L. Newman, eds. Contemporary Africa: Geography and Change (Englewood Cliffs, NJ: Prentice-Hall) pp. 466-477.

370 Marsaudon, Alain. 1984. Guide pratique des marchés publiques en Côte d'Ivoire. Le Vésinet (France): EDITM.

371 Meillassoux, Claude. 1958. "Social and Economic Factors Affecting Markets in Guro Land." In Paul Bohannon and George Dalton, eds. Markets in Africa (Evanston: Northwestern University Press).

372 Meissonnier, Georges. 1983b. Le guide pratique des douanes de la Côte d'Ivoire. Le Vésinet (France): EDITM.

373 Michel, Gilles. 1984. Short-term Responses to Trade and Incentive Policies in the Ivory Coast: Comparative Static Simulations in a Computable General Equilibrium Model. Washington, D.C.: World Bank.

374 Michel, Gilles and Michel Noel. 1984. "The Ivoirian Economy and Alternative Trade Regimes." In I. William Zartman and Christopher Delgado, eds. The Political Economy of Ivory Coast (New York: Praeger) pp. 77-114.

375 Michelini, Philip. 1976. Marketing in Ivory Coast. Washington: U.S. Domestic and International Business Administration.

376 Michotte, J. 1970. "Les marchés du pays baoule de la zone dense: Typologie, organisation et fonctionnement." ORSTOM: Sciences humaines 3 (5). Petit Bassam, Ivory Coast.

377 Monson, Terry D. 1977. "La politique du commerce extérieur de la Côte d'Ivoire et son impact sur l'emploie." CIRES 15/16 (Sept.-Dec.): 103-138.

378 _____. 1981. "Trade strategies and employment in the Ivory Coast." In A. O. Krueger et al., eds. Trade and Employment in Developing Countries, vol. 1: Individual Countries (Chicago: University of Chicago Press): 239-290.

379 Montgomery, R. D. 1975. "Baisse de la consommation de viande de boeuf à Abidjan: raisons économiques." CIRES 7/8 (Oct./Dec.): 29-68.

380 N'cho, Anet M. 1978. "Le droit des sociétés et la promotion de la petite et moyenne entreprise en Côte d'Ivoire." RJPIC 32 (1, Jan.-March): 517-528.

381 La Publicité en Côte d'Ivoire. 1980. Abidjan: Université nationale de Côte d'Ivoire, Centre d'enseignement et de recherche audio-visuels.

382 Ruf, François. 1981. "Le déterminisme des prix sur les systèmes de production en économie de plantation ivoirienne." CIRES 28/29 (March-June): 89-114.

383 Ryan, Peter and Renee Hancher. 1985. Marketing in Ivory Coast. Washington: U.S. Department of Commerce.

384 Staatz, John M. 1980. "Commercialisation du bétail et de la viande en Côte d'Ivoire." CIRES 24/25 (Mar.-June): 10-43.

385 _____. 1978. "Intégration des commerçants et bouchers traditionnels dans le système moderne en Côte d'Ivoire." CIRES 19 (Dec.): 101-109.

386 Tricart, J. 1956. "les échanges entre la zone forestière de la Côte d'Ivoire et les savanes soudaniennes." <u>COM</u> 9 (35): 209-238.

C. CONSTRUCTION

387 "Batiments et travaux publics en Côte d'Ivoire." 1977. <u>Afrique industrie infrastructure</u> 147 (Oct. 1): 18-137.

388 Meissonnier, Georges. 1983a. <u>Guide Pratique de la Construction et de l'Urbanisme en Côte d'Ivoire.</u> Le Vésinet (France): EDI-TM.

D. DEVELOPMENT AND PLANNING

389 Almroth, S. and T. Greiner. 1979. <u>The Economic Value of Breast-feeding.</u> Rome: Food and Agriculture Organization.

390 Amagou, V. 1980. "La capacité de la Côte d'Ivoire à répondre aux besoins alimentaires de sa population." <u>CIRES</u> 27 (December): 13-29.

391 Amin, Samir. 1970. "Capitalism and Development in the Ivory Coast." In I. L. Markovitz, ed., <u>African Politics and Society</u> (New York, Free Press), pp. 277-288.

392 _____. 1967. <u>Le développement du capitalisme en Côte d'Ivoire.</u> Paris: Editions de Minuit.

393 Arnaud, Jean-Claude. 1978. "Agriculture traditionnelle et problèmes de développement dans la région d'Odienné (Côte d'Ivoire)." <u>L'information géographique</u> 42 (5, Nov.-Dec.): 223-228.

394 Atsain, Achi. 1984. "Regional Economic Integration and Foreign Policy." In Zartman and Delgado, <u>The Political Economy of the Ivory Coast</u>, pp. 175-218.

395 Aubertin, Catherine. 1980a. "Histoire et création d'une région 'sous-développée': Le Nord ivoirien." <u>Cahiers ORSTOM, Sciences Sociales et Humaines</u> 19 (1): 23-57.

396 Badouin, R. 1977. "Le rôle de l'agriculture dans l'accession au développement de la Côte d'Ivoire." <u>CIRES</u> 15/16 (Sept.-Dec.): 7-28.

397 Berg, Elliot J. 1971. "Structural Transformation versus Gradualism: Recent Economic Development in Ghana and Ivory Coast." In Philip Foster and Aristide R. Zolberg, eds.,

Ghana and Ivory Coast: Perspectives on Modernization (Chicago, University of Chicago Press).

398 Boelman, Wirte. 1981. "Rural growth and distribution in Ivory Coast." Development and Change 12 (4, October): 619-628.

399 Bra Kanon, D. 1978. "Pour une nouvelle problématique du développement agricole ivoirien." RFEPA 150/151 (June-July), pp. 17-28.

400 Brayton, Abbott A. 1979. "Stability and Modernization: The Ivory Coast Model." World Affairs 141 (3): 235-249.

401 Cacheux. P. and Y. Cogoluegnes. 1975. "L'aide au développement de la Cote d'Ivoire." Cahiers de recherche économique et sociale 5: 83-106.

402 Campbell, Bonnie. 1983. "Etat et développement du capitalisme en Côte d'Ivoire." In Entreprises et Entrepreneurs en Afrique, XIXe et XXe siècles, vol. 2 (Paris: L'Harmattan), pp. 301-314.

403 _____. 1976. "L'idéologie de la croissance: Une analyse du plan quinquennal de développement 1971-1975 de la Côte d'Ivoire." Canadian Journal of African Studies 10 (2): 211-233.

404 Catrisse, Benoit. 1984. "Dossier Côte d'Ivoire: Les bienfaits de la diversification." Afrique Agriculture 104: 29-45.

405 Charbonneaux, Rene. 1971. "Planning in the Ivory Coast," Marchés Tropicaux et Mediterranéens 1361 (11 December).

406 Chenery, Hollis, et al. 1974. Redistribution with Growth. London: Oxford University Press.

407 Christopher, Garland. 1979. "Urbanization, Rural to Urban Migration, and Development Policies in the Ivory Coast." In R. A. Obudho and S. El-Shakh, eds., Development of Urban Systems in Africa (New York: Praeger), pp. 157-176.

408 Comeliau, Christian and Jacques Loup. 1983. "La planification dans les pays en développement: Quelques réflexions à partir de l'expérience ivoirienne." Stateco 36 (December): 28-47.

409 "Côte d'Ivoire: Le Plan Quinquennal de développement (1981-1985)." 1983. Afrique Agriculture 90: 41-63 and 91: 32-43.

410 Coulibaly, A. 1978. "L'insertion des organisations coopératives dans le développement rural en Côte d'Ivoire." RJPIC 32 (1, Jan-March): 239-256.

411 Daniel, Kadja M. 1981. "La problématique de l'eau en milieu

rural ivoirien: Aspects méthodologiques et pédagogiques." *Africa Development* 6 (1): 71-79.

412 Den Tuinder, Bastiaan A. 1978. *Ivory Coast, The Challenge of Success.* Baltimore: Johns Hopkins University Press.

413 de The, Marie-Paule. 1968. *Participation féminine au développement rural de la region de Bouake.* Aix-en-Provence: Centre Africain des Sciences Humaines Appliquées.

414 Diabaté, Moustapha. 1973. *Le modèle ivoirien du développement.* Abidjan: Institut d'Ethno-sociologie.

415 Diarrassouba, V. C. 1973. "Le plan quinquennal 1971-1975 et la problématique de l'éducation en Côte d'Ivoire." *CIRES* 4: 43-66.

416 Diawara, Mohammed T. 1973. "Management et développement ivoirien." *CIRES* 4: 29-41.

417 _____. 1976. "Le plan 1976-1980." *RFEPA* 11 (131, Nov.): 22-39.

418 Dick, H., et al. 1983. "The short-run impact of fluctuating primary commodity prices on three developing economies: Columbia, Ivory Coast and Kenya." *World Development* (May): 405-416.

419 Dienot, J. 1985. "Les devises touristiques: Bénéfice ou leurre pour la Côte d'Ivoire?" *COM* 149 (January-March): 65-80.

420 Dobrska, Zofia. 1966. "Economic Development of the Ivory Coast from the Winning of Independence." *Africana Bulletin* 5 (29).

421 Drabo, Yaya Karim. 1984. "Côte d'Ivoire: Ni mirage, ni miracle, ni modèle?" *Peuples noirs--Peuples africains* 7 (39, May-June): 45-74.

422 Eshag E. and J. Richards. 1967. "A Comparison of Economic Development in Ghana and the Ivory Coast since 1960." *Bulletin of the Oxford University Institute of Statistics* (Dec.): 353-371.

423 Fache, Edmée. 1974. *Les Incidences Economiques du Complèxe de Kossou.* University of Abidjan, Faculté des Sciences Economiques.

424 Foster, Philip and Aristide R. Zolberg, eds. 1971. *Ghana and the Ivory Coast: Perspectives on Modernization.* Chicago: University of Chicago Press.

425 France, Republic of. Ministry of Foreign Affairs. 1982.
Côte d'Ivoire Décembre 1982: Analyse et Conjoncture. Paris:
Coopération et Développement.

426 Frelastre, Georges. 1983. "En Côte d'Ivoire: Prudente mise
en oeuvre de la nouvelle politique de développement rural intégré." Le Mois en Afrique 18 (213-214, October-November):
52-62.

427 Gbaka, G. K. 1983. "Aspects régionaux de la planification
ivoirienne." AUA:K 6: 155-210.

428 Gbetibouo, Mathurin and Christopher L. Delgado. 1984.
"Lessons and Constraints of Export Crop-Led Growth: Cocoa
in Ivory Coast." In I. William Zartman and Christopher Delgado, eds. The Political Economy of Ivory Coast (New York:
Praeger), pp. 115-147.

429 Glardon, M. and P. Picard. 1969. L'animation de la jeunesse
rurale en Côte d'Ivoire. Paris: Culture et Développement.

430 Goreux, Louis M. 1977. Interdependence in Planning: Multi-
level Programming Studies of the Ivory Coast. Baltimore: The
Johns Hopkins University Press.

431 Gouffern, Louis. 1982. "Les limites d'un modèle? A propose
d'Etat et bourgeoisie en Côte d'Ivoire." Politique africaine 2
(6, May): 19-34.

432 Gouvernal, Elisabeth. 1983. "Développement économique de la
Côte d'Ivoire: Le Plan 1981-1985, les conditions politiques
et sociales." Afrika Spectrum 18 (1): 87-96.

433 Granier, Roland, et al. 1981. Disparités de revenus ville-
campagne Côte d'Ivoire et Haute-Volta. Addis Ababa: International Labor Organization.

434 Green, Reginald H. 1971. "Reflections on Economic Strategy,
Structure, Implementation and Necessity: Ghana and the Ivory
Coast, 1957-67." In Philip Foster and Aristide R. Zolberg,
eds., Ghana and the Ivory Coast: Perspectives on Modernization. Chicago: University of Chicago Press.

435 Hauhouot, Asseypo D. 1982. "Problématique du développement
dans le pays Lobi (Côte d'Ivoire)." COM 35 (140): 307-334.

436 Hecht, Robert M. 1983. "The Ivory Coast Economic 'Miracle':
What Benefits for Peasant Farmers?" JMAS 21 (March) 25-53.

437 _____. 1984. "The transformation of lineage production in
Southern Ivory Coast, 1920-1980." Ethnology 23 (4): 261-277.

438 Hinderink, J. and Tempelman, G. J. 1979. Development Policy and Development Practice in Ivory Coast: A Miracle or a Mirage? Utrecht (Netherlands): Institute of Geography, Royal University of Utrecht.

439 Ikonicoff, Moises and Silvia Sigal. 1978. "'L'état relais': Un modèle de développement des sociétés périphériques?" Tiers-Monde 19 (76, Oct.-Dec.): 683-706.

440 Ivory Coast. Conseil Economique et Social. 1965. Rapport sur l'Evolution économique et sociale de la Cote d'Ivoire: 1960-64. Abidjan: Imprimerie Nationale.

441 _____. Direction de l'Animation et de la Productivité. 1968. Eléments pour une politique de développement social et culturel. Abidjan.

442 _____. Ministère des Affaires Economiques et Financières. 1967. Situation Economique de la Cote d'Ivoire. Abidjan.

443 _____. Ministère du Plan et de l'Industrie. 1983. Plan quinquennal de développement économique, social et culturel, 1981-1985. Abidjan: Le Ministère.

444 _____. 1975. Summary of the Five Year Economical Social and Cultural Plan 1976-1980. Abidjan: SAE.

445 Johns, Sheridan. 1982. "Reform of State Enterprises in the Ivory Coast: Reorganization or Redirection." Paper delivered to the Annual Meeting of the African Studies Association, Washington, D.C.

446 Kadja Mianno, Daniel. 1981. "La problématique de l'eau en milieu rural ivoirien: Aspects méthodologiques et pédagogiques." AUA:F 9: 35-46.

447 Kobben, A. J. F. 1958. "The Development of an Under-Developed Territory." Sociologus 8 (1) pp. 29-40.

448 Kouamé, Luc Koli. 1981. "Problèmes fonciers et développement rural en Cote d'Ivoire: L'exemple du Centre Bandama." CIRES 28/29 (Mar.-June): 37-48.

449 Koby Assa, Théophile. 1979. "Agriculture, développement et intégration nationale." AUA:G 8: 33-55.

450 Kouamé, Luc Koli. 1977. "Regional Statistics and the Structure of Regional Planning in the Ivory Coast." In A. L. Mabogunje and A. Faniran, eds. Regional Planning and National Development in Tropical Africa (Ibadan: Ibadan University Press), pp. 222-226.

451 Kouadio, Konan. 1979. "Situation et objectif du plan quinquennal ivoirien (1976-1980)." RFEPA 159 (March): 14-27.

452 Launay, Robert. 1977. "The Birth of a Ritual: The Politics
of Innovation in Dyula Islam." Savanna (Zaria) 2 (Dec.): 145-
154.

453 Lassailly-Jacob, Véronique. 1984. "La Charge de population
planifiée des rives du Lac de Kossou en Côte d'Ivoire." In
C. Blanc-Pamard, ed. Le Développement Rural en Questions
(Paris: ORSTOM), pp. 403-416.

454 _____. 1979. "Une opération de développement intégré en
Côte d'Ivoire centrale: l'opération Kossou." L'Espace géographique 8 (1, Jan.-Mar.): 57-63.

455 Lee, Eddy. 1980. "Export-led Rural Development: The Ivory
Coast." Development and Change (Netherlands) 11 (4): 607-
642.

456 _____. 1980. "Export-led Rural Development: The Ivory
Coast." In Agrarian Policies and Rural Poverty in Africa, pp.
99-127.

457 Lefournier, P. 1973. "La Côte d'Ivoire ou la croissance à l'en-
droit." L'Expansion (68, November): 102-109.

458 Lena, Philippe, 1981. "Quelques aspects du processus de différenciation économique en zone de colonisation récente (région
de Soubré...)." CIRES 30 (Sept.): 65-95.

459 _____. 1979. Transformation de l'espace rurale dans le front
pionnier du Sud-Ouest Ivoirien. Abidjan: ORSTOM.

460 Lesourd, M. 1984. "Mise en valeur agricole et organisation
de l'espace en zone pionnier: Les baoulés dans le sud-ouest
de la Côte d'Ivoire." In Chantal Blanc-Pamard, ed. Le Dévelop-
ment Rural en Questions. Paris: ORSTOM.

461 Ley, Albert. Le régime domanial et foncier et le développement
économique de la Côte d'Ivoire. Paris: R. Pichon et R. Durand-
Auzias.

462 Lister, Douglas W. 1976. "European Economic Presence in
Francophone Africa: The Ivory Coast." In C. Gregory Knight
and James L. Newman, eds. Contemporary Africa: Geography
and Change (Englewood Cliffs, NJ: Prentice-Hall), pp. 466-477.

463 Le Livret Vert de la croisade pour l'autosuffisance alimentaire.
Abidjan: Fraternité-Hebdo.

464 Marcussen, Henrik S. and Jens E. Torp. 1982. "The Ivory Coast: transcending blocked development?" (and) "The socio-economic consequences of economic development in the Ivory Coast." In their The internationalization of capital (London: Zed Press), pp. 66-121, 122-138.

465 _____. 1978. "The Ivory Coast--Towards Self-Centered Development?" In Kirsten Worm, ed. Industrialization, Development and the Demands for a New International Economic Order. Copenhagen: Samfundsvidenskabeligt Forlag).

466 Masini, Jean, et al. 1979. Multinationals and development in Black Africa: A case study in the Ivory Coast. Farnborough: Saxon House.

467 McCord, William. 1984. "A Wager in West Africa: Third World Report--II." New Leader 67 (September 3): 6-11.

468 McFarlane, George. 1984. "Ivory Coast: Hard times for an African success story." Africa Report 29 (March-April): 20-23.

469 Meister, Ulrich. 1982. "Ivory Coast Bottlenecks." Swiss Review of World Affairs 32 (October): 23-25.

470 M'lan, O. 1978. "Le rôle des entreprises publiques dans le développement de la Côte d'Ivoire." RJPIC 32 (1, Jan.-March): 69-83.

471 Montgomery, B. 1976. "Le rôle économique de la femme ivoirienne." CIRES 9 (March): 25-57; 10 (June): 7-26.

472 Mytelka, Lynn Krieger. 1984. "Foreign Business and Economic Development." In I. William Zartman and Christopher Delgado, ed. The Political Economy of the Ivory Coast (New York; Praeger): 149-173.

473 Nebo, Paul. 1973. "Côte d'Ivoire au dynamisme étonnant." France Eurafrique 242 (September): 6-7.

474 Ngango, Georges. 1973. Les investissements d'origine extérieure en Afrique noire francophone: Statut et incidence sur le développement. Paris.

475 Nyong'o, P. A. 1978. "Liberal models of capitalist development in Africa: Ivory Coast." Africa Development 3 (2, Apr.-June): 5-20.

476 N'zembele, L. 1984. "Côte d'Ivoire: L'envers du Miracle." Peuples Noire--Peuples Africains 7 (38, April): 69-87.

477 O'Connor, Michael. 1972. "Guinea and the Ivory Coast, Contrast in Economic Development." JMAS 10 (3): 409-426.

478 Pegatienan-Hiby, J. 1978. "Le rôle des instituts de recherche dans les pays africains à économie de marché: Le cas du Centre Ivoirien de Recherches Economiques et Sociales." Africa Development 3 (4, Oct.-Dec.): 109-121.

479 _____. 1980. "Le rôle du marché dans le développement économique de la Côte d'Ivoire." CIRES 26 (Sept.): 99-116.

480 Peltre-Wurtz, Jacqueline. 1984. "Gérer son terroir: Adaptation paysanne d'une projet de développement (Nord-ouest Côte d'Ivoire)." In Chantal Blanc-Pamard, ed. Le Développement Rural en Questions (Paris: ORSTOM).

481 Peltre-Wurtz, Jacqeline and Benjamin Steck. 1979. "Influence d'une société de développement sur le milieu paysan: Coton et culture attelée dans la région de la Bagoué (Nord Côte d'Ivoire)."

482 Priovolos, Theophilos. 1981. Coffee and the Ivory Coast: An Econometric Study. Lexington, MA: Lexington Books.

483 Problèmes économiques et humains du développement rural. 1978. Abidjan: CIRES.

484 Prowizur, E. 1976. "Les effets humains du barrage Kossou sur le Bandama blanc." Civilisations 26 (3/4): 232-258.

485 _____. 1979. "Les effets humains du barrage de Kossou (Côte d'Ivoire): Evolution depuis 1975." Civilisations 29 (3/4): 340-358.

486 Rondos, Alexander G. 1979. "The Price of Development: Ivory Coast." Africa Report 24 (March-April): 4-9.

487 Sawadogo, Abdoulaye, 1981. "Tradition et développement en agriculture: Le cas ivoirien." AUA:G 10: 115-130.

488 Sawadogo, Patrice. 1980. Impact de la croissance démographique sur le développement économique et social en République de Cote d'Ivoire. Addis Ababa: United Nations Economic Commission for Africa.

489 Schwartz, Alfred. 1979. "La dimension humaine des grandes opérations de développement: L'exemple de l'opération San Pedro." L'Espace Géographique 8 (1, Jan.-Mar.): 64-70.

490 Secher Marcussin, Henrik. 1979. The Development of Capitalist Relations of Production in Agriculture: The Case of Sodepalm in the Ivory Coast. Copenhagen: Institute for International Economics and Management.

491 Shabtai, Sabi H. 1975. "Army and Economy in Tropical Africa."
     Economic Development and Cultural Change 23 (4): 687-701.

492 "The short-run impact of fluctuating primary commodity prices
     on three developing economies: Colombia, Ivory Coast and
     Kenya." World Development 11 (May): 405-416.

493 Sinsou, J.-P. 1980. "Croissance autonome et aide étrangère:
     Le cas de la Côte d'Ivoire." AUA:K 3: 83-96.

494 Soumia, G. 1978. "Aménagement du territoire et stratégie
     du développement en Côte d'Ivoire." L'Information Géographique
     (5, November-December): 218-222.

495 Stryker, J. D. 1974. Exports and Growth in the Ivory Coast:
     Timber, Cocoa and Coffee. In S. R. Pearson and J. Counie,
     eds. Commodity Exports and African Economic Development
     (Lexington, MA: D. C. Heath).

496 Stryker, Richard Ellis. 1971. "A Local Perspective on Develop-
     ment Strategy in the Ivory Coast." In Michael F. Lofchie, ed.
     The State of the Nations: Constraints on Development in In-
     dependent Africa (Berkeley: University of California Press).

497 Teal, Francis. 1986. "The Foreign Exchange Regime and
     Growth: A Comparison of Ghana and the Ivory Coast." African
     Affairs 85 (339): 267-282.

498 Thibault, J. 1978. "Le développement ivoirien." RFSPA
     (150/151, June-July): 57-78.

499 Thomas, Tayib. 1984. "La formation coopérative en Côte
     d'Ivoire." Communautés 70 (October-December): 171-174.

500 Torp, Jens Erik. 1979. The Textile Industry in France and
     the Ivory Coast: Case Study of the Internationalization of
     Capital, the Nation State, and the Development of Peripheral
     Capitalism. Copenhagen: Institute for International Economics
     and Management.

501 Traore, A. 1983. "La problématique de l'auto-suffisance alimen-
     taire en Cote d'Ivoire." AUA:K 6: 49-127.

502 Vellas, François. 1981. "La fonction de pays relais dans les
     échanges Nord-Sud: Le cas de la Cote d'Ivoire." Tiers Monde
     22 (85): 121-139.

503 Woronoff, Jon. 1979. "The Value of Development." Africa Re-
     port 24 (July-August 1979): 13-19.

504 _____. 1972. West African Wager. Metuchen, N.J.: Scare-
     crow Press.

505   Yansane, Aguibou Y. 1984. Decolonization in West African
      States with French Colonial Legacy. Comparison and Contrast:
      Development in Guinea, the Ivory Coast and Senegal (1945-1980).
      Cambridge, MA: Schenkman.

E. ENERGY

506   Ivory Coast. 1972. Kossou: Aujourd'hui et demain. Abidjan.

507   Laigroz, J. 1974. "Tiers-Monde et crise petrolière: Le cas
      de la Côte d'Ivoire." Revue de l'Energie (25, 265, August-
      September): 93-94.

F. FINANCE

508   Arditi, Claude and J.-M. Young. 1983. "L'épargne en milieu
      rural ivoirien." Etudes pour le développement 2: 128-158.

509   Bello, Toyidi. 1980. "La demande de financement extérieur
      en Côte d'Ivoire." AUA:K 3: 21-36.

510   Chevassu, Jean. 1974. "Which Countries Are Best for Invest-
      ment?" International Management (August).

511   Dick, Hermann and David P. Vincent. 1984. "Export taxation
      by marketing boards in developing countries: Some macroecono-
      mic and distributional aspects with reference to the Ivory Coast."
      In Recent German research in international economics (Bonn:
      Deutsche Forschungsgemeinschaft), pp. 80-105.

512   Garity, Monique P. 1972. "The 1969 Franc Devaluation and the
      Ivory Coast Economy." JMAS 10 (4): 627-633.

513   Glasman, Monique. 1983. "Analyse de la loi des finances de
      la Côte d'Ivoire." Afrique Contemporaine 22 (127, July-
      September): 19-27.

514   Gourvez, J. Y. 1983. "Epargne et investissement des ménages
      de l'agglomération d'Abidjan: Résultats d'une première approche."
      Etudes pour le développement 2: 159-173.

515   Kouadio, Lambert. 1984. "L'endettement extérieur de la Côte
      d'Ivoire." Peuples noirs--Peuples Africains 7 (41-42, December):
      30-45.

516   _____. 1984. "La Zone Franc et la Côte d'Ivoire: Le tribut
      financier à payer à la France." Peuples noirs--Peuples Africains
      7 (41-42, December): 60-75.

517 Koumoue Koffi, Moise. 1980. La taxe sur la valeur ajoutée
dans le développement économique de la Côte d'Ivoire. Paris:
Librairie Générale de Droit et de Jurisprudence.

518 Miras, Claude de. 1982. "L'entrepreneur ivoirien ou une bour-
geoisie privée de son état." In Y.-A. Faure and Jean-François
Ménard, eds. Etat et bourgeoisie en Côte d'Ivoire (Paris,
Karthala).

519 _____. 1984. "De la formation de capital privé à l'économie
populaire spontanée: Itinéraire d'une recherche en milieu urbain africain." Politique Africaine 14 (June): 92-109.

520 Mytelka, Lynn Krieger. 1981. "Direct foreign investment and
technological choice in the Ivoirian textile and wood industries."
Vierteljahresberichte (Bonn) 83: 61-79; also (in French) in
Revue Canadienne d'Etudes du Développement 4 (1): 95-123.

521 Schwartz, André. 1966. "Etude de comptabilité nationale:
Les opérations financières des entreprises en Côte d'Ivoire sur
la période 1963-1965." Abidjan: ORSTOM.

522 Wellons, P. A. 1977. "Eager borrowers: Ivory Coast." In
Wellons, ed. Borrowing by Developing Countries on the Euro-
currency Market (Paris: OECD), pp. 131-143.

G. HOUSING

523 Ducharme, Michel. 1968. "L'Habitat, Outil d'Urbanisation."
Bulletin du Secretariat des Missions d'Urbanisme et d'Habitat.
(No. 54, Paris: S.M.U.H.): 1-15.

524 Grootaert, Christiaan and Jean-Luc Dubois. 1986. The Demand
for Urban Housing in the Ivory Coast. Washington, D.C.:
World Bank

525 _____. Ministère de l'Information. Sous-Direction de la
Documentation Générale et de la Presse. 1968. Town Planning
and Rural Housing Modernization in the Ivory Coast. Abidjan.

526 Martin, R. P. and J. L. Boutillier. 1956. "L'Amélioration de
l'Habitat dans la subdivision de Bongouanou." Etudes Eburnéennes (5): 191-215.

527 Mermet, Louis-Félix. 1979. Habitats traditionnels en Côte
d'Ivoire. Paris: Ministère de la Coopération.

H. INDUSTRY

528 Ahua, Antoine and Jean-Thomas Bernard. 1985. Structure

de la demande d'énergie dans les pays de l'Afrique de l'ouest.
Quebec: Department of Economics, Laval University.

529 Alfthan, Torkel. 1982. "Industrialisation in the Ivory Coast:
Impact on employment and basic-needs satisfaction." International Labour Review 121 (November-December): 761-774.

530 Chevassu, Jean and Alain Valette. 1975. "Les industriels de
la Côte d'Ivoire: Qui et pourquoi?" Abidjan: ORSTOM.

531 _____. 1975. "Les relations intermédiaires dans le secteur
industriel ivoirien." Abidjan: ORSTOM.

532 _____. 1975. "Les revenus distribués par les activités industrielles en Côte d'Ivoire." Abidjan: ORSTOM.

533 _____. 1973. "Le système de production industrielle de la
Côte d'Ivoire: Type d'analyse et premiers résultats." Abidjan:
ORSTOM.

534 Deniel, Raymond. 1981. "Du sucre et des hommes: La SODE-
SUCRE de Sérébou-Comoé (Côte d'Ivoire)." Cultures et Développement (Belgium) 13 (4): 575-631.

535 Deniel, Raymond and J. H. Moulignot. 1984. "Evaluation 'ex-
post' du complèxe de Borotou-Koro (SODESUCRE--République de
Côte d'Ivoire)." Paris: Ministry of Foreign Affairs.

536 Dubresson, Alain. 1984. "Régionalisation de l'industrie et
croissance urbaine: Un 'mammouth' à Agboville (Côte d'Ivoire)."
In De Caracas à Kinshasa, pp. 91-108.

537 Gboizo, Josette. 1978. L'industrie textile en Côte d'Ivoire:
Emploi et qualifications. Abidjan: Office National de Formation
Professionnelle.

538 Ismail, Toufik. 1970. "L'industrie dans l'économie de l'Afrique
Centrale, Sénégal, Côte d'Ivoire, Cameroun, Congo (Kinshasa)."
Louvain: Université Catholique de Louvain.

539 Lecallo, Denis. 1982. Les entreprises publiques en Côte
d'Ivoire. Paris: Ministry of Foreign Affairs.

540 Maex, Rudy and Alan Read. 1982. International division of
labour programme: A comparative analysis of local processing for
exports in Niger and the Ivory Coast. Geneva: International
Labor Office.

541 Masini, J., et al. 1979. Les multinationales et le développement:
Trois entreprises et la Côte d'Ivoire. Paris: Presses Universitaires de France.

542 Miras, Claude de. 1980. "Le secteur de subsistance dans les branches de production à Abidjan." Tiers Monde 21 (82): 353-372; also in De Caracas à Kinshasa (1984): 237-258.

543 Monson, Terry D. 1975. "Evolution des prix dans le secteur industriel ivoirien." CIRES 5: 43-67.

544 Mytelka, Lynn Krieger. 1983. "The Limits of Export-Led Development: The Ivory Coast's Experience with Manufactures." In J. G. Ruggie, ed. The Antinomies of Interdependence (New York: Columbia University Press), pp. 239-270.

545 Pegatienan-Hiby, Jacques. 1980. "Système et structure de production de l'industrie manufacturière: implications pour une politique des revenus." CIRES 24/25 (Mar.-June): 45-120.

I. LABOR

546 Atta, Koffi. 1981. "La situation de l'emploi dans une ville moyenne africaine: Le cas de Bouaké (Côte d'Ivoire)." AUA:G 10: 131-149.

547 Centre Ivoirien de recherche économique et sociale (CIRES). 1979. "La mobilité de la main d'oeuvre agricole en forêt." Abidjan: University of Abidjan, Centre réprographique de l'enseignement supérieur.

548 Convention collective interprofessionnelle de la République de Côte d'Ivoire. 1983. Abidjan: Association interprofessionnelle des employeurs de Côte d'Ivoire.

549 Coulibaly, Aly. 1978. L'emploi dans les entreprises libano-syriennes de Côte d'Ivoire: Analyse de documents. Abidjan: Ministry of Technical Instruction and Professional Training.

550 Coulibaly, Aly and Michel Firmin-Guion. 1978. Etude de synthèse de la région Ouest: Emploi/formation. Abidjan: Ministry of Technical Instruction and Professional Training.

551 Dessallien, C. and A. Hauser. 1976. "Les jeunes déscolarisés sans qualification inscrits à l'Office de la Main d'Oeuvre d'Abidjan en 1975." Abidjan: ORSTOM.

552 _____. 1978. "Attitudes à l'égard de l'emploi: Les jeunes déscolarisés sans qualification inscrits à l'Office de la Main d'Oeuvre de San Pedro et Bouaké en 1977." Abidjan: ORSTOM.

553 France. Secrétariat d'état aux affaires étrangères, Direction de l'aide au Développement. 1974. Evolution des structures de l'emploi en Côte d'Ivoire 1965-1971. Paris.

554 Gastellu, Jean-Marc. 1979. "Disparition de la main-d'ouevre etrangère?" CIRES 23 (Dec.): 17-45.

555 Hauser, André. 1983. "Cent mille personnes devant les grilles: Les demandeurs et demandeuses d'emploi d'Abidjan." Cahiers ORSTOM, Série Sciences Humaines 19 (4): 397-413.

556 Joshi, Heather, Harold Lubell and Jean Mouly. 1976. Abidjan: Urban Development and Employment in Ivory Coast. Geneva: International Labor Office.

557 Koné, Zobila. 1984. "Les formes d'importation de technologie et leurs effets sur la formation et l'emploi: Le cas de la Côte d'Ivoire." Perspectives (UNESCO) 14 (4): 545-558.

558 Lena, Philippe. "1979. Le problème de la main d'oeuvre en zone pionnière, quelques points de repère." CIRES 23 (Dec.): 89-98.

559 Monson, Terry D. and Garry G. Pursell. 1979. "The use of DRC's to evaluate indigenization programs: The case of the Ivory Coast." Journal of development Economics 6 (1, March): 119-139.

560 Pegatienan-Hiby, J. 1975. "Les qualifications de la main-d'oeuvre et le développement économique de la Côte d'Ivoire." CIRES 5: 9-42.

561 _____. 1978. "Technologie industrielle et création d'emplois modernes: Le cas de la Côte d'Ivoire." CIRES 17 (March): 5-21.

562 Sanoh, L. 1978. "Essai sur les déterminants de l'emploi agri-cole permanent sur les grandes exploitations et exploitations agricoles modernes de Côte d'Ivoire." CIRES 17 (March): 23-49.

563 Savignac, Chantal. 1979. "Approche des conditions de travail en agriculture dans le Nord de la Côte d'Ivoire." CIRES 22 (Sept.): 13-38.

564 Schwartz, Alfred. "1976. La problématique de la main-d'oeuvre dans le sud-ouest ivoirien et le projet pâte à papier: Bilan et perspectives." Abidjan: ORSTOM.

565 Skinner, Elliott P. 1965. "Labor Migration among the Mossi of the Upper Volta." In Kuper, Hilda, ed. Urbanization and Migration in West Africa (Berkeley: University of California Press), pp. 60-84.

J. MINING AND MINERALS

566   Société pour le développement minier de la Côte d'Ivoire. 1978.
      Liste des publications, rapports et notes documentaires diffuses
      par SODEMI de juin 1962 à janvier 1978. Abidjan: SODEMI.

K. TOURISM

567   Mehou-Loko, Victor. 1978. Tourisme et ressources locales dans
      les pays en développement: Dimbokro, Côte d'Ivoire, 5 avril-30
      juin 1977. Abidjan: Ministère du Tourisme.

568   Nedelec, Michel. 1974. Equipements touristiques et récréatifs
      dans la région d'Abidjan. University of Abidjan: Centre de re-
      cherches architecturales et urbaines.

L. TRANSPORT AND COMMUNICATIONS

569   Beenhakker, Henri L. and Nils Bruzelius. 1987. Transport
      and Marketing of Agricultural Products in the Ivory Coast.
      Washington, D.C.: World Bank.

570   Benveniste, C. 1974. La boucle du cacao (Côte d'Ivoire):
      Etude régionale des circuits de transport. Paris: ORSTOM.

571   Bisilliat, Jeanne. 1979. "Présentation d'une expérience de
      télévision communautaire à Bonoua, Côte d'Ivoire." Tiers-
      Monde 20 (79, July-Sept.): 563-570.

572   Bouthier, M. 1969. Le Port d'Abidjan. COM 87 (July-
      September): 288-312.

573   Equipement et Transports en République de Côte d'Ivoire 1960-
      1980: Bilan et Perspectives. 1980. Malesherbes (Loiret,
      France): Imprimerie Maury.

574   Ivory Coast. Service d'études économiques. 1980. Equipement
      et transports, 1960-1980: Bilan et perspectives. Abidjan.

HISTORY

575   Cangah, Guy and Ekanza, Simon-Pierre. 1978. La Côte d'Ivoire
      par les textes: De l'aube de la colonisation à nos jours. Abid-
      jan: NEA.

576   Chauveau, J.-P. 1980. "Agricultural Production and Social

Formation: The Baule Region of Toumodi-Kokumbo in Historical Perspective." In Martin A. Klein, ed. Peasants in Africa (Beverly Hills, CA: Sage), pp. 142-174.

577 Clerici, A., (director) 1962. Histoire de la Côte d'Ivoire. Abidjan: CEDA.

578 Duprey, Pierre. 1962. Histoire des Ivoiriens. Abidjan: Imprimerie de la Côte d'Ivoire.

579 Loucou, Jean-Noël. 1982. Bibliographie de l'histoire de Côte d'Ivoire (1960-1980). Abidjan: University of Abidjan, Publications of the History Department.

580 _____. 1984. Histoire de la Côte d'Ivoire. Vol. 1: La formation des peuples. Abidjan: CEDA.

581 Welch, Ashton Wesley. 1982. The National Archives of the Ivory Coast. History in Africa (9): 377-380.

A. PRE-COLONIAL

582 Agyeman, E. A. 1966. "A Note on the Foundation of the Kingdom of Gyaman." Ghana Notes and Queries 9: 36-39.

583 Aka, Kouamé. 1980. "Origine et évolution du Ngatianou jusqu'à la colonisation." AUA:I 8: 211-236.

584 Arhin, Kwame. 1970. "Aspects of the Ashanti Northern Trade in the Nineteenth Century." Africa 40 (4, Oct.): 363-373.

585 _____. 1980. "The Economic and Social Significance of Rubber Production and Exchange on the Gold and Ivory Coasts, 1880-1900." CEA 20 (77-78): 63-82.

586 Augé, Marc. 1971. "L'organisation du commerce précoloniale en basse Côte d'Ivoire et ses effets sur l'organisation sociale des populations cotières." In Claude Meillassoux, ed. The Development of Indigenous Trade and Markets in West Africa (London: Oxford University Press), pp. 153-167.

587 Azarya, Victor. 1980. "Traders and the Center in Massina, Kong, and Samori's State." IJAHS 13 (3): 420-456.

588 B., J. S. 1979. "Les civilisations sénoufo en Afrique de l'ouest: Espoirs et limites de la tradition orale." Entente africaine 39 (Dec.): 58-61.

589 Bernus, Edmond. 1960. "Kong et sa region." Etudes Eburnéennes 8: 239-323.

590 _____. 1961. "Notes sur l'histoire de Korhogo." Bulletin de l'IFAN (B, 23, 1-2): 284-290.

591 Bertho, Père Jacques. 1952. "Nouvelles ruines de pierre en pays lobi." Notes Africaines 54 (April): 33-34.

592 Binger, Louis-Gustave. 1892. Du Niger au golfe de Guinée par le pays de Kong et le Mossi (2 vols.). Paris: Hachette.

593 Boutillier, J.-L. 1971. "La cité marchande de Bouna dans l'ensemble économique ouest-africain pré-colonial." In C. Meillassoux, ed. The Development of Indigenous Trade and Markets in West Africa (London: Oxford University Press), pp. 240-252.

594 _____. 1971. "Les effets de la disparition du commerce précolonial sur le système de production koulango." Cahiers ORSTOM 8 (3): 243-253.

595 _____. 1975. "Les trois esclaves de Bouna." In Claude Meillassoux, ed. L'Esclavage en Afrique précoloniale (Paris: François Maspero), pp. 253-280.

596 _____. 1969. "La ville de Bouna: De l'époque précoloniale à auhourd'hui." Cahiers ORSTOM 6 (2): 3-20.

597 Chauveau, J. P. 1978. "Contribution à la géographie historique de l'or en pays baule (Côte d'Ivoire)." Journal des Africanistes 48 (1): 15-70.

598 _____. 1984. "Le fer, l'outil et la monnaie: Hypothèses à partir du jede, ancien couteau à débrousser baule (Côte d'Ivoire)." Cahiers ORSTOM, séries sciences humaines 20 (3-4): 471-484.

599 _____. 1979. "Note sur l'histoire économique et sociale de la région de Kokumbo (Baoulé-Sud, Côte d'Ivoire)." Abidjan: ORSTOM.

600 _____. 1971. "Note sur l'histoire du peuplement de la région de Kokumbo (Cote d'Ivoire)." Abidjan: ORSTOM.

601 _____. 1973. "Note sur la morphologie matrimoniale de Kokumbo (pays baoulé; Côte d'Ivoire): Perspective historique." Abidjan: ORSTOM.

602 _____. 1972. "Note sur la place du Baoulé dans l'ensemble économique ouest-africain précolonial." Abidjan: ORSTOM.

603 _____. 1976. "Note sur les echanges dans le Baule precolonial." CEA 16 (63-64): 567-602.

604 _____. 1977. "Societe baule precoloniale et model segmentaire: Le cas de la region de Kokumbo." CEA 17 (68): 415-434.

605 Cotten, A. M. 1969. "Odienné, notes d'histoire." Abidjan: ORSTOM.

606 Delafosse, Maurice. Kong. Encyclopedia of Islam, 1st ed.

607 Dérive, Jean. 1978. "Le chant de Kurubi à Kong." AUA:J 2: 85-114.

608 Diabaté, Henriette. 1975. Aniaba: Un Assinien à la cour de Louis XIV. Paris: ABC; Dakar: NEA.

609 Dumett, R. E. 1979. "Precolonial Goldmining and the State in the Akan Region." In G. Dalton, ed. Research in Economic Anthropology (Greenwich, CT: JAI Press), pp. 37-68.

610 Ekanza, Simon-Pierre. 1981. "Le Moronou à l'époque de l'administrateur Marchand: Aspects physiques et économiques." AUA:I 9: 53-70.

611 Fynn, J. K. 1971. Asante and its Neighbours. London: Longman.

612 Goody, Jack R. 1964. "The Mande and the Akan Hinterland." In Jan Vansina, R. Mauny, and L. Thomas, ed. The Historian in Tropical Africa (London: Oxford Univ. Press), pp. 193-218.

613 Green, Kathryn L. 1985. "Dyula and Sonongui Roles in the Islamization of Kong." Asian and African Studies.

614 _____. 1984. "The Foundation of Kong: A Study of Dyula and Sonongui Ethnic Identity." Ph.D. diss., Indiana University.

615 _____. 1982. "Kong: Lost City of the Ivory Coast." Craft International (Summer): 33-35.

616 Griffeth, Robert R. 1971. "The Dyula Impact on the Peoples of the West Volta Region." In Carleton T. Hodge, Ed. Papers on the Manding (Bloomington, IN: Indiana University Press), pp. 167-181.

617 Guyader, Josseline. 1979. "Une royauté agni à l'aube de la conquête coloniale: Le pouvoir politique dans la société Sanwi depuis 1843 jusqu'à 1893." AUA:I 7: 28-114.

618 Handloff, Robert E. 1982a. "The Dyula of Gyaman: A Study of Politics and Trade in the Nineteenth Century." Ph.D. diss., Northwestern University.

619 Holden, Jeff. 1970. "The Samorian Impact on Buna: An Essay in Methodology." In C. Allen and R. W. Johnson, eds. African Perspectives (Cambridge: Cambridge University Press), pp. 83-108.

620 Jamain, E. 1973. "Introduction à l'histoire précoloniale du pays Neyo d'aprés la tradition orale." Abidjan: ORSTOM.

621 Kipre, Pierre. 1967. "De la tradition orale chez les Bété: La conversion de la tradition orale." Bulletin d'information et de liaison des Instituts d'Ethno-Sociologie et de Geographie Tropicale. Abidjan: University of Abidjan.

622 Kodjo, N. G. 1983. "Les précurseurs de Séku Watara (1600-1670)." AUA:I 11: 61-83.

623 Kouroubari, Amadou. 1959. "Histoire de l'Imam Samori." BIFAN B (31): 544-571.

624 Loucou, Jean-Noël. 1976. "L'exode des Baule." BIFAN 38 (3, Série B, Sciences Humaines, July): 506-516.

625 Loucou, Jean-Noël and Françoise Ligier. 1977. La reine Pokou, fondatrice du royaume baoulé. Paris: ABC.

626 Louhoy, Tety Gauze. 1969. "Contribution à l'histoire du peuplement de la Côte d'Ivoire." AUA:F 1, fasc. 1: 7-24.

627 Mauny, R. 1977. "A propos de perles anciennes ('agris') recueillies par Maurice Delafosse avant 1914 en Côte d'Ivoire." Notes africaines (Dakar: IFAN) 154 (April): 38-40.

628 M'bra-Ekanla, S.-P. 1984. "Mutations d'une société rurale: Les Agnis de Moronou 18e siècle-1939." AUA:I 12: 217-227.

629 McCall, Daniel F. 1981. "Probing Lo Bir History." In 2000 Ans d'Histoire Africaine: Le sol, la Parole, et l'Ecrit (Paris: Société Française d'Histoire d'Outre-Mer), pp. 361-373.

630 McIntosh, Susan Keech. 1981. "A Reconsideration of Wangara/Paolus, Island of Gold." Journal of African History 22: 145-158.

631 Mouezy, Henri. 1954. Assinie et la royaume de Krinjabo: Histoire et coutumes, 2d ed. Paris: Larose.

632 Muhammad, Akbar. 1977. "The Samorian Occupation of Bondoukou: An Indigenous View." IJAHS 10 (2): 242-258.

633 Olivier de Sardan, Jean-Pierre. 1982. "Le cheval et l'arc." In Jean Bazin and Emmanuel Terray, eds. Guerres de lignages

et guerres d'états en Afrique (Paris: Editions des Archives Contemporaines), pp. 189-234.

634 O'Sullivan, John M. 1976. "Developments in the Social Stratification of Northwest Ivory Coast during the 18th and 19th Centuries." Ph.D. dissertation, University of California at Los Angeles.

635 _____. 1980. "Slavery in the Malinke Kingdom of Kabadougou (Ivory Coast)." IJAHS (13, 4): 633-650.

636 Perinbam, B. Marie. 1980. "The Julas in Western Sudanese History: Long-Distance Traders and Developers of Resources." In B. K. Swartz, Jr. and Raymond E. Dumett, eds. West African Culture Dynamics (The Hague: Mouton), pp. 455-475.

637 Perrot, Claude-Hélène. 1982a. Les Anyi-Ndenye et le pouvoir politique au XVIIIe et XIXe siecles. Paris: Publications de la Sorbonne.

638 _____. 1985. "L'appropriation de l'espace: un enjeu politique --Pour une histoire du peuplement." Annales: économies, sociétés, civilisations 40 6: 1289-1306.

639 _____. 1979. "Femmes et pouvoir politique dans l'ancienne société anyi-ndenye (Côte d'Ivoire)." CEA 19 (73-76): 219-223.

640 _____. 1982. "Formation d'Etats et formation d'une ethnie: Le cas des Anyi-Ndenye." CEA 22 (87-88): 455-463.

641 _____. 1969. "Hommes libres et captifs dans le royaume agni de l'Indenie." CEA 9 (35): 482-501.

642 _____. 1978. "Or, richesse et pouvoir chez les Anyi-Ndenye aux XVIIIe et XIXe siècles." Journal des Africanistes 48 (1): 101-126.

643 _____. 1981. "Le processus de formation d'une ethnie: Les Anyi-Ndenye de Côte d'Ivoire." RFHOM 68 (250-253): 427-429.

644 _____. 1976. "De la richesse au pouvoir: Les origines d'une chefferie du Ndenye (Côte d'Ivoire)." CEA 16 (61-62): 173-187.

645 Person, Yves. 1963. "Les ancêtres de Samori." CEA 3 (4, 1): 125-156.

646 _____. 1972-73. "The Atlantic Coast and the Southern Savannahs, 1800-1880." In J. F. Ade Ajayi and Michael Crowder, eds. History of West Africa (New York: Columbia University Press), Vol. 2, pp. 262-307.

647 _____. 1964. "En queste d'une chronologie ivoirienne." In Jan Vansina, R. Mauny, and L. V. Thomas, eds. The Historian in Tropical Africa. London.

648 _____. 1970. "Samori and Resistance to the French." In Robert I. Rotberg and Ali A. Mazrui, eds. Power and Protest in Black Africa (New York: Oxford University Press), pp. 80-112.

649 _____. 1968-1975. Samori: une révolution dyula, 3 vols. Dakar: IFAN.

650 Schwartz, Alfred. 1968. La Mise en Place des Populations Guéré et Wobe: Essai d'interprétation historique des données de la tradition orale. Adiopodoume, Ivory Coast: ORSTOM, Sciences Humaines, vol. 5 (4): 1-38; vol. 6 (1): 1-31.

651 Sugy, Catherine. 1975. "Economic Growth and Secular Trends in the Pre-Colonial Sudanic Belt." Ph.D. diss., Columbia University.

652 "Table ronde sur les origines de Kong." 1977. AUA:J (1).

653 Terray, Emmanuel. 1974. "Bondoukou avant la conquête coloniale: Le témoignage des visiteurs britanniques." In Les populations communes de la Côte d'Ivoire et du Ghana. Colloque Inter-Universitaire, Ghana-Côte d'Ivoire. Universities of Abidjan and Legon, Bondoukou, Jan. 4-9.

654 _____. 1975. "La captivité dans le royaume abron du Gyaman." In C. Meillassoux, ed. L'esclavage en Afrique précolonial (Paris: Maspero), pp. 221-250.

655 _____. "Class and Class Consciousness in the Abron Kingdom of Gyaman." In M. Bloch, ed. Marxist Analysis and Social Anthropology (London: Malaby Press), pp. 85-135.

656 _____. 1982. "L'economie politique du royaume abron du Gyaman." CEA 22 (87-88): 251-275.

657 _____. 1977. "Event, structure and history: the formation of the Abron kingdom of Gyaman (1700-1780)." In J. Friedman and M. J. Rowlands, eds. The Evolution of Social Systems (London: Duckworth), pp. 279-301.

658 _____. 1974. "Long-distance Exchange and the Formation of the State." Economy and Society 3 (3): 315-345.

659 _____. 1979. "Un mouvement de réforme religieuse dans le royaume abron précolonial: Le culte de Sakrobundi." CEA 19 (73-76): 143-176.

660 Toungara, Jeanne Maddox. 1980. "The Pre-Colonial Economy of Northwestern Ivory Coast and its Transformation under French Colonialism, 1827-1920." Ph.D. dissertation, University of California at Los Angeles.

661 Touré, M. 1974. "Dominance de la langue koulango dans le Royaume Abron." In Les Populations communes de la Côte d'Ivoire et du Ghana. Colloque Inter-Universitaire, Ghana-Côte d'Ivoire. Universities of Abidjan and Legon, Bondoukou, Jan. 4-9.

662 Traoré, Dominique. 1950. "Les relations de Samory avec l'Etat de Kong." Notes Africaines 47: 96-97.

663 Weiskel, Timothy C. 1976. "L'histoire socio-economique des peuples baoulé: Problèmes et perspectives de recherche." CEA 16 (61-62): 357-395.

664 _____. 1978. "The Precolonial Baule: A Reconstruction." CEA 18 (72) 503-560.

665 Wondji, Christophe. 1972. "Commerce du cola et marchées pré-coloniales dans la région de Daloa." AUA:I :33-61.

B. COLONIAL

666 Angoulvant, G. 1916. La Pacification de la Côte d'Ivoire (1908-1915). Paris: Larose.

667 Anouma, René-Pierre. 1978. "L'impot de capitation en Côte d'Ivoire de 1901 à 1908: Modalités et implications d'un instrument de politique et d'économie coloniales." Afrika zamani (Yaoundé) 8/9 (December): 132-155; also in AUA:I 3: 121-139.

668 _____. 1976. "Une modalité du travail forcé: La prestation en Côte d'Ivoire de 1912 à la veille de la seconde guerre mondiale." AUA:I 4: 61-86.

669 _____. 1977. "Les sociétés indigènes de prévoyance, la caisse centrale de crédit agricole mutuel: Organisation, fonctionnement et rôle en Côte d'Ivoire jusqu'à la veille de la 2e guerre mondiale." AUA:I 5: 55-80.

670 Asiwaju, A. I. 1976. "Migrations as Revolt: The Example of the Ivory Coast and the Upper Volta before 1945." JAH 17 (4): 577-594.

671 Atger, P. 1962. La France en Côte d'ivoire de 1843 a 1893: Cinquante ans d'hésitations politiques et commerciales. Dakar.

672 Bening, R. B. 1974. "Definitions of the Ghana-Ivory Coast
Boundary North of the Ninth Parallel 1890-1898." In Les Populations communes de la Côte d'Ivoire et du Ghana. Colloque
Inter-Universitaire, Ghana-Côte d'Ivoire: Universities of Abidjan and Legon, Bondoukou, Jan. 4-9.

673 Bony, Joachim. 1980. "La Côte d'Ivoire sous la colonisation
française et le prélude à l'émancipation 1920-1947: Genèse d'une
nation." Thèse de doctorat de l'état, Université de Paris.

674 Chaput, J. 1949. "Treich-Laplene et la naissance de la Côte
d'Ivoire française." Revue d'Histoire des Colonies 36: 110.

675 Dadié, Bernard Binlin. Carnet de Prison. Abidjan: CEDA.

676 Delafosse, Louise. 1976. Maurice Delafosse: Le Berrichon
conquis par l'Afrique. Paris.

677 Delafosse, Maurice. 1908. Les Frontières de la Côte d'Ivoire
et de la Côte d'Or. Paris: Masson et Cie.

678 Delpech, Bernard. 1984. "Qui a trahi Badiegoro? Un chant
de Bolia sur la conquête française en pays Gouro, Côte d'Ivoire."
Genève-Afrique 22 (2): 119-135.

679 Derou, J. 1984. "Notes sur les traités entre la France et les
entités politiques de la Côte d'Ivoire pré-coloniale (1884-1893)."
AUA:I 12: 153-187.

680 Diabaté, Henriette. 1975. "Le role des femmes dans l'histoire
du R.D.A." In Fondation Houphouet-Boigny, Revue de l'Institut
Africain de Recherches historiques et politiques, 2: 88-102.

681 _____. 1975. La marche des femmes sur Grand-Bassam.
Abidjan: NEA.

682 Diallo, Abdoulaye. 1980. "Financement de l'infrastructure
routière en Côte d'Ivoire, 1946-1953." AUA:I: 257-282.

683 Domergue, Danielle. 1976. "La Côte d'Ivoire de 1912 à 1920."
AUA:I 4: 35-59.

684 _____. 1981. "Essai sur l'alcoolisme en Côte d'Ivoire,
1900-1958." AUA:I 9: 99-120.

685 _____. 1983. "Un gouverneur pas comme les autres: Gabriel
Angoulvant." AUA:I 11: 231-242.

686 _____. 1981. "La Lutte contre la Trypanosomiase en Côte
d'Ivoire, 1900-1945." JAH 22 (1): 63-72.

687 _____. 1978. "Les Vingt Primières Années de l'Action Sanitaire en Côte d'Ivoire." RFHOM 65 (1): 40-63.

688 Ekanza, Simon-Pierre. 1981. "La main-d'oeuvre ivoirienne des entreprises privées pendant l'entre-deux-guerres 1921-1939." AUA:I 9: 71-97.

689 _____. 1975. "Le méssianisme en Côte d'Ivoire au début du siècle: une tentative de réponse nationaliste à l'état de situation coloniale." AUA:I 3: 55-71.

690 _____. 1975. "L'oppression administrative en Côte d'Ivoire (1908-1920)." BIFAN Série B 37 (3, July): 667-84.

691 Forlacroix, C. 1968. "La pénétration française dans l'Indénié (1887-1901)." AUA:F 1, fasc. 1: 91-136.

692 Gbagbo, Laurent. 1982. Côte d'Ivoire: Economie et Société à la veille de l'Indépendence: 1944-1960. Paris: Harmattan.

693 _____. 1983. "Les entreprises coloniales en Côte d'Ivoire à la veille de la Séconde Guerre Mondiale." In Entreprises et entrepreneurs en Afrique, XIXe et XXe siècles (Paris: L'Harmattan), vol. 1, pp. 477-487.

694 Groff, David Huston. 1980. "The Development of Capitalism in the Ivory Coast: The Case of Assikasso, 1880-1940." Ph.D. Dissertation, Stanford University.

695 Houphouët-Boigny, Félix. 1957. "Black Africa and the French Union." Foreign Affairs (23, July): 543-599.

696 Kipre, Pierre. 1976. "La crise économique dans les centres urbains en Côte d'Ivoire, 1930-1935." CEA 16 (61-62): 119-146.

697 _____. 1983. "Grandes sociétés et entreprises individuelles dans la ville coloniale en Côte d'Ivoire à la veille de la Seconde Guerre Mondiale." In Entreprises et entrepreneuirs en Afrique, XIX et XXe siècles (Paris: L'Harmattan), 229-240.

698 _____. 1975. "La place des centres urbains dans l'économie de la Côte d'Ivoire de 1920 à 1930." AUA:I 3: 93-120.

699 Knops, P. 1981. Les Anciens Sénufo: 1923-1935. Berg en Dal: Afrika Museum.

700 Landraud, M. 1978. "Justice 'indigène' et politique coloniale: L'exemple de la Côte d'Ivoire (1903-1940)." Penant 87, 759 (Jan.-March): 5-42; 760 (Apr.-June): 205-249.

701 Loucou, Jean-Noël. 1980. "La Deuxième Guerre Mondiale et ses effets en Côte d'Ivoire." AUA:I 8: 183-207.

702 _____. 1976. "Les premières élections de 1945 en Côte d'Ivoire." AUA:I 4: 5-33.

703 Mamdou, C. 1976. "Mentalités africaines et colonisation." AUA: I 4: 105-122.

704 Manso, M. Eyui J. Marie. "Le mouvement coopératif ivoirien; Regard sur la commune d'Agboville: Synthèse de l'histoire de la coopération éburnéenne en agriculture de la colonisation à l'indépendance." CIRES 28/29 (March-June): 147-177.

705 Mortimer, Edward. 1969. France and the Africans, 1944-1960: A Political History. New York: Walker.

706 Olivier, R. 1976. "L'organisation judiciare de la Côte d'Ivoire pendant la période coloniale." RID 1/2: 4-31.

707 O'Sullivan, John M. 1978. "The Franco-Baoule War, 1891-1911: The Struggle against the French Conquest of Central Ivory Coast." JAS 5(3): 329-356.

708 _____. 1983. "The French Conquest of Northwest Ivory Coast: The Attempt of the Rulers of Kabadugu to Control the Situation." CEA (89-90): 121-138.

709 Perrot, Claude-Hélène. 1982. "Ecrits coloniaux et crise dynastique anyi-ndenye: Essai d'analyse critique." In Etudes africaines offertes à Henri Brunschwig (Paris: Ecoles des hautes études en sciences sociales).

710 Person, Yves. 1981. "Colonisation et décolonisation en Côte d'Ivoire." Le Mois en Afrique (188-189, August-September): 15-30.

711 _____. 1983. "La crise de l'exploitation du diamant dans la région de Séguéla (Côte d'Ivoire), 1955-1962." In Entreprises et entrepreneurs en Afrique (Paris: Harmattan), vol. 1, pp. 411-422.

712 Picciola, Andre. 1973. "Quelques aspects de la Côte d'Ivoire en 1919." CEA 13 (50): 239-274.

713 Savonnet, G. 1962. "La colonisation du pays Koulango (haute Côte d'Ivoire) pars les Lobi de Haute Volta." COM 15 (57).

714 Semi-Bi, L. 1983. "Equipement public et changements socio-économiques en Côte d'Ivoire (1930-1957)." AUA:I 11: 245-255.

715 Semi-Bi, Zan. 1976. "L'infrastructure routière et ferroviaire coloniale, source de mutations sociales et psychologiques: Le cas de la Côte d'Ivoire, 1900-1940." CEA 16 (61-62): 147-158.

716 _____. 1975. "La politique coloniale des travaux publiques en Côte d'Ivoire (1900-1940)." AUA:I.

717 _____. 1979. "Les projets d'infrastructure ferroviaire abandonnés en Côte d'Ivoire (1904-1940)." AUA:I 7: 115-136.

718 Tirefort, Alain. 1980. "La Côte des Males Gens ou l'anti-hospitalité de l'enfer vert ivoirien: Une image de la colonie dans le premier quart du XXe Siècle." Genève-Afrique 18 (1): 91-100.

719 _____. 1983. "Un monde policé en terre ivoirienne: Le cercle toubabou, 1904-1939." CEA 23 (1-2, 89-90): 97-119.

720 Toure, Abdoulaye Jamil. 1984. Les Batisseurs de l'Enseignement en Côte d'Ivoire (1942-1958): Témoignage. Abidjan: CEDA.

721 Villamur, R. and Richard, L. 1903. Notre colonie de Côte d'Ivoire. Paris: Challamel.

722 Vrih, Gbazah. 1981. "La culture du café et du cacao dans la subdivision de Gagnoa de 1920 à 1940." AUA:I 9: 139-152.

723 Wallerstein, Immanuel. 1964. The Road to Independence. The Hague: Mouton.

724 Weiskel, Timothy C. 1980. French Colonial Rule and the Baule Peoples: Resistance and Collaboration, 1889-1911. Oxford: Clarendon Press.

725 _____. 1979. "Labor in the Emergent Periphery: From Slavery to Migrant Labor among the Baule Peoples, 1880-1925. In W. L. Goldfrank, ed. The World-System of Capitalism (Beverly Hills, CA: Sage), pp. 207-233.

726 Wondji, Christophe. 1976. "Bingerville, naissance d'une capitale 1899-1909." CEA 16 (61-62): 83-102.

727 _____. 1963. "La Côte d'Ivoire Occidentale, période de pénétration pacifique (1890-1908)." RFHOM 178.

728 Yayat d'Alépé, Hubert. 1979. "Une économie coloniale de transition: La Côte d'Ivoire de 1893 à 1919." Thèse de 3e cycle (Histoire), Université de Paris 7.

729 Zinsou, J.-V. 1979. "L'or en Côte d'Ivoire coloniale: 1890--milieu du 20e siècle." AUA:D 12: 7-25.

730 _____. 1981. "Remarques sur la guerre coloniale en pays baoulé." AUA:I 9: 155-171.

C. INDEPENDENCE

731 Amon d'Aby, F. J. 1968. Le problème des chefferies traditionnelles en Côte d'Ivoire. Abidjan: Institut d'Ethno-sociologie.

732 Campbell, Bonnie. 1982. L'état post-colonial en Côte d'Ivoire.
Paris: Centre d'études africaines.

733 "Complots de 1963." 1984. Peuples Noirs--Peuples Africains
7 (41-42, Dec.): 144-226.

734 Semi-Bi, L. 1984. "L'ascension d'une catégorie socio-
professionelle: Les commerçants-transporteurs africains en Côte
d'Ivoire au second moitié du XXe Siècle (de 1945 à nos jours)."
AUA:I 12: 189-212.

735 Thompson, Virginia. 1962. "The Ivory Coast." In Gwendolen
M. Carter, ed. African One-Party States (Ithaca, NY: Cornell
University Press), pp. 237-324.

736 Wright, J. B. 1981. Francophone Black Africa since Independence. London: Institute for the Study of Conflict.

POLITICS

A. CONSTITUTION

737 Aggrey, Albert. 1982. La Constitution. Abidjan: Editions
Juris conseil.

738 _____. 1982. La Cour Suprême: Composition, organisation,
attributions et fonctionnement. Abidjan: Editions Juris conseil.

739 Ivory Coast. 1980. Constitution de la République de Côte
d'Ivoire. Abidjan: Imprimerie Nationale.

B. GOVERNMENT

740 Boni, Alphonse. 1961. "La nouvelle organisation judiciaire de
la République de Côte d'Ivoire." Penant (689, November-
December): 659-664.

741 Derycke, P.-H. 1983. Le système financier local de deux villes
africaines, Tunis et Abidjan: Une étude exploratoire. Nanterre:
Université de Paris X, Centre d'études et recherches économiques
sur la ville et l'espace.

742 Dje Bi Dje, C. and Thirot, A. 1980. Introduction à l'étude des institutions politiques ivoiriennes. Abidjan: Faculté de Droit.

743 Ekra, Mathieu. 1961. "L'organisation de la fonction publique de la Côte d'Ivoire." Penant (689, November-December): 659-664.

744 Ekue, A. K. 1976. Le Centre de Perfectionnement des Cadres d'Abidjan. RFEPA 11 (131, Nov.): 40-49.

745 Essienne, Dieudonné. 1974. Le Ministère des Affaires Etrangères de Côte d'Ivoire. Paris: Librairies Techniques.

746 Ette, M. 1980. "La criminologie en Côte d'Ivoire." Revue internationale de criminologie et de police techniques 33: 350-360.

747 Hoimian, A. 1972-73. "Le cadre institutionnel de la politique touristique en Côte d'Ivoire." RID 3/4: 4/17.

748 Hug, Jean-Marie. 1969. L'Organisation Judiciaire en Côte d'Ivoire. Abidjan: Ministere de la Fonction Publique.

749 _____. 1982? Organisation municipale en Côte d'Ivoire. Abidjan: Imprimerie Nationale.

750 _____. Journal Officiel de la République de Côte d'Ivoire. 1959- . Abidjan: Imprimerie Nationale.

751 _____. Journal Officiel de la République de Côte d'Ivoire, Débats de l'Assemblée Nationale. Abidjan: Imprimerie nationale.

752 Schrike, H. 1976. "L'administration locale ivoirienne: L'exemple de la sous-préfecture d'Agnibilékrou." RJPIC 30 (2, Apr-June): 32-54.

753 Staniland, Martin. 1971. "Colonial Government and Populist Reform: The Case of the Ivory Coast." Journal of Administration Overseas (10, 1/2, January/April): 33-42, 113-126.

754 Tay, Hugues. 1974. L'administration Ivoirienne. Paris: Berger-Levrault.

755 Tice, Robert D. 1974. "Administrative Structure, Ethnicity, and Nation-Building in the Ivory Coast." JMAS 12 (2): 211-229.

756 Wodié, Francis and Bleou D. Martin. 1981. La Chambre administrative de la Cour suprême et sa jurisprudence (commentaires d'arrêts). Paris: Economica.

757 Yacé, Philippe. 1973. "La Côte d'Ivoire et son Parlement." Bulletin Interparlementaire 53 (1): 25-31.

C. INSTITUTIONS AND POLITICAL PROCESS

758 Asiwaju, A. I. 1977. "Political Aspects of Migrations in West Africa." Afrika zamani (Yaoundé) 6/7 (December): 73-101.

759 Bakary, Tessy D. 1985. "Côte d'Ivoire: Logiques du recrutement politique et éventuels changements à la tête de l'état." Le mois en Afrique 237/238: 3-32.

760 Bakary, Tessilimi. 1984. "Elite Transformation and Political Succession." In I. William Zartman and Christopher Delgado, eds. The Political Economy of Ivory Coast (New York: Praeger), pp. 21-55.

761 Cohen, Michael. 1973. "The Myth of the Expanding Centre: Politics in the Ivory Coast." JMAS 2 (2): 227-46.

762 Delpech, Bernard. 1973. "Réflexions sur la fonction politique chez les Islamisés et des animistes Malinké, Sia, Guro de Côte d'Ivoire." L'Homme 13: 83-96.

763 Fauré, Y.-A. 1983. "Le complexe politico-économique." In Fauré and J.-F. Médard, eds. Etat et Bourgeoisie en Côte d'Ivoire (Paris: Editions Karthala).

764 _____. "Classe dominante ou classe dirigeante?" In Fauré and J.-F. Médard, eds. Etat et Bourgeoisie en Cote d'Ivoire (Paris: Editions Karthala).

765 Fauré, Y.-A. and Médard, J-F., eds. 1983. Etat et Bourgeoisie en Côte d'Ivoire. Paris: Editions Karthala.

766 _____. 1982. "Le pouvoir d'être riches." Politique Africaine 2 (6, May).

767 Gbagbo, Laurent. 1983. La Côte d'Ivoire: Pour une alternative démocratique. Paris: Harmattan.

768 Jackson, Robert H. and Carl G. Rosberg. 1982. Personal Rule in Black Africa: Prince, Autocrat, Prophet, Tyrant. Berkeley: University of California Press.

769 Kourouma, Mamadi. 1984. "Le contentiex électoral municipal en Côte d'Ivoire." Penant 94 (785, July-September): 290-306.

770 Médard, J.-F. 1982. "La régulation socio-politique." In Y.-A. Fauré and Médard, eds. Etat et bourgeoisie en Côte d'Ivoire (Paris: Karthala).

771 Potholm, Christian. 1970. Four African Political Systems. Englewood Cliffs, N.J.: Prentice-Hall.

772 Salem, Claude I. 1975. "Pluralism in the Ivory Coast: The Persistence of Ethnic Identities in a One-Party State." Ph.D. dissertation, University of California at Los Angeles.

773 Stryker, Richard Ellis. 1970. "Center and Locality: Linkage and Political Change in the Ivory Coast." Unpublished Ph.D. dissertation, University of California, Los Angeles.

774 Sy, Seydou Madani. 1965. Recherches sur l'Exercise du Pouvoir Politique en Afrique Noire (Côte d'Ivoire, Guinée, Mali). Paris: Pedone.

775 Wolf, Jean. 1970. "Evolution politique en Côte d'Ivoire." Remarques africaines 12 (350, 20 January): 43.

776 Zolberg, Aristide R. 1966. Creating Political Order. Chicago: Rand-McNally.

777 _____. 1967. Patterns of National Integration." JMAS 5 (4): 449-467.

778 _____. 1971. "Political Development in the Ivory Coast since Independence." In Philip Foster and Aristide Zolberg, eds. Ghana and the Ivory Coast: Perspectives on Modernization (Chicago: University of Chicago Press), pp. 9-31.

779 _____. "1975. Political Generations in Conflict: The Ivory Coast Case." In W. J. Hanna et al, eds. University Students and African Politics (New York), pp. 103-133.

D. LAW

780 Abitbol, Eliette. 1966. "La Famille conjugale et le droit nouveau du mariage en Côte d'Ivoire." Penant 76 (712-714, July-December): 303-316, 455, 467.

781 Aggrey, Albert. 1983. Code des sociétés. Abidjan: Editions Juris Conseil.

782 Blaise, J-B and J. Mourgeon. 1970. Lois et decrets de Côte d'Ivoire. Paris: Libraire Technique.

783 Code Civil. 1981. Abidjan: Juris Conseil.

784 Code de Commerce. 1981. Abidjan: Juris Conseil.

785 Code de Procédure Civile, Commerciale et Administrative. 1981. Abidjan: Juris Conseil.

786 Code des Sociétés. 1981. Abidjan: Juris Conseil.

787 Code du Travail. 1982. Abidjan: Juris Conseil.

788 Code Penal. 1983. Abidjan: Imprimerie Nationale.

789 Code Penal: Code de la Route. 1981. Abidjan: Juris Conseil.

790 Coulibaly, Lazeni. 1967. "Les Traits Principaux du Nouveau Droit Ivoirien de la Famille." RJPIC 21 (1, January-March): 76-95.

791 Dumetz, Marc. 1974. Le droit du mariage en Côte d'Ivoire. Paris: Librairie Générale de Droit et de Jurisprudence.

792 Dutheil de la Rochère, Jacqueline. 1972/73. "Le nouveau Code des investissements touristiques." RID 3/4: 18-28.

793 Ellovich, Risa S. 1985. "The law and Ivoirian women." Anthropos (Fribourg) 80: 185-197.

794 Emané, J. 1967. "Les droits patrimoniaux de la femme mariée ivoirienne." Annales Africaines: 89-126.

795 Fadika, M. and R. Arthur. 1977. "Commentaires du Code ivoirien de procédure civile, commerciale et administrative." Penant 86 (755, Jan.-March): 85-102.

796 Francoul, André. 1982. Le manuel pratique de droit fiscal de la Côte d'Ivoire. Le Vesinet (France): EDITM.

797 Gaye, L.-G. 1982. "Le droit de l'enfant en Afrique noire: La Côte d'Ivoire." AUA: F 10: 63-100.

798 Ivory Coast. Ministère de la Justice. 1980. Lois civiles: Aide-Mémoire. Abidjan: Le Ministère.

799 Landraud, Daniel. 1977. "Remarques sur le mandat domestique de la femme mariée en droit ivoirien." RID 1/2: 4-11.

800 Lazerges-Rothé, C. 1977. "Droit du travail." RID 1/2: 103-141.

801 Levasseur, Alain A. 1971. "The Modernization of Law in Africa with Particular Reference to Family Law in the Ivory Coast." In Philip Foster and Aristide R. Zolberg, eds. Ghana and the Ivory Coast: Perspectives on Modernization (Chicago: University of Chicago Press), pp. 151-166.

802 Meissonnier, Georges. 1976. "Le droit des sociétés en Côte d'Ivoire." Penant 752 (April-June): 187-226; 753 (July-Sept.): 351-372.

803 Mescheriakoff, Alain Serge. 1982. Le droit administratif ivorien. Paris: Economica.

804 _____. 1979. "La jurisprudence, source de droit administratif ivoirien." RID 80 (1/2): 4-14.

805 Mundt, Robert J. 1972. "Family Structure, Polity, and Law: The Implementation of the Civil Code in the Ivory Coast." Ph.D. dissertation, Stanford University.

806 _____. 1975. "The Internalization of Law in a Developing Country: The Ivory Coast's Civil Code." African Law Studies 12: 60-101.

807 _____. 1978. "The Racial Integration of Legal Systems in Africa and the American South: Participation in Micro-Policy." In Lucian W. Pye and Sidney Verba, eds. The Citizen and Politics (Stamford, CN: Greylock Publishers), pp. 65-85.

808 N'guessan, M. 1978. "La lutte contre les aventuriers du développement: Le droit pénal des sociétés en Côte d'Ivoire." RJPIC 32 (1, Jan.-March): 517-528.

809 Oble-Lohoues, A. Jacqueline. 1984. Le droit des successions en Côte d'Ivoire: Traditions et modernité. Abidjan: NEA.

810 Raulin, Henri. 1968. "Le Droit des personnes et de la famille en Côte d'Ivoire." In Le Droit de la famille en Afrique noire et à Madagascar: Etudes préparées à la requete de l'UNESCO. Association Internationale des Sciences Juridiques (Paris: Maisonneuve et Larose), pp. 221-241.

811 Revue Ivoirienne de Droit. Abidjan.

812 Sarassoro, Yacinthe. 1984. L'enfant naturel en droit ivoirien. 1984. Abidjan: NEA.

813 Vangah, Désiré. 1967. "Le Statut de la femme mariée dans le nouveau droit de la famille en Côte d'Ivoire." RJPIC 21 (1, January-March): 96-101.

814 Veaux-Fournerie, Paulette. 1977. "Droit commercial." RID 1/2: 22-102.

815 _____. 1979/80. "Droit judiciare privé." RID 3/4: 4-104.

816 Vellenga, Dorothy Dee. 1971. "Attempts to Change the Marriage Laws in Ghana and the Ivory Coast." In Philip Foster and Aristide R. Zolberg, eds. Ghana and the Ivory Coast: Perspectives on Modernization (Chicago: University of Chicago Press), pp. 125-150.

817 Wodié, Francis and Bléou D. Martin. 1981. La Chambre ad-
     ministrative de la Cour suprème et sa jurisprudence (commen-
     taires d'arrets). Paris: Economica, and AUA:A (6).

E. MASS ORGANIZATIONS

818 Chazan, Naomi. 1976. "The Manifestation of Youth Politics in
     Ghana and the Ivory Coast." Genève Afrique 15 (2): 38-63.

819 Lewis, Barbara C. 1970. "The Transporters' Association of
     the Ivory Coast: Ethnicity, Occupational Specialization, and
     National Integration." Unpublished Ph.D. dissertation, North-
     western University.

F. POLITICAL PARTIES

820 Amondji, Marcel. 1986. Côte d'Ivoire: Le PDCI et la vie poli-
     tique de 1944 à 1985. Paris: Harmattan.

821 _____. 1984. "Le Parti démocratique de la Côte d'Ivoire."
     Peuples Noirs--Peuples Africains 7 (41-42, December): 46-59.

822 French, Howard. 1985. "One-Party State at a Crossroads."
     Africa Report 30 (July-August) 14-18.

823 Glasman, Monique. 1981. "La Côte d'Ivoire aprés le VIIe con-
     grès du PDCI-RDA." Afrique Contemporaine 20 (118): 11-15.

824 Schachter-Morgenthau, Ruth. 1974. Political Parties in French-
     Speaking West Africa. Oxford: Clarendon.

825 Semi-Bi, Zan. 1973. "Le parti démocratique de Côte d'Ivoire."
     RFEPA 8 (94, October): 61-75.

826 Staniland, Martin. 1969. "Single-Party Regimes and Political
     Change: The PDCI and Ivory Coast Politics." In Colin Leys,
     ed. Politics and Change in Developing Countries (London:
     Cambridge University Press), pp. 135-175.

827 Wodié, Francis. 1968. "Le parti démocratique de Côte d'Ivoire."
     RJPIC 22 (4, October-December): 987-1018.

828 Zolberg, Aristide R. 1969. One-Party Government in the Ivory
     Coast, rev. ed. Princeton, N.J.: Princeton University Press.

G. FOREIGN AFFAIRS

829 Alalade, F. O. 1975. "President Felix Houphouët-Boigny, the Ivory Coast and France." JAS 6 (3, Autumn): 122-131.

830 Bach, D. 1982. "L'insertion dans les rapports internationaux." In Y.-A. Fauré and J.-F. Médard, eds. Etat et bourgeoisie en Côte d'Ivoire (Paris, Karthala).

831 Baulin, Jacques F. 1980. La politique africaine d'Houphouët-Boigny. Paris: Eurafor Press.

832 Chipman, John. 1985. French Military Policy and African Security. London: International Institute for Strategic Studies.

833 Cornevin, Robert. 1976. Dix huit ans de politique extérieure. RFEPA 11 (131, Nov.): 50-74.

834 Fadika, L. 1978. "Stratégie Ivoirienne et nouvel order maritime international." RFEPA 150/151 (June-July): 29-56.

835 _____. 1971. "Houphouët Boigny et la diplomatie Ivoirienne." RFEPA 68 (August): 23-36.

836 Harshe, Rajen. 1984. Pervasive Entente: France and Ivory Coast in African Affairs. Atlantic Highlands, N.J.: Humanities Press.

837 Monouan. 1974. "L'Evolution du Conseil de l'Entente." Penant (October-December): 447-74.

838 Novicki, Margaret A. 1986. "The CEAO and 'L'Affaire Diawara.'" Africa Report 31 (May-June): 65-67.

839 Secher Marcussin, Henrik and Jens Erik Torp. 1979. The European Economic Community, France, and the Ivory Coast 1958-1976: A Study of the Internationalization of Capital, the Nation State, and the Development of Peripheral Capitalism. Copenhagen: Institute for International Economics and Management.

840 Skurnik, W. A. E. 1979. "Ivoirien Student Perceptions of U.S. Africa Policy." JMAS 17 (3): 409-432.

841 Tance, Appagny. 1979. "La Politique extérieure de la Côte d'Ivoire. France Eurafrique (216, April-May): 12-15.

H. PUBLIC POLICY

842 Amara Cissé, Daniel and Y. Fassassi. 1981. "Houphouët-Boigny, homme de la terre: Une approche économique." AUA: K 4: 35-90.

843 Amondji, Marcel. 1984. Felix Houphouët-Boigny et la Côte d'Ivoire: L'envers d'une Légende. Paris: Karthala.

844 Baulin, Jacques. 1982. La politique intérieure d'Houphouët-Boigny. Paris: Eurafor Press.

845 Campbell, Bonnie. 1978 "The Ivory Coast." In J. Dunn, ed. West African States: Failures and Promises (Cambridge: Cambridge University Press).

846 Cohen, Michael. 1974. Urban Policy and Political Conflict in Africa. Chicago: University of Chicago Press.

847 _____. 1974. "Urban Policy and the Decline of the Machine: Cross-Ethnic Politics in the Ivory Coast." Journal of Developing Areas 8 (2): 227-234.

848 _____. 1984. "Urban Policy and Development Strategy." In I. William Zartman and Christopher Delgado, eds. The Political Economy of Ivory Coast (New York: Praeger), pp. 57-75.

849 Damachi, U. G. 1976. "Houphouët-Boigny: The Ivory Coast--An Extension of the West. In U. G. Damachi, ed. Leadership Ideology in Africa: Attitudes toward Socio-Economic Development (New York), pp. 21-36.

850 Dessart, Francis. 1983. "Dossier Côte d'Ivoire: Félix Houphouët-Boigny, l'Humanisme et le réalisme au service d'un grand pays." Remarques arabo-africaines 25 (535-536): 59-62.

851 Dutheil de la Rochère, Jacqueline. 1976. L'Etat et le Développement Economique de la Côte d'Ivoire. Paris: Editions A. Pedone.

852 Fadika, L. 1978. "La stratégie maritime ivoirienne et le nouvel order maritime international." RFEPA 150/151 (June-July): 29-56.

853 Fauré, Y.-A. and J.-F. Médard. 1982. Hommage à Houphouët-Boigny, homme de la terre. Paris: Présence Africaine.

854 Hinderink, J. and Tempelman, G. J. 1978. "Rural inequality and Government Policy: A Case Study of the River Basin of the Bou in Northern Ivory Coast." Tijdschrift voor Economische en Sociale Geografie (1/2): 58-67.

855 Hommage à Houphouët-Boigny: Homme de la terre. 1982. Paris: Présence Africaine.

856 Houphouët, un combat en image: 40 ans de vie publique. 1984. Abidjan: SAE.

857 Houphouët-Boigny, Félix. 1978. Anthologie des discours, 1946-1978. Abidjan: Editions CEDA.

858 _____. 1984. "J'ai des milliards en Suisse" (text of speech). Peuples noirs--Peuples africains 7 (41-42, December): 76-103.

859 Présence Africaine. 1982. "Hommage à Houphouët-Boigny, Homme de la Terre."

860 Rake, Alan. 1962. "Mr. Ivory Coast." Africa Report 7 (4, April): 3-4.

861 Siriex, P. H. 1975. Houphouët-Boigny: L'Homme de la Paix. Paris: Seghers.

862 Turcotte, Denis. 1981. La politique linguistique en Afrique francophone: Une étude comparative de la Côte d'Ivoire et de Madagascar. Quebec: Presses de l'Université de Laval.

863 Wolf, Jean. 1973. "Tête-à-tête avec le Président Ivoirien: Echapper à la loi des nantis." Remarques africaines (427, September): 3-7.

864 Zartman, I. William and Christopher Delgado, eds. 1984. The Political Economy of the Ivory Coast. New York: Praeger.

865 Zolberg, Aristide. 1983. "La Rédécouverte de la Côte d'Ivoire." Politique Africaine 9 (March): 118-131.

SCIENCES

A. GEOGRAPHY

866 Arnaud, Jean-Claude and Jean-Charles Filleron. 1980. "Eléments pour une géographie du peuplement dans le nord-ouest de la Côte d'Ivoire." AUA:G 9: 233-257.

867 Bigot, Y. 1981. "Assolement stable et pluviosité incertaine dans le centre de la Côte d'Ivoire." Agronomie tropicale 36 (2, April-June): 110-121.

868 Blanc-Pamard, Chantal and R. Spichiger. 1973. "Contact forêt-savane et recru forestier en Côte d'Ivoire." L'Espace Géographique 3: 199-206.

869 Camus, H. et al. 1976. "Analyse et modélisation de l'écoulement superficiel d'un bassin tropical; influence de la mise en culture: Côte d'Ivoire, Korhogo, 1962-1972." Paris: Travaux et Documents de l'ORSTOM.

870 Diambra-Hauhouot, Asseypo. 1973. "Etude géographique des migrations quotidiennes de travailleurs à Abidjan." AUA:G 5: 147-266.

871 Dosso, Henri. 1984. "Large-scale land development and conservation in the Tai forest region of the Ivory Coast." In F. di Castri, et al, eds. Ecology in practice (Paris: UNESCO), part 1, pp. 127-143.

872 Effron, L. 1975. "Les conséquences de la sécheresse en Côte d'Ivoire." CIRES 7/8 (Oct.-Dec.) 87-116.

873 Fargues, Phillipe. 1981. "Les migrations en Côte d'Ivoire d'après le recensement de 1975." Abidjan: National University of the Ivory Coast (CIRES).

874 Filleron, J. Ch. and J.-F. Richard. 1974. "Recherches sur les paysages subsoudanais: Les géosystèmes de la région d'Odienné (Nord-Ouest de la Côte d'Ivoire)." AUA:G 6: 103-68.

875 Koby Assa, Théophile. 1981. "Le système spatial de l'Odjoukrou." AUA:G 10: 93-114.

876 Mangenot, Georges. 1955. "Etudes sur les forets, des plaines, et plateaux de la Côte d'Ivoire." Etudes Eburnéennes (4): 5-61.

877 Menaut, J. C. and J. Cesar. 1979. "Structure and Primary Productivity of Lamto Savannas, Ivory Coast." Ecology (Durham, NC) 60 (6): 1197-1210.

878 Monnier, Yves and H. Berron. 1973. "Pour une découverte aérienne de la Côte d'Ivoire." AUA:G 5: 285-306.

879 Rancurel, P. 1968. Topographie générale du plateau continental de la Côte d'Ivoire et du Libéria. Paris: ORSTOM.

880 Répertoire des photographies aeriennes (par degré carré) 1982. Abidjan: Institut géographique de Côte d'Ivoire.

B. GEOLOGY

881 Angoran, Y. and E. Kadio. 1984. "Review of the Precambrian of the Ivory Coast: Geology and Metallogeny." Journal of African Earth Sciences (2).

882 Arens et al. 1971. "The Continental Margin of the Ivory Coast and Ghana." Report 70/16, Institute of Geological Sciences (London), pp. 63-78.

883 Avenard, J.-J. 1977. "Cartographie géomorphologique dans l'ouest de la Côte d'Ivoire." Paris: ORSTOM.

884 Bertrand, R., G. Bourgeon, and A. Ange. 1984. "Les paysages morphopédologiques du complexe sucrier de Borotou-Koro (Côte d'Ivoire): Caracteristique et genése." Agronomie Tropicale 39 (2, April-June): 107-120.

885 Dabin, B. et al. 1965. Carte pédologique de Côte d'Ivoire à 1:200 000. Paris: ORSTOM.

886 Davies, O. 1964. The Quaternary in the Coastlands of Guinea. Glasgow: Jackson, Son and Company.

887 Delestre, T. 1973. "Note sur les falaises de Fresco (Côte d'Ivoire)." AUA:G 5: 307-320.

888 Delvigne, J. 1965. Pédogénèse en zone tropicale: La formation des minéraux sécondaires en milieu ferralitique. Paris: Dunod.

889 Eschenbrenner, V. 1978. "Inventaire des études pédologiques effectuées dans le bassin du fleuve Niger (Bénin, Côte d'Ivoire, Haute-Volta, Mali, Niger, Cameroun et Tchad)." Paris: ORSTOM.

890 _____ and L. Badarello. 1978. Etude pédologique de la région d'Odienné (Cote d'Ivoire). Paris: ORSTOM.

891 Ivory Coast. SODEMI. 1964. Carte géologique de la République de Côte d'Ivoire (1/100,000). Abidjan: Direction des Mines et de la Géologie.

892 Lafforgue, A. 1982. "Etude hydrologique des bassins versants de Sakassou, Côte d'Ivoire, 1972-1977." Paris: ORSTOM.

893 LeBourdiec, Paul. 1958. "Contribution à l'étude géomorphologique du bassin sédimentaire et des régions littorales de Côte d'Ivoire." Abidjan: IFAN, Centre de Côte d'Ivoire, Etudes Eburnéennes.

894 Leneuf, N. 1959. L'altération des granites calco-alcalins et des granodiorites en Côte d'Ivoire forestière et les sols qui en sont dérivés. Paris: ORSTOM.

895 Lévêque, A. 1983. Etude pédologique et des ressources en sols de la région du nord du 10e parallèle en Côte d'Ivoire. Paris: ORSTOM.

896 Martin, L. 1973. Carte sédimentologique du plateau continental de Côte d'Ivoire à 1:200 000. Paris: ORSTOM.

897 _____. 1977. Morphologie, sédimentologie et paléogéographie au Quaternaire récent du plateau continental ivoirien. Paris: ORSTOM.

898 Mpiana, Kenababo. 1981. Contribution à l'étude de profils bauxitiques de Côte d'Ivoire et du Cameroun: Relations entre les microstructures et la minéralogie. Marseille: Laboratoire de sedimentologie, Faculté des sciences et techniques de Saint-Jerome.

899 Peltre, P. 1978. Le 'V' Baoulé (Côte d'Ivoire Centrale): Héritage géomorphologique et paléoclimatique dans le tracé du contact foret-savane. Paris: ORSTOM.

900 Poss, R. 1982. Etude morpho-pédologique de la région de Katiola (Côte d'Ivoire). Paris: ORSTOM.

901 Rougerie, Gabriel. 1951. "Etude morphologique du bassin français de la Bia et des régions littorales de la Lagune Aby (Basse Côte d'Ivoire orientale)." Abidjan: IFAN.

902 Verheye, W. 1979. "Le profil d'altération pédogéologique sur granodiorites en Côte d'Ivoire centrale." Revue de géomorphologie dynamique 23 (2): 49-60.

C. MEDICINE

903 Corrain, Cleto and Capitanio, Mariantonia. 1980. "Quelques observations hémotypologiques sur les Koulango (Côte d'Ivoire)." Anthropologie 84 (3): 448-454.

904 Coulibaly, A. et al. 1984. "Utilisation des structures de santé modernes et traditionnelles au niveau de trois dispensaires ruraux de Côte d'Ivoire." Afrique médicale 23 (223, Oct.): 573-577.

905 Deluz, Ariane. 1981. "Perception de la maladie à travers un suicide manqueé. Psychopathologie Africaine 19 (2): 193-200.

906 Kerharo, J. and A. Bouquet. 1950. Plantes médicinales et toxiques de la Côte d'Ivoire--Haute Volta. Paris: Vigot Frères.

907 Koffi, J. K., et al. 1983. "La lêpre en Côte d'Ivoire." Médecine d'Afrique noire 38 (8/9, August): 367-371.

908 Lhuillier, M. et al 1985. "Epidémie rurale de fièvre jaune avec transmission interhumaine en Côte d'Ivoire en 1982." Bulletin of the World Health Organisation 63 (3): 527-536.

909 Remy, Gérard. 1984. "Paysages et milieux épidémiologiques dans l'espace ivoiro-voltaique: Etude géographique des principales maladies transmissibles." Marseille: Centre d'étude des espaces epidémiologiques en milieu tropical et sub-tropical.

D. NATURAL SCIENCES

910 Adjanohoun, E. 1964. Végétation des savanes et des rochers découverts en Côte d'Ivoire centrale. Paris: ORSTOM.

911 Alexandre, Daniel Y. 1980. "Caractère saisonnier de la fructification dans une forêt hygrophile de Côte d'Ivoire." Revue d'écologie 34 (3): 335-359.

912 _____. 1980. "Le régime des éléphants du centre de la Côte d'Ivoire." Revue d'écologie 34 (4): 655-657.

913 _____. 1982. "Pénétration de la lumière au niveau du sous-bois d'une forêt dense tropicale." Annales des sciences forestières 39 (4): 419-438.

914 Arnaud, Jean-Claude and Gérard Sournia. 1980. "Les forêts de Côte d'Ivoire: Essai de synthèse géographique." AUA:G 9: 5-93.

915 _____. 1979. "Les forêts de Côte d'Ivoire: Une richesse naturelle en voie de disparition." COM 32 (127, July-September): 281-301.

916 Avenard, J.-J. 1972. "La répartition des formations végétales en relation avec l'eau du sol dans la région de Man-Touba (Côte d'Ivoire)." Paris: Travaux et Documents de l'ORSTOM.

917 _____, et al. 1974. Aspects du contact Forêt-Savane dans le Centre et l'Ouest de la Côte d'Ivoire. Paris: ORSTOM.

918 _____. 1971. Le milieu naturel de la Côte d'Ivoire. 2 vols. Paris: ORSTOM.

919 Caverivière, A. 1983. Les espèces démersales du plateau continental ivoirien: Biologie et exploitation. Paris: ORSTOM.

920 Coulibaly, S. 1977. "La problématique de la reconstitution du couvert arbore dans la zone dense de Korhogo." AUA:G 7: 5-39.

921 Daget, J. and A. Iltis. 1965. Poissons de Côte d'Ivoire (eaux douces et saumâtres). Dakar: IFAN.

922 Debray, M. 1971. Contribution à l'étude du genre Epinetrum (Ménispermacées) de Côte d'Ivoire. Paris: ORSTOM.

923 Fauquet, C. and J.-C. Thouvenel. 1980. Viral Diseases of Crop Plants in Ivory Coast. Paris: ORSTOM.

924 Fortuner, Renaud. 1981. "Les nématodes associeés au riz pluvial en Côte d'Ivoire." Agronomie tropicale 36 (1, Jan-Mar): 70-77.

925 Givord, L. and L. Den Boer. 1980. "Insect transmission of okra mosaic virus in the Ivory Coast." Annals of applied biology (UK) 94 (2, March): 235-241.

926 Guillaumet, J.-L. 1967. Recherches sur la végétation et la flore de la région du Bas-Cavally, Côte d'Ivoire. Paris: OR-STOM.

927 Guillamet, J-L., G. Couturier and H. Dosso. 1984. Recherche et aménagement en milieu forestier tropical humide: Le Projet Tai de Côte d'Ivoire. Paris: UNESCO.

928 Hervouet, J.-P. and C. Laveissiére. 1983. "Les interrelations homme/milieu/glossines et leurs répercussions sur le développement de la maladie du sommeil en secteur forestier de Côte d'Ivoire." In De l'épidémiologie à la géographie humaine (Paris: Agence de la coopération culturelle et technique), pp. 139-147.

929 Hoffmann, O. 1985. Pratiques pastorales et dynamique du couvert végétal en pays lobi (Nord-Est de la Côte d'Ivoire). Paris: ORSTOM.

930 Kahn, Francis. 1982. La reconstitution de la forêt tropicale humide (Sudouest de la Côte d'Ivoire). Paris: ORSTOM.

931 Lamy, D., et al. 1980. "Quelques viroses du mais en Côte d'Ivoire." L'Agronomie Tropicale 35 (2, Apr-June): 192-196.

932 Langellier, P. 1980. "Détermination du régime hydrique d'une culture de canne à sucre de milieu, en période de maturation, dans le Nord de la Côte d'Ivoire." L'agronomie tropicale 35 (3, July-Sept.): 232-239.

933 Laveissière, C. 1981. La répartition des glossines en Côte d'Ivoire. Paris: ORSTOM.

934 Lepesme, Pierre. 1953. Coléoptères Cérambycides (Longicornes) de Côte d'Ivoire. Dakar: IFAN.

935 Lorougnon, G. 1972. Les cypéracées forestières de Côte d'Ivoire. Paris: ORSTOM.

936 Miege, Jacques. 1955. "Les savanes et forêts claires de Côte d'Ivoire." Etudes Eburnéennes (4): 62-83.

937 Monnier, Yves. 1968. "Les effets des feux de brousse sur une savane préforestière de Côte d'Ivoire." Etudes Eburnéennes (9).

938 Pollet, A. 1981. Maliarpha separatella Ragonot (Pyralidae, Phycitinae) sur riz irrigué en Côte d'Ivoire centrale (Kotiessou). Paris: ORSTOM.

939 Quillevere, D. 1979. Contribution à l'étude des caractéristiques taxonomiques bioécologiques et vectrices des membres du complexe Simulium damnosum présents en Côte d'Ivoire. Paris: ORSTOM.

940 Rancurel, P. 1971. Les 'Teredinidae' (mollusques lamellibranches) dans les lagunes de Côte d'Ivoire. Paris: ORSTOM.

941 Rinaudo, G. 1970. Fixation biologique de l'azote dans trois types de sols de riziéres de Côte d'Ivoire. Paris: ORSTOM.

942 Rognon, Pierre. 1970. "Un massif montagneux en région tropicale aride: l'Atakor--relations entre le milieu naturel et le peuplement." AUA:G 2, fasc. 2.

943 Tran, M. 1981. Reconnaissance des principaux foreurs des tiges du riz, du mais et de la canne à sucre en Côte d'Ivoire. Paris: ORSTOM.

ANTHROPOLOGY, ETHNOLOGY, AND SOCIOLOGY

A. ANTHROPOLOGY

944 Abel, A. 1973. "Utilisation des poids à peser l'or en Côte d'Ivoire." Journal de la Société des Africanistes 43 (1): 33-109.

945 Angoulvant, G. 1916. "Les coutumes indigènes de la Côte d'Ivoire." BCAF-RCD 7 (July): 211-12.

946 Augé, Marc. 1979. "Un jeune homme de bonne famille: Logique de l'accusation et de la confession en Côte d'Ivoire." CEA 19 (73-76): 177-218.

947 Berron, Henri. 1980. Tradition et Modernisme en Pays Lagunaires de Basse Côte d'Ivoire. Paris: Editions Ophrys.

948 Blanc-Pamard, Chantal. 1979. Un jeu écologique différentiel: Les Communauteés Rurales du Contact Forêt-Savane au Fond du "V Boulé" (Côte d'Ivoire). Paris: ORSTOM.

949 Blanc-Pamard, Chantal and Pierre Peltre. 1984. "Dynamique
des paysages préforestières et pratiques culturelles en Afrique
de l'Ouest (Côte d'Ivoire centrale)." In C. Blanc-Pamard, et
al, eds. Le Développement Rural en Questions (Paris: ORSTOM),
pp. 55-74.

950 Deluz, Ariane. 1984. "Deuil et Alcool." In Collectif Champ
Social et Inconscient, eds. Actes du Colloque Champ Social
et Inconscient (Paris: Editions du Centre d'Etudes Sociologi-
ques), pp. 119-125.

951 _____. 1973. "Deux avatars d'une ethnologue." Psychiatrie
aujourd'hui (Sept.): 42-44.

952 _____. 1978. "Féminin Nocturne." In A. Deluz, C. Le
Cour Grandmaison, and A. Retel-Laurentin, eds. La Natte et
le Manguier, les carnets d'Afrique des trois ethnologues (Paris:
Editions du mercure de France), pp. 187-246

953 _____. 1973. "Variations ivoiriennes sur un thème omaha."
L'Homme 13 (4): 31-44.

954 Handloff, Robert E. 1982. "Prayers, amulets, and charms:
Health and social control." African Studies Review 25 (2/3):
185-194.

955 Hauenstein, A. 1981. "Chefferies en Côte d'Ivoire." Ethnographie 77 (84): 7-36.

956 _____. 1978. "L'excision en Afrique Occidentale." Ethnol.
Z. Zürich 2: 83-103.

957 _____. 1979. "Le palmier dans les rites et coutumes de
certaines populations ivoiriennes." Genève-Afrique 17 (2):
83-110.

958 _____. 1978. "Le serpent dans les rites, cultes et coutumes
de certaines ethnies de Côte d'Ivoire." Anthropos (Fribourg)
73 (1/4): 525-558.

959 _____. 1975. "La couleur blanche dans certains rites et
costumes en Côte d'Ivoire." Archs. suisses Anthrop. gèn. 39
(1): 7-41.

960 _____. 1981. "Lundi, mardi, mercredi ... chez les Yakouba,
Wobé et Baulé (Côte d'Ivoire)." In M. Centlivres-Demont,
et al, eds. Symboles et société en Afrique (Berne: Société
Suisse d'Ethnologie), pp. 45-64.

961 _____. 1984. "Roles que sont appelés à jouer les neveux
dans certaines ethnies ivoiriennes." Zeitschrift für Ethnologie
109 (2): 247-271.

962 Holas, Bohumil. 1960. Cultures Materielles de la Côte d'Ivoire. Paris: Presses Universitaires de France.

963 _____. 1965. Industries et cultures en Côte d'Ivoire. Abidjan: Centre des Sciences Humaines.

964 Kerharo, J. and A. Bouquet. 1949. "La chasse en Côte-d'Ivoire et en Haute-Volta: Rites, plantes, fetiches et poisons de fleche." Acta Tropica 6 (3): 193-220.

965 _____. 1950. Sorciers, feticheurs et guerisseurs de la Côte d'Ivoire et Haute Volta: Les hommes, les croyances, les pratiques. Paris: Vigot.

966 Kobben, A. J. F. 1964. "Social Change and Political Structure --a Comparative Study of Two West African Societies." In W. Frohlich, ed. Afrika im Wandel Siener Gesellschaftsformen (Leiden: Brill), pp. 71-83.

967 Koehl, B. 1983. "Notes sur quelques incompréhensions en mathématiques dues au contexte culturel ivoirien." Bulletin de l'Observatoire du français contemporain en Afrique noire 4: 125-138.

968 Kokora, P. D. 1983. "La culture comme approche globale de la société ivoirienne." CIRL 13: 204-214.

969 Meillassoux, Claude. 1978. "Kinship relations and relations of production." In D. Seddon, ed. Relations of production: Marxist approaches to economic anthropology (London: Frank Cass), pp. 289-330.

970 Memel-Fote, H. 1967. "Un guerisseur de la basse Côte d'Ivoire: Josue Edjro." CEA 7 (28): 547-605.

971 _____. 1980. Le système politique de Lodjoukrou. Paris: Présence Africaine.

972 Paulme, Denise. 1971. "Les classes d'age dans le sud-est de la Côte d'Ivoire." In Denise Paulme, ed. Classes et Associations d'age en Afrique de l'Ouest (Paris), pp. 205-285.

973 Rahm, U. 1979. "Pièges indigènes de la forêt tropicale d'Afrique (Côte d'Ivoire et Zaire)." Africa Tervuren 25 (1): 19-25.

974 Rey-Hulman, Diana. 1978. "L'or et les différenciations sociales dans l'Anno, ou la création de l'espace politique de l'Anno." Journal des Africanistes 48 (1): 71-88.

975 Richard, J. 1972. "Le contact forêt-savane dans le centre-ouest ivoirien (Séguéla-Vavoua): Aspects et significations." Abidjan: ORSTOM.

B. DEMOGRAPHY AND POPULATION

976 Antoine, Philippe and Claude Herry. 1981. Implications du déséquilibre de la structure par age et par sexe, le cas d'une métropole africaine: Abidjan. Abidjan: ORSTOM.

977 _____. 1984. Mortalité infantile et juvénile à Abidjan. Cahiers ORSTOM: Sciences Sociales et Humaines 20 (2): 141-155.

978 _____. 1983. "La Population d'Abidjan dans ses murs: Dynamique urbaine et évolution des structures démographiques entre 1955 et 1978." Cahiers ORSTOM, Série Sciences Humaines 19 (4): 371-395.

979 Assa, K. 1977. "Effets d'un investissement massif sur les déplacements de populations en Cote d'Ivoire." AUA:G 7:41-84.

980 Dittgen, Alfred. 1979. "Aspects de la mortalité des jeunes enfants à Abidjan en 1975 à partir des décès déclarés à l'état civil." CIRES 22 (Sept.): 69-104.

981 _____. 1979. "L'état civil comme source de données du mouvement naturel de la population: Etude des naissances et des décès déclarés dans la commune d'Abidjan en 1975." CIRES 22 (Sept.): 39-68.

982 _____. 1978. "Etude de la fécondité à partir des intervalles entre naissances." CIRES 18 (Sept.): 37-57.

983 _____. 1978. "Evolution de la population rurale en Côte d'Ivoire entre 1965 et 1975." CIRES 17 (March): 55-84.

984 Fargues, Phillipe. 1981. "Les migrations en Côte d'Ivoire d'après le recensement de 1975." Abidjan: National University of the Ivory Coast (CIRES).

985 Ivory Coast. Ministère de l'Economie et des Finances. 1984. Enquête ivoirienne sur la fécondité, 1980-81: Rapport principal, 2 vols. Abidjan: Le Ministère.

986 _____. Ministere des Finances, des Affaires Economiques et du Plan. "Direction de la Statistique et des Etudes Economiques et Demographiques. 1960." Recensement d'Abidjan 1955.

987 _____. _____. (et de l'industrie). 1980. Enquete démographique à passages répétés, 1978-1979: Résultats définitifs. Abidjan: Direction de la Statistique.

988 Koffi Koffi, Paul and Touré Aboumediane. 1980. Croissance démographique et prévisions des effectifs scolaires et de la

population active en Côte d'Ivoire, 1980, 1985, 1990. Abidjan: Ministry of Economics, Finance and Planning.

989 Kouadio, L. 1976. "Estimation de la fécondité des femmes de la ville de Bouaké en 1969." CIRES 9 (March): 9-26.

990 Saint-Vil, Jean. 1975. "L'immigration scolaire et ses conséquences sur la démographie urbaine en Afrique Noire: L'exemple de Gagnoa (Côte d'Ivoire)." COM 28 (112, Oct.-Dec.): 376-387.

991 United States. Agency for International Development. 1981. Africa, Ivory Coast: Selected Statistical Data by Sex. Washington, D.C.: USAID.

992 Vedrenne-Villeneuve, E. 1975. "Fécondité dans le Sud-Ouest Ivoirien: Essai d'application d'une méthode d'estimation de la fécondité à partir d'un recensement." CIRES 6 (June): 57-88.

C. EDUCATION

993 Bloch-Lemoine, Michel. 1978. "Développement et transformation de l'éducation en Côte d'Ivoire." RFEPA 150/151 (June-July): 79-94.

994 Benveniste, Annie. 1979. "Côte d'Ivoire: Télévision extra-scolaire pour l'éducation des adultes ruraux, bilan critique." Tiers-Monde 20 (79, July-Sept.): 465-478.

995 Cerych, Ladislav. 1967. L'aide extérieure et la planification de l'éducation en Côte d'Ivoire. Paris: UNESCO.

996 Charlick, Robert B. 1978. "Access to 'elite' education in the Ivory Coast--the importance of socio-economic origins." Sociology of Education 51 (July): 187-200.

997 Clignet, Remi and Philip Foster. 1966. The Fortunate Few: A Study of Secondary Schools and Students in the Ivory Coast. Evanston: Northwestern University Press.

998 Coirault, Claudine and Conturie, Christiane. 1978. "Etude du roman 'Le monde s'effondre': Conte rendu de travaux faits dans les lycées de Côte d'Ivoire." Recherche, pédagogie et culture 6 (33, Jan.-Feb.): 32-37.

999 Comoe-Krou, Barthélémy. 1982. "L'éducation de l'enfant en milieu villageois." AUA:F 10: 29-37.

1000 Dadier, K. 1982. "La dépendance du contenu de l'enseignement en Côte d'Ivoire." AUA:D 15: 205-220.

1001 Dédy, Séri. 1981. "La place de l'art musical dans l'éducation ivoirienne." AUA:F 9: 5-34.

1002 Desalmand, Paul. 1983. Histoire de l'Education en Côte d'Ivoire. Vol. 1: Des Origines à la Conférence de Brazzaville (1944).

1003 Faujas, Alain. 1971. "L'Université d'Abidjan." RFEPA 71 (November): 40-53.

1004 Ferrari, Antoine. 1969. La mutation scolaire et le développement de l'enseignement à Lakota: Résultats d'Enquêtes. Abidjan: Université d'Abidjan, Institut d'Ethno-sociologie.

1005 La Formation Professionnelle Continue en Côte d'Ivoire. 1978. Paris: Imprimerie C. Adam.

1006 Grisay, Aletta. 1984. "Analyse des inégalités du rendement lié au sexe de l'élève dans l'enseignement primaire ivoirien." International Review of Education 30 (1): 25-39.

1007 Hallak, Jacques and Raymond Poignant. 1966. "Les aspects financiers de l'éducation en Côte d'Ivoire." Paris: UNESCO (African Research Monographs, no. 8).

1008 Hoftijzer, Dirk A. 1980. L'organisation du programme d'éducation télévisuelle en Côte d'Ivoire: Une Etude de Cas. The Hague: Center for the Study of Education in Developing Countries.

1009 Iturrioz, Martina. 1983. Ville d'Abidjan, équipements scolaires (primaire et sécondaire): Contribution à l'atlas des équipements. Abidjan: Bureau central d'études techniques.

1010 Ivory Coast. "Ministère de l'Education Nationale (et de la recherche scientifique)." 1984. Education morale. Yamoussoukro.

1011 _____. 1971. Programme d'Education Télévisuelle 1968-1980, 15 vols. Abidjan.

1012 _____. Office Nationale de Formation Professionnelle. 1978-79. Bibliographie, La formation professionnelle en Côte d'Ivoire. Abidjan.

1013 Keita, G. 1983. "Enseignement du français et biculturelisme en Côte d'Ivoire." Bulletin de l'Observatoire du français contemporain en Afrique noire 4: 141-156.

1014 Kokora, P. D. 1977. "Enseignement et langues maternelles en Côte d'Ivoire." AUA:D 10: 231-246.

1015 _____. 1983b. "Pourquoi parle-t-on tant de la promotion des langues nationales dans le système éducatif? Le point de vue de l'Institut de linguistique appliquée de l'Université d'Abidjan." CIRL 13: 93-102.

1016 Konan-Daure, N'Guessan, et al. 1980. Guide professionnel de l'instituteur. Abidjan: CEDA.

1017 Monson, Terry D. 1979. "Educational Returns in the Ivory Coast." Journal of Developing Areas 13 (July): 415-430.

1018 Muncie, P. C. 1973. Torches in the Night: Educational Experiences in Tanzania and the Ivory Coast. London.

1019 Odi Assamoi, Georgette. 1984. "L'enseignement de l'anglais en Côte d'Ivoire (1946-1977)." Afram Newsletter 18 (January): 5-10.

1020 Pairault, Claude. 1977. "Des étudiants parlent de l'enseigne-ment." AUA:F 6:61-131.

1021 Ravel, Jean-Louis and André Jacques Martin. 1984. "Les enseignants du secondaire en Côte d'Ivoire: Représentations sociales de la fonction enseignante." Paris: Ministry of Foreign Affairs.

1022 Sigel, Efrem. 1967. "Ivory Coast Educaiton: Brake or Spur?" Africa Report (January): 48-51.

1023 Soulez, Philippe. 1969. "Sociologie de la population scolaire en Côte d'Ivoire." CEA 9 (36): 527-545.

1024 Tchimou, Edi. 1984. Répertoire des moyens de formation en République de Côte d'Ivoire. Abidjan: Office national de form-ation professionnelle.

1025 Thomas, P. 1977. "L'alphabétisation en Côte d'Ivoire: Situa-tion actuelle." CIRL 1 (April): 51-86.

1026 Touré, K. 1975. "Primary education by television in the Ivory Coast." UNESCO Chronicle 21 (11, Nov.): 308-314.

1027 Yao, Faustin Kouadjo. 1983. "Communication Technology Transfer for Development: Issues from the Ivory Coast Edu-cational Television Program." Ph.D. dissertation, Stanford University.

D. ETHNOLOGY

1028 Clozel, F. J. and R. Villamur, eds. 1902. Les Coutumes In-digènes de la Côte d'Ivoire. Paris.

Abron

1029 Alland, Alexander, Jr. 1964. "Native Therapists and Western Medical Practitioners among the Abron of Ivory Coast." Transactions of the New York Academy of Sciences 26 (6): 714-25.

1030 _____. 1965. "Abron witchcraft and social structure." CEA 5 (20: 495-502.

1031 Alland, Alexander, Jr. When the Spider Danced.

1032 Koby, A. T. 1974. "Milieu physique et implantations humaines dans le 'Pays Abron.'" In Les Populations communes de la Côte d'Ivoire et du Ghana. Colloque Inter-Universitaire Ghana-Côte d'Ivoire. Univs. of Abidjan and Legon, Bondoukou Jan. 4-9.

1033 Terray, Emmanuel. "Class and Class Consciousness in the Abron Kingdom of Gyaman." In M. Bloch, ed. Marxist Analysis and Social Anthropology (London: Malaby Press), pp. 85-135.

Abure

1034 Niangoran Bouah, Georges. 1965. "Les Aboure, une société lagunaire de Côte d'Ivoire." AUA:F 1: 37-166.

Adjukru

1035 Dupire, Marguerite and Jean-Louis Boutillier. 1958. Le pays Adioukrou et sa palmeraie (Basse-Côte d'Ivoire): Etude Socio-Economique. Paris: ORSTOM.

1036 Mémel-Fote, Harris. 1978. "L'ethnie et l'histoire à propos de l'histoire culturelle des Adjoukrou." AUA:F 7: 5-19.

Aizi

1037 Bonnefoy, C. 1954. Tiagba--Notes sur un Village Aizi. Etudes Eburnéennes (3): 7-129.

1038 Verdeaux, François. 1981. "L'Aizi pluriel: Chronique d'une ethnie lagunaire de Côte d'Ivoire." Abidjan: ORSTOM.

1039 _____. 1977. "Appartenance et dependance: L'exemple du systeme de classes d'age des Aizi (basse Côte d'Ivoire)." CEA 17 (68): 435-461.

Akan

1040 Eschlimann, Jean-Paul. 1984. "La culture akan: Ouverture sur l'universel de la vie." Spiritus 25 (97): 383-390.

1041 Konan, F. 1983. "L'esthétique akan." AUA:F 11: 5-12.

1042 Niangoran Bouah, Georges. 1978. "Idéologie de l'or chez les Akan de Côte d'Ivoire et du Ghana." Journal des Africanistes 48 (1): 127-140.

1043 _____. 1981. Introduction à la Drummologie. Abidjan: Editions GNB.

1044 _____. 1979. "Le mariage nsoyahin." CEA 19 (73-76): 315-322.

1045 _____. 1973. "Symboles institutionnels chez les Akan." L'Homme 13 (1-2): 207-232.

1046 Terray, Emmanuel. 1978. "L'or dans les sociétés akan: Bibliographie." Journal des Africanistes 48 (1): 141-165.

Alladian

1047 Augé, Marc. 1969. Le Rivage Alladian: Organisation et Evolution des Villages Alladian. Paris: ORSTOM.

1048 _____. 1978. "Status, power and wealth: Relations of lineage, dependence and production in Alladian society." In D. Seddon, ed. Relations of production: Marxist approaches to economic anthropology (London: Frank Cass), pp. 388-412.

Anyi

1049 Amon d'Aby, F. J. 1960. Croyances Religieuses et Coutumes Juridiques des Agni de la Côte d'Ivoire. Paris: Larose.

1050 Brou-Tanoh, A. 1967. "La tradition orale chez les Agni Ahali du Moronou." Bulletin d'information et de liaison des Instituts d'Ethno-sociologie et de Geographie Tropicale (Abidjan: University of Abidjan) 2: 45-48.

1051 Diabaté, Henriette. 1977. "Mlan Alua, blahima du Sanvi." Bulletin IFAN 39B (2, April): 304-340.

1052 Eschlimann, Jean-Paul. 1985. Les Agni devant la mort (Côte d'Ivoire). Paris: Karthala.

1053 _____. 1982. Naitre sur la terre africaine. Abidjan: IN-ADES.

1054 _____. 1979. "Quand on te donne un mari, ne le refuse pas." CEA 19 (73-76): 517-547.

1055 Gastellu, J. M. 1980. Une économie de trésor: les grands planteurs du Moronou, 2 vols. Abidjan: ORSTOM.

1056 Kadja Mianno, Daniel. 1978. "Mythe Sanwi de l'origine des clans: Essai d'interprétation sociologique." AUA:F 7: 21-32.

1057 Kobben, A. J. F. 1954. "L'Heritage chez les Agni: L'influence de l'economie de profit." Africa (24, 4): 359-363.

1058 _____. 1956. "Le Planteur Noir." Etudes Eburnéennes (5): 7-190.

1059 Lystad, Robert A. 1959. "Marriage and Kinship among the Ashanti and the Agni: A Study of Differential Acculturation." In William R. Bascom and Melville J. Herskovits, eds. Continuity and Change in African Cultures (Chicago: University of Chicago Press), pp. 187-204.

1060 Perrot, Claude-Hélène. 1967. "'Be Di Murua': un rituel d'inversion sociale dans le royaume agni de l'Indenie." CEA 7 (27): 434-443.

1061 Rougerie, Gabriel. 1957. "Les Pays Agni du Sud-Est de la Côte d'Ivoire Forestière." Etudes Eburnéennes (6): 7-211.

1062 Tauxier, Louis. 1932. Religion, moeurs, et coutumes des Agni de la Côte d'Ivoire (Indenie et Sanwi). Paris: Paul Geuthner.

1063 Villamur, R. and Delafosse, M. 1904. Les coutumes agni. Paris: Challamel.

Attié

1064 Affou Yapi, Simplice. 1979. "Le grand planteur villageois dans le procès de valorisation du capital social: Une introduction à l'organisation socio-économique Akyé." Abidjan: ORSTOM.

1065 Boni, Dian. 1970. Le Pays Akye (Côte d'Ivoire): Etude de l'Economie Agricole. Abidjan: AUA:G II, fasc. 1.

1066 Paulme, Denise. 1965. "Mission en Pays Atié, Côte d'Ivoire." Homme (5, 1): 105-109.

1067 _____. 1966. "Première approche des Atié (Côte d'Ivoire)." CEA 6 (21): 86-120.

1068 Vincenti, M. J. 1914. Coutumes attie. Paris: Larose.

Baule

1069 Arbelbide, Cyprien. 1975. Les Baoulés d'aprés leurs dictons et proverbes. Paris: CEDA.

1070 Bamba, Sekou Mohammed. 1981. "Le processus de formation et de consolidation d'un Etat Baule: l'Etat Elomwen..." RFHOM 68 (250/253): 233-250.

1071 Chauveau, J.-P. 1977. "Réussite économique et statut social en milieu de plantations villageoises: Résultats d'enquête sur 8 villages baoulé de la Préfecture de Toumodi." Abidjan: ORSTOM.

1072 Etienne, Mona. 1979. "Maternité sociale, rapports d'adoption et pouvoir des femmes chez les Baoulé." L'homme 19 (3/4, Jul-Dec): 63-107.

1073 _____. 1980. "Women and Men, Cloth and Colonization: The Transformation of Production-Distribution Relations among the Baule (Ivory Coast)." In Mona Etienne and Eleanor Leacock, eds. Women and Colonization (New York), pp. 214-38. Also in CEA 1977 (17 (1): 41-64.

1074 Etienne, Pierre. 1968. "Les aspects ostentatoires du système économique baoulé." Economies et Sociétés 2(4).

1075 _____. 1968. "Les Baoulé et le temps." Cahiers ORSTOM, (série sciences humaines) 5 (3): 17-37.

1076 _____. 1971. "Les Baoulés face aux rapports de salariat." Cahiers ORSTOM (série sciences humaines) 8 (3): 235-242.

1077 _____. 1971. Le fait villageois baulé. Abidjan: ORSTOM.

1078 _____. 1973. "L'individu et le temps chez les Baoule: Un cas de contradiction entre la représentation d'un phénomène social et sa pratique." CEA 13 (52): 631-648.

1079 _____. 1966. "Phénomènes religieux et facteurs socio-economiques dans un village de la region de Bouake (Côte d'Ivoire)." CEA 6 (23): 367-401.

1080 Etienne, Pierre and Mona. 1971. "'A qui mieux mieux' ou le mariage chez les Baoule." Cahiers ORSTOM (Série sciences humaines 8 (2): 165-186.

1081 _____. 1968. "L'émigration Baoulé actuelle." COM 21: 155-195.

1082 _____. 1964. "L'organisation sociale des baoulé." In Etude Régionale de Bouaké (Abidjan: Ministère du Plan), pp. 125-195.

1083 _____. 1967. "Terminologie de la parenté et de l'alliance chez les Baoulé." L'Homme 7 (4): 50-76.

1084 Guerry, Vincent. 1975. Life with the Baoule. Washington: Three Continents Press.

1085 Kofi, J.-K. 1983. "Une journée d'activités de la femme africaine en pays baoulé (République de Côte d'Ivoire)." L'enfant en milieu tropical 146: 31-35.

1086 Kouakou, Albert. 1979. "Un exercice de tension et de détente en pays baoulé: Le Goli des esprits." AUA:F 8: 121-127.

1087 Kouassi, Kouakou. 1985. "Naître en pays Baoulé, ou les bébés esprits." Nouvelle revue d'ethnopsychiatrie (Grenoble) 4: 59-67.

1088 Lassailly-Jacob, Véronique. 1983. "Structures villageois et caractères migratoires de la société baule-kode, dans la région de Béoumi (Côte d'Ivoire centrale)." CEA 23 (89-90): 73-95.

1089 Lombard, Chantal. 1978. Les jouets des enfants baoulé: Essai sur la créativité enfantine dans une société rurale africaine. Paris: Quatre Vents.

1090 MARCOMER, 1968-1969. Les Jeunes Baoulés: Besoins culturels et développement, 2 vols. Paris: Secrétariat d'Etat chargé de la Coopération.

1091 Marie, Alain. 1973. "Structures, pratique et ideologies chez les Baoulé." CEA 13 (50): 363-376.

1092 Mercier, Paul. 1968. "Baoulé." In Georges Balandier and Jacques Maquet, eds. Dictionnaires des Civilisations Africaines (Paris: Fernand Hazan).

1093 Monnier, Yves. 1969. "Il était une fois, à Ayérémou ... un village du Sud-Baoule." AUA:G I, fasc. 1.

1094 Peltre-Wurtz, Jacqueline. 1971. Adiamprikofikro-Douakoukro: Etude géographique d'un terroir baoulé de Côte d'Ivoire. Paris: Mouton.

Beng

1095 Gottlieb, Alma. 1987. "Cousin Marriage, Birth Order, and Gender: Alliance Models among the Beng of Ivory Coast." Man 21 (4).

1096 _____. 1986. "Dog: Ally or Traitor? Mythology, Cosmology, and Society among the Beng of Ivory Coast." American Ethnologist 13 (3): 477-488.

1097 _____. 1982. "Sex, Fertility and Menstruation among the Beng of the Ivory Coast: A Symbolic Analysis." Africa 52 (4): 34-47.

1098 _____. 1987. "Witches, Kings, and the Sacrifice of Identity; or, the Power of Paradox and the Paradox of Power among the Beng of Ivory Coast." In Ivan Karp and William Arens, eds. The Creativity of Power (Washington, D.C.: Smithsonian Institution Press).

Bété

1099 Dozon, Jean-Pierre. 1977. "Economie marchande et structures sociales: Le cas des Bété de Côte d'Ivoire." CEA 17 (68): 463-483.

1100 _____. 1981. Ethnicité et histoire: Productions et métamorphoses sociales chez les Bété de Côte d'Ivoire. Paris: ORSTOM.

1101 _____. 1981. "Les métamorphoses urbaines d'un 'double' villageois." CEA 21 (81-83): 389-403.

1102 _____. 1979. "La parenté mise à nu, ou Pandore chez les Bété de Côte d'Ivoire." CEA 19 (73-76) 101-110.

1103 _____. 1985. La Société Bété: Histoires d'une 'ethnie' de Côte d'Ivoire. Paris: Karthala.

1104 _____. 1978. "Les transformations des structures de parenté bété dans le cadre de l'économie marchande." In C. Oppong, et al, eds. Marriage, fertility and parenthood in West Africa (Canberra: Australian National University), pp. 827-848.

1105 Gronner, Joël. 1982. Les Bété de Soubré et le développement régional (Sud-ouest de la Côte d'Ivoire). Paris: ORSTOM.

1106 Holas, Bohumil. 1968. L'image du monde Bété. Paris: PUF.

1107 Kobben, A. F. K. 1960. "Land as an object of gain in a non-literate Society: Land tenure among the Bete and Dida (Ivory Coast, West Africa)." In Daniel Biebuyck, ed. African Agrarian Systems (London: Oxford University Press), pp. 245-266.

1108 Paulme, Denise. 1962. Une Société de Côte d'Ivoire: Les Bété. Paris: Mouton.

1109 Zunon Gnobo, Julien. 1979. "La religion bété traditionnelle." AUA:I 7: 5-27.

Dan

1110 Marie, Alain. 1972. "Parenté, échange matrimonial et réciprocité: Essai d'interpretation à partir de la société Dan et de quelques autres sociétés de Côte d'Ivoire." L'Homme 12 (3, 4): 6-46, 5-36.

1111 Paulme, Denise. 1968. "Dan." In Georges Balandier and Jacques Maquet, eds. Dictionnaire des Civilisations Africaines (Paris: Fernand Hazan).

Dida

1112 Beke, P. Zeze. 1981. "Origine et mise en place des populations Dida." AUA:I 9: 123-137.

1113 Bernus, E. 1957. "Ahouati, Notes sur un Village Dida." Etudes Eburnéennes 6: 213-229.

1114 Dobe, Lobognon. 1980. "Les Dida-Godié et leur cadre de vie." AUA:G 9: 95-196.

1115 Terray, Emmanuel. 1969. "L'Organisation sociale des Dida de Côte d'Ivoire." AUA:F 1.

Djimini

1116 Suthers, Ellen. 1987. "Perception, Knowledge and Divination in Djimini Society, Ivory Coast." Ph.D. dissertation, University of Virginia.

1117 Thoret, Jean-Claude. 1969. Les Djimini: Elements d'organisation sociale. Abidjan: Institut d'Ethno-sociologie.

Dyula

1118 Akasaka, M. 1976. "A review on Dyula town: Culture and society of a trader in West Africa." Kyoto University African Studies 10: 295-334.

1119 Bernus, E. 1969. "Kong et sa region." Etudes Eburnéennes 8: 239-323.

1120 Green, Kathryn L. 1984. "Dyula." In Richard V. Weekes, ed. Muslim Peoples: a World Ethnographic Survey (Westport, CN: Greenwood Press).

1121 Launay, Robert. 1977. "Joking slavery." Africa 47 (4): 413-422.

1122 _____. 1982. Traders without Trade: Responses to Change in Two Dyula Communities. Cambridge: Cambridge University Press.

1123 Lewis, Barbara C. 1971. "The Dioula in the Ivory Coast." In Carleton T. Hodge, ed. Papers on the Manding (Bloomington, Indiana).

1124 Perinbam, B. M. 1974. "Notes on Dyula origins and nomenclature." BIFAN 36 (B), (4, Oct.): 676-690.

1125 Prouteaux, M. 1918-19. "Une eclipse de lune chez les Dioula de Bondoukou." L'Anthropologie 29: 337-339.

1126 Tauxier, Louis. 1921. Le Noir de Bondoukou: Koulangos, Dyoulas, etc.. Paris: E. Leroux.

Ebrié

1127 Niangoran Bouah, Georges. 1969. "Les Ebrié et leur organisation politique traditionnelle." AUA F: I: 51-89.

French

1128 Bonnet, P. 1978. "La minorité française en Côte d'Ivoire: pouvoir économique et indépendance nationale." Afrique et Asie Moderne 118: 29-40.

Fula (Peul)

1129 Barry, M. B. 1975. "Les Peuls en Côte d'Ivoire." CIRES 5: 75-81.

1130 Bernardet, Philippe. 1984a. Assocation agriculture-élévage en Afrique: Les Peuls semi-transhumants de Côte d'Ivoire. Paris: Harmattan.

Gagu

1131 Holas, Bohumil. 1975. Le Gagou: Son Portrait Culturel. Paris: PUF.

1132 Tauxier, Louis. 1924. Nègres gouro et gagou. Paris: Paul Geuthner.

Gban

1133 Chauveau, J.-P. 1983. Bodiba en Côte d'Ivoire: du terroir à l'Etat: Petite production paysanne et salariat agricole dans un village Gban. Paris: ORSTOM.

1134 Parenko, Paley and R. P. J. Hébert. 1962. "Une famile ethnique: Les Gan, les Padoro, les Dorobé, les Komono." BIFAN B (24, 3-4): 414-448.

Godie

1135 Degri de Djagnan, Raymond. 1967. "Organisation familiale des Godié de Côte d'Ivoire." CEA 7 (27, 3e cahier): 399-433.

1136 Kouassi-Lowa, J. 1967. "Origine des Godié du Tigrou." Bulletin d'information et de liaison des Instituts d'Ethno-sociologie et de Geographie Tropicale (Abidjan: University of Abidjan): 13-39.

Guere

1137 Boulnois, J. 1933. Gnon-Sua: Dieu des Guérés. Paris: L. Fournier.

1138 Holsoe, Svend E. and Lauer, Joseph. 1976. "Who are the Kran/Guere and the Gio/Yacouba? Ethnic Identifications along the Liberia-Ivory Coast Border." African Studies Review 19 (1): 139-149.

1139 Paulme, Denise. 1968b. "Guéré." In Georges Balandier and Jacques Maquet, eds. Dictionnaire des Civilisations Africaines (Paris: Fernand Hazan).

1140 Schwartz, Alfred. 1971. "Tradition et Changements dans la société guéré (Côte d'Ivoire)." Paris: ORSTOM.

1141 Viard, R. 1934. Les Guéré, peuple de la fôret. Paris: Société d'éditions géographiques, maritimes et coloniales.

Guro

1142 Coulibaly, Bakary. 1967. "Essai sur la Dot en Pays Gouro." Penant (718, October-December): 425-446.

1143 Deluz, Ariane. 1982. "L'air de la calomnie: L'esclavage et son héritage chez les Gouro (Côte d'Ivoire)." Ethnologica Helvetica 5: 25-44.

1144 _____. 1968. "Gouro." In Georges Balandier and Jacques Maquet, eds. Dictionnaire des Civilisations Africaines (Paris: Fernand Hazan).

1145 _____. 1985. "Histoire inattendue; insultes et récit épique." Journal de la Société des Africanistes 55 (1-2): 187-202.

1146 _____. 1965. "Mariage et économie monétaire chez les Guro de Côte d'Ivoire." L'Afrique et l'Asie 70: 3-16.

1147 _____. 1965. "Mission en Pays Gouro, Côte d'Ivoire." L'Homme 5 (1): 110-112.

1148 _____. 1985. "Des nourritures comme indicateurs des rapports sociaux (versions traditionnelle, transitionnelle et moderne) chez les Gouro de Côte d'Ivoire." Recherches et Travaux de l'Institut d'Ethnologie (Neuchatel) 6.

1149 _____. 1970. Organisation sociale et tradition orale: Les Gouro de Côte d'Ivoire. Paris: Mouton.

1150 _____. 1984. "Qui a trahi Badiegoro?' Un chant de Bolia sur la conquête française en pays Gouro, Côte d'Ivoire." Genève-Afrique 22 (2): 119-135.

1151 _____. 1986. "Social and Symbolic Value of Feminine Kne Initiation among the Guro of Ivory Coast." In D. Parkin and D. Niamwaya, eds. Transformations of African Marriage.

1152 _____. 1965. "La société du gyè chez les Gouro." Musées de Genève 55 (May): 10-14.

1153 _____. 1985. "Villages et lignages chez les Gouro de Côte d'Ivoire." CEA 5 (19, 3e cahier): 388-452.

1154 _____. 1985. "Zan, tourbillon de poussière: Histoire d'un homme qui n'a pu enterrer sa mère." Psychiatrie Française 4: 7-12.

1155 Kacou, Venance. 1978. "Les masques et leur fonction sociale chez les Gouro." AUA:F 7: 77-84.

1156 Meillassoux, Claude. 1964. Anthropologie Economique des Gouro de Côte d'Ivoire. Paris: Mouton.

1157 _____. 1958. Social and Economic Factors Affecting Markets in Guro Land. In Paul Bohannon and George Dalton, eds. Markets in Africa (Evanston: Northwestern University Press).

1158 Tauxier, Louis. 1924. Nègres gouro et gagou. Paris: Paul Geuthner.

Kru

1159 Behrens, Christine. 1974. Les Kroumen de la côte occidentale de l'Afrique. Talence (France): Centre d'études de géographie tropicale.

1160 _____. 1982. "Les Kroumen et le développement du Sud-Ouest ivoirien." COM 35: 335-361.

1161 Holas, Bohumil. 1976. "Krou popular traditions in the Ivory Coast." In A. Bharati, ed. The Realm of the Extra-Human: Ideas and Actions (The Hague), pp. 365-377.

1162 _____. 1980. Traditions Krou. Paris: F. Nathan.

1163 Lafage, Suzanne. 1982. Etude sociolinguistique de l'aire kru de Côte d'Ivoire. Paris: Agence de la coopération culturelle et technique.

1164 Lauer, Joseph J. 1978/79. "A Konobo Group in the Ivory Coast and Chronology in the Kru Cultural Zone." Liberian Studies Journal 8 (1): 35-47.

1165 Massing, Andreas. 1980. The Economic Anthropology of the Kru (West Africa). Wiesbaden; F. Steiner.

1166 Schwartz, Alfred. 1978. "Fécondité et mortalité avant l'age de 3 ans chez les Krou de Côte d'Ivoire." In Christine Oppong, et al., eds. Marriage, fertility and parenthood in West Africa (Canberra: Australian National University), pp. 453-472.

1167 _____. 1979. "Images de la femme Kru à travers une cérémonie de funerailles (Côte d'Ivoire)." CEA 19 (73-76): 323-327.

Kulango

1168 Prouteaux, M. 1918-1919. "Un enterrement chez les Koulangos de Bouna." L'Anthropologie 29.

1169 Tauxier, Louis. 1921. Le Noir de Bondoukou: Koulangos, Dyoulas, etc.. Paris: E. Leroux.

Lagoon Peoples

1170 Dugast, Stephan. 1985. "Pour une nouvelle interprétation des systèmes de classes d'âge des peuples lagunaires." L'ethnographie 81 (95): 51-83.

1171 Manso, M. Eyui. 1975. "Les rites d'initiation dans les sociétés lagunaires de Côte d'Ivoire: L'exemple des Odjukru." CIRES 5: 69-74.

1172 Niangoran Bouah, Georges. 1964. "La Division du temps et le calendrier rituel des peuples lagunaires de Côte d'Ivoire." Paris: Université de Paris, Travaux et mémoires de l'Institut d'Ethno-sociologie.

Lebanese

1173 Gayet, Georges. 1957. "Les libanais et les syriens dans l'Ouest Africain." In Ethnic and Cultural Pluralism in Intertropical Communities (Brussels: International Institute of Differing Civilizations).

Lobi

1174 Boutillier, J.-L. 1968. Notes préliminaries à l'étude de la ville de Bouna. Abidjan: ORSTOM.

1175 Fieloux, Michèle. 1980. Les Sentiers de la Nuit: Les migrations rurales Lobi de la Haute-Volta vers la Côte d'Ivoire. Paris: ORSTOM.

1176 Labouret, H. 1931. Les Tribus de Rameau Lobi. Paris.

1177 _____. 1958. Nouvelles Notes sur les Tribus du Rameau Lobi. Dakar.

1178 Savonnet, G. 1962. "La colonisation du pays Koulango (haute Côte d'Ivoire) pas les Lobi de Haute Volta." COM 15 (57).

Manding

1179 Dalby, David. 1971. "Introduction: Distribution and Nomenclature of the Manding People and Their Language." In Carleton T. Hodge, ed. Papers on the Manding (Bloomington: Indiana University Press), pp. 1-13.

Maninka

1180 Arnaud, Jean-Claude. 1980. "Dabadougou Maféléni, un village
malinké de la région d'Odienné." AUA:G 9: 197-231.

1181 Deluz, Ariane. 1973. "Réflexion sur la fonction politique
chez des islamisés et des animistes (Malinké Sia, Guro de Côte
d'Ivoire)." L'Homme 13 (1-2): 83-96.

1182 Haidara, Ibrahim. 1983. "Les Malinkés d'Odienné en haute
Côte d'Ivoire." In Les communautés rurales. Première Partie:
Sociétés sans écriture (Afrique, Amérique, Europe) (Paris:
Dessain and Tolra), pp. 171-184.

1183 Sanogo, Moustapha. 1983. "La part sacrificielle et l'alliance
chez les Worodougou de Côte d'Ivoire." Systèmes de pensée
en Afrique noire 6: 103-116.

M'Batto

1184 Kihm, J.-M. and G. Tape. 1977. "Le langage des amulettes
en pays M'Batto." AUA:D 10: 121-152.

Mossi

1185 Deniel, Raymond. 1970. De la Savane à la Ville: Essai sur
La migration des Mossi vers Abidjan et sa region. Paris:
Editions Aubier-Montaigne.

Nzima

1186 Paulme, Denise. 1970. "Un rituel de fin d'année chez les
Nzema de Grand-Bassam." CEA 10 (38): 189-202.

1187 Verdeaux, François. 1979. "La Tradition n'est plus ce qu'elle
était ... Deux cas d'héritage chez les Nzima Aduvle, Côte
d'Ivoire." CEA 19 (73-76): 69-85.

Senufo

1188 Coulibaly, Sinali. 1961. "Les paysans senoufo de Korhogo."
COM 14: 26-59.

1189 _____. 1978. Le Paysan Senoufo. Abidjan: NEA.

1190 Dembele, N.U. 1977. "Société traditionnelle minianka--philoso-
phie et rites de la mort." Etudes Maliennes (Bamako) 20
(Jan.): 1-49.

1191 Eckert, H.-E. 1974. "Les fondeurs de Koni: Enquête sur
la métallurgie du fer chez les Sénoufos du Nord de la Côte
d'Ivoire." AUA:G 169-189.

1192 Holas, Bohumil. 1966. Les Senoufo (y compris les Minianka).
Paris: PUF.

1193 _____. 1956. "Fondements spirituels de la société sénoufo."
Journal de la Société des Africanistes 26: 9-31.

1194 Jespers, Philippe. 1983. "L'arc et le sang des chiens."
Systèmes de pensée en Afrique noire 6: 65-102. (Minianka)

1195 Jonckers, D. 1976. "Contribution à l'étude du sacrifice chez
les Minyanka." Systèmes de pensée en Afrique noire 2: 91-110.

1196 Keletigui, Jean-Marie. 1978. Le Sénoufo face au cosmos.
Abidjan: NEA.

1197 Kientz, Albert. 1979. Dieu et les génies: Récits étiologiques
senoufo, Côte d'Ivoire. Paris: Société d'études linguistiques
et anthropologiques de France.

1198 Kientz, Albert, et al. 1976. "Optimalisation de la communication
et agencement de l'espace: Le modèle senufo." CEA 16 (63-64):
541-552.

1199 Knops, P. 1958. "Aspect de la vie agricole des Senoufo de
l'Afrique occidentale." Bulletin de la Société royale belge
d'anthropologie et de préhistoire 69: 105-129.

1200 _____. 1958. "Critique de 'Fondements spirituels de la
vie Sénoufo' de M. Bohumil Holas." Bulletin de la Société
royale belge d'anthropologie et de préhistoire 69: 130-138.

1201 Paulme, Denise. 1968. "Senoufo." In Georges Balandier and
Jacques Maquet, eds. Dictionnaire des Civilisations Africaines
(Paris: Fernand Hazan).

1202 Peltre-Wurtz, Jacqueline. 1976. "Inventaire des villages et
campements du pays senoufo occidental." Abidjan: ORSTOM.

1203 Richter, Dolores. 1980. "Further Considerations of Caste
in West Africa: The Senufo." Africa 50 (1): 37-54.

1204 Sindzingre, Nicole. 1984-85. "Une société matrilinéale (les
Senufo Fodonon)." Les Cahiers du GRIF (29, Winter): 37-51.

Tura

1205 Holas, Bohumil. 1962. Les Toura: Esquisse d'une civilisation
montagnarde de Côte d'Ivoire. Paris: PUF.

Ubi

1206 Holas, Bohumil. 1957. "Le Paysannat Africain devant le
problème des cultures industrielles: L'exemple des Oubi (Côte
d'Ivoire)." Revue de l'Institut de Sociologie Solvay 2: 219-233.

Wan

1207 Ravenhill, Philip L. 1978. "The Interpretation of Symbolism
in Wan Female Initiation." Africa 48 (1): 66-78.

1208 _____. 1975. "The Social Organization of the Wan: A
Patrilineal People of the Ivory Coast." Unpublished Ph.D.
dissertation, the New School for Social Research, New York.

Wobe

1209 Girard, J. 1967. "Dynamique de la société ouobé: Loi des
masques et coutumes." Memoires de l'IFAN 78.

1210 Hauenstein, A. 1976. "Quelques formes de divination parmi
les Wobé et les Guéré de Côte d'Ivoire." Anthropos (Fribourg)
71 (3/4): 473-507.

1211 _____. 1981. "La société secrète des hommes panthères
chez les Wobé de Côte d'Ivoire." Anthropos (Fribourg) 76
(1/2): 67-88.

E. PSYCHOLOGY

1212 Parin, Paul, et al. 1980. Fear Thy Neighbour as Thyself:
Psychoanalysis and Society among the Anyi of West Africa.
Chicago: Univ. of Chicago Press.

1213 Partmann, Gayle H. 1979. "Socioeconomic rivalry and national
competence in Ivory Coast." Journal of Social Psychology
107 (2, Apr.): 149-160.

1214 Petitto, Andrea L. 1982. "Practical arithmetic and transfer:
a study among West African tribesmen." Journal of Cross-
Cultural Psychology 13 (1, March): 15-28.

F. RELIGION

1215 Deniel, Raymond. 1982. Croyants dans la ville. Abidjan:
INADES.

1216 _____. 1976. "Religions traditionnelles et religions révél-
ées." RFEPA 11 (131, Nov.): 75-84.

Animism and Traditional Belief

1217 Augé, Marc. 1976. "Savoir voir et savoir vivre: Les croyances à la sorcellerie en Côte d'Ivoire." Africa 46 (2): 128-
136.

1218 _____. 1971. "Sorciers noirs et diables blancs: La notion
de personne, les croyances à la sorcellerie et leur évolution
dans les lagunaires de basse Côte d'Ivoire (Alladian et Ebrié)."
In La notion de personne en Afrique noire (Paris: Colloques
Internationaux du Centre national de la Recherche Scientifique),
no. 544 (Oct.).

1219 Grottanelli, V. L. 1961. "Asonu Worship among the Nzema:
A Study in Akan Art and Religion." Africa 31 (1): 46-60.

1220 Himmelheber, H. 1965. "Le système de la religion des Dan."
In H. Himmelheber, ed. Les Religions Africaines Traditionnelles
(Paris: Seuil) pp. 75-96.

1221 Holas, Bohumil. 1969. "Les Dieux d'Afrique noire." Eburnea
21: 6-11.

1222 Kientz, Albert, et al. 1979. Dieu et les génies: Récits étiologiques Senoufo, Côte d'Ivoire. Paris: Société d'études linguistiques et anthropologiques de France.

1223 Surgy, Albert. 1981. "La divination dite ngonjoma dans la
préfecture d'Aboisso." AUA:F 9: 47-90.

Christianity

1224 Bianquis, Jean. 1924. "Dix ans d'histoire religieuse à la

Côte d'Ivoire." Foi et Vie 1 (16 November): 1086-1106; 2 (1 December): 1144-1158.

1225 Cauvin, J. 1983. "Célébrations dominicales sans prêtre: La Côte d'Ivoire." Spiritus 24 (91, May): 153.

1226 Eschlimann, Jean-Paul. 1979. "Evangélisation: Réponse de l'amour de Dieu aux aspirations d'un peuple." Z. f. Missions-Wiss. und ReligionsWiss. (Münster) 63 (1, Jan.): 35-51.

1227 Gorju, Joseph. 1915. La Côte d'Ivoire chrétienne. Lyon: Librairie Catholique Emmanuel Vitte.

1228 Mouezy, Henri. 1954. "Le Christianisme en Côte d'Ivoire." Cahiers Charles de Foucauld, 3e trimestre, 91-102.

1229 Thompson, E. W. 1928. "The Ivory Coast: A Study in Modern Missionary Methods." International Review of Missions 17 (68): 630-644.

Harrism and Other Syncretism

1230 Amos-Djoro, Ernest. 1966. "Les Eglises Harristes et le nationalisme ivoirien." Le Mois en Afrique 5: 26-47.

1231 Augé, Marc. et al. 1975. Prophétisme et thérapeutique: Albert Atcho et la Communauté de Bregbo. Paris: Hermann.

1232 Babi, Rene. 1969. "L'Eglise Harriste de Côte d'Ivoire: Les Continuateurs de W. W. Harris." Eburnea 29 (October): 16-20.

1233 _____. 1969. "L'Eglise Harriste de Côte d'Ivoire: Naissance et expansion." Eburnea 28 (September): 2-7.

1234 Bureau, Rene. 1971. "Le Prophète Harris et la religion Harriste." Institut d'Ethno-sociologie, University of Abidjan.

1235 Girard, Jean. 1973-74. Deima. Vol. I: Prophètes Paysans de l'environment noir (1973); Vol. 2: Les évangiles selon la prophétesse Bagué Honoyo (1974). Grenoble: Presse Universitaire de Grenoble.

1236 Greschat, Hans-Jürgen. 1981. "A book of revelations from Ivory Coast." Africana Marburgensia 14 (1): 66-78.

1237 Haliburton, Gordon Mackay. 1973. The Prophet Harris: A Study of an African Prophet and his Mass Movement in the

Ivory Coast and the Gold Coast 1913-1915. New York: Oxford University Press.

1238 Hayford, Joseph E. Casely. 1915. William Waddy Harris: The West African Reformer--The Man and His Message. London: C. M. Phillips.

1239 Holas, Bohumil. 1954. "Bref aperçu sur les principaux cultes syncrétiques de la basse Côte d'Ivoire." Africa 24 (1): 55-60.

1240 _____. 1965. Le Séparatisme religieux en Afrique Noire: L'Exemple de la Côte d'Ivoire. Paris: PUF.

1241 Paulme, Denise. 1963. "Une religion syncrétique en Côte d'Ivoire: Le culte déima." CEA 3 (9): 5-90.

1242 Piault, Colette, ed. 1975. Prophétisme et thérapeutique: Albert Atcho et la communauté de Bregbo. Paris: Hermann.

1243 Pritchard, John. 1973. "The Prophet Harris and Ivory Coast." Journal of Religion in Africa 5 (1): 23-32.

1244 Roux, Andre. 1971. L'Evangile dans la forêt. Paris: Les Editions du Cerf.

1245 _____. 1950. "Un Prophète: Harris." Présence Africaine, special issue (8-9) of Le Monde Noir, pp. 133-140.

1246 Shank, David A. 1983. "The Prophet Harris: A historiographical and bibliographical survey." Journal of Religion in Africa 14 (2): 130-160.

1247 Walker, Sheila S. 1983. "African Initiative and Indigenous Christianity in the Ivory Coast." In Pearl T. Robinson and Elliott P. Skinner, eds. Transformation and Resiliency in Africa (Washington: Howard University Press), pp. 191-209.

1248 _____. 1979. "The Message as the Medium: The Harrist Churches of the Ivory Coast and Ghana." In George Bond, Walton Johnson, and Sheila S. Walker, eds. African Christianity: Patterns of Religious Continuity (New York: Academic Press), pp. 9-64.

1249 _____. 1977. "Religion and Modernization in an African Context: The Harrist Church of the Ivory Coast." Journal of African Studies 1977 4 (1): 77-85.

1250 _____. 1983. The Religious Revolution in the Ivory Coast: The Prophet Harris and the Harrist Church. Chapel Hill, N.C.: The University of North Carolina Press.

1251 _____. 1980. "Witchcraft and Healing in an African Christian Church." Journal of Religion in Africa 11 (2): 127-138.

1252 _____. 1979. "Women in the Harrist Movement." In Bennetta Jules-Rosette, ed. The New Religions of Africa (Norwood, N.J.: Ablex Publishing Corp.), pp. 87-97.

1253 _____. 1980. "Young Men, Old Men, and Devils in Aeroplanes: The Harrist Church, the Witchcraft Complex, and Social Change in Ivory Coast." Journal of Religion in Africa 11 (2): 106-123.

1254 Zarwan, J. 1975. "William Wade Harris: the genesis of an African religious movement." Missiology (Pasadena) 3 (4, Oct.): 431-450.

Islam

1255 Delval, Raymond. 1980. Les Musulmans d'Abidjan. Paris: Foundation natonale des sciences politiques, Centre de hautes études sur l'Afrique et l'Asie modernes.

1256 Gouilly, Alphonse. 1952. L'Islam dans l'Afrique Occidental Française. Paris: Larose.

1257 Marty, Paul. 1922. Etudes sur l'Islam en Côte d'Ivoire. Paris: Leroux.

1258 Person, Yves. 1982. "Islam et décolonisation en Côte d'Ivoire." Le mois en Afrique 188/189 (May-June): 14-30.

1259 Quimby, Lucy Gardner. 1972. "Transformations of Belief: Islam among the Dyula of Kongbougou from 1880 to 1970." Ph.D. diss., University of Wisconsin.

1260 Triaud, Jean-Louis. 1974. "Un cas de passage collectif à l'Islam en Basse Côte d'Ivoire: Le village d'Ahua au début du siècle." CEA 14 (54): 316-337.

1261 _____. 1974. "Lignes de force de la pènètration islamique en Côte d'Ivoire." Revue des Etudes Islamiques 42 (1): 121-160.

1262 Yacoob, May Mirza. 1980. "The Ahmadiyya: Urban Adaptation in the Ivory Coast." Ph.D. dissertation, Boston University.

G. SOCIOLOGY

1263 Amon d'Aby, F. J. 1959. "Côte d'Ivoire." In Women's Role in the Development of Tropical and Sub-Tropical Countries (Brussels: INCIDI), pp. 44-64.

1264 Antoine, Philippe and Claude Herry. 1984. "Du célibat féminin à la polygamie masculine: Les situations matrimoniales à Abidjan." In Antoine, et al. La Nuptualité en Afrique: Etudes de cas (Paris: ORSTOM).

1265 _____. 1984. "Urbanisation et dimension du mariage: Le cas d'Abidjan." In De Caracas à Kinshasa: Bonne Feuilles de Recherches, pp. 337-354.

1266 _____. 1983. "Urbanisation et dimension du ménage: Le cas d'Abidjan." Cahiers ORSTOM, série sciences humaines 19 (3): 295-310.

1267 Antoine, Philippe, et al. (forthcoming). Habitat populaire à Abidjan. Paris: Karthala/ORSTOM.

1268 Augé, Marc. 1975. Théorie des pouvoirs et idéologie. Etude de cas en Côte d'Ivoire. Paris: Hermann.

1269 Aujac, Henri. 1983. "Culture nationale et aptitude à l'indus-trialisation. (1)." Revue d'Economie Politique 93 (1): 1-28.

1270 Bebel-Grand, E. 1983-84. "Problèmes de délinquance juvénile sur fond de développement: Le cas de la Côte d'Ivoire." Cahiers de pédagogie africaine (4-5): 110-139.

1271 Bonnassieux, Alain. 1983. "Fragmens d'une précarité: La difficile condition des immigrés voltaiques dans l'agglomération abidjanaise." Cahiers ORSTOM, Série Sciences Humaines 19 (4): 459-469.

1272 Campbell, Bonnie. 1978. "Social Change and Class Formation in a French West African State." Canadian Journal of African Studies, 8 (2): 285-306.

1273 Chambard, Paul. 1979. "La modification en profondeur des conditions de vie de la population." Europe outremer 57 (588/9, Jan.-Feb.): 27-31.

1274 Christopher, Garland. 1976. "Les causes de la migration de la campagne à la ville: Le cas de la Côte d'Ivoire." CIRES 10 (June): 43-71.

1275 _____. 1978. "Revenus, éducation et exode rural vers les petits centres urbains en Côte d'Ivoire." CIRES 18 (September): 5-36.

1276 Clignet, Remi. 1964. "Les attitudes de la société à l'égard

des femmes en Côte d'Ivoire." In Paul-Henry Chombart de
Lauwe, ed. Images de la femme dans la société (Paris: Editions
Ouvrières), pp. 204-221.

1277 _____. 1967. "Ethnicity, Social Differentiation, and Secondary Schooling in West Africa." CEA 4 (26, 2e cahier): 360-
378.

1278 _____. 1970. Many Wives, Many Powers: Authority and
Power in Polygynous Families. Evanston: Northwestern University Press.

1279 _____. 1977. "Social Change and Sexual Differentiation
in the Cameroun and the Ivory Coast." Signs: Journal of
Women in Culture and Society 3 (1): 244-260.

1280 _____. 1966. "Urbanization and Family Structure in the
Ivory Coast." Comparative Studies in Society and History 8
(4, July): 385-401.

1281 Clignet, Remi and Philip Foster. 1964. "Potential Elites in
Ghana and the Ivory Coast: A Preliminary Comparison."
American Journal of Sociology 70 (3, November): 349-362.

1282 de la Vaissière, P. de. 1978. Typologie selon l'âge et l'origine
de chefs d'exploitations paysannes du sud de la Côte d'Ivoire.
CIRES 18 (Sept.): 77-108.

1283 Delpech, Bernard. 1983. "Les nouveaux Abidjanais et leurs
racines, ou l'idéologie du citadin-planteur." Cahiers ORSTOM,
série sciences humaines 19 (4): 567-584.

1284 _____. 1983. "La solidarité populaire abidjanaise."
Cahiers ORSTOM, série sciences humaines 19 (4): 551-566.

1285 Dupire, Marguerite. 1960. "Planteurs Autochtones et Etrangers
en Basse-Côte d'Ivoire Orientale." Etudes Eburneennes (8):
7-237.

1286 Duponchel, Maryse. 1971. "Enquête socio-sanitaire sur un
quartier d'Adjamé." Abidjan: Ministére de la santé publique
et de la population.

1287 Ferrari, Antoine. 1970. La Situation des Jeunes à Lakota:
Méthodologie et Recensement. Abidjan, Université d'Abidjan,
Institut d'Ethno-sociologie.

1288 Ferrari, Antoine and Jean-Claude Thoret. 1970. Atiekwa: Un
village de Côte d'Ivoire. Abidjan, Universite d'Abidjan: Institut d'Ethno-sociologie.

1289 Gastellu, J. M. and S. Affou Yapi. 1982. "Un mythe à décomposer: La bourgeoisie des planteurs." In Y. A. Fauré and J. F. Médard, eds. Etat et Bourgeoisie en Côte d'Ivoire (Paris: Karthala).

1290 Gibbal, Jean-Marie. 1969. Adaptation à la vie urbaine et différenciation sociàle dans deux quartiers récents d'Abidjan. Paris: ORSTOM.

1291 _____. 1974. Citadins et villageois dans la ville africaine: L'exemple d'Abidjan. Paris: Maspero.

1292 _____. 1979. "Les collégiens de Côte d'Ivoire en famille." CEA 19 (73-76) 87-100.

1293 _____. 1974. "La magie à l'école." CEA 14 (56): 627-650.

1294 _____. 1973. "Le retour au village des nouveaux citadins: Résultats d'enquete et amorce de réflexion méthodologique." CEA 13 (51): 549-574.

1295 Glasman, Monique. 1983b. "Côte d'Ivoire: Une Société Ebranlée." Esprit (2): 124-132.

1296 Haeringer, Philippe. 1973. "Cheminemonts et migrations maliens, voltaiques et nigeriens en Côte d'Ivoire." Cahiers ORSTOM, série sciences humaines (Paris), 10 (2-3): 195-201.

1297 Hecht, Robert M. 1981. "Cocoa and the Dynamics of Socioeconomic Change in Southern Ivory Coast." Ph.D. dissertation, Cambridge University.

1298 Hinderink, J. and Tempelman, G. J. 1978. "Rural Change and Types of Migration in Northern Ivory Coast." African Perspectives (Netherlands) (1): 93-108.

1299 Holas, Bohumil. 1961. Changements Sociaux en Côte d'Ivoire. Paris: PUF.

1300 Keita, Sarangbé. 1983. "Deux cours et un immeuble: Témoignage de vingt femmes d'Abidjan sur leur vie quotidienne." Cahiers ORSTOM, série sciences humaines 19 (4): 513-532.

1301 Kobben, A. F. K. 1964. "Social Change and Political Structure --a Comparative Study of Two West African Societies." In W. Frohlich, ed. Afrika im Wandel Siener Gesellschaftsformen (Leiden: Brill), pp. 71-83.

1302 Kouakou, N'Guessan Francois. 1970. Etude d'un Famille de Bidonville à Marcory 3: Monographie de Type Familial. Abidjan: University of Abidjan, Institute of Ethno-sociology.

1303 Launay, Robert. 1978. "Transactional Spheres and Inter-Societal Exchange in the Ivory Coast." CEA 18 (72): 561-573.

1304 LePape, Marc and Claudine Vidal. 1984. "Libéralisme et vécus sexuels à Abidjan." Cahiers internationals de Sociologie 76 (January-June): 111-118.

1305 Lewis, Barbara C. 1981. "Aspects socio-économiques de la fécondité dans un cadre urbain africain: Abidjan." CIRES 28/29 (March-June): 3-35.

1306 _____. 1977. "Economic Activity and Marriage among Ivoir-ian Urban Women." In A. Schlegel, ed. Sexual stratification: a cross-cultural view (New York: Columbia University Press), pp. 161-191.

1307 _____. 1980. "Ethnicity and occupational specialization in the Ivory Coast: The Transporters' Association." In J. N. Paden ed. Values, Identities, and National Integration (Evanston: Northwestern University Press), pp. 75-87.

1308 Leymarie, P. 1977. "Un jésuite converti à la sociologie: Une 'enquete-autopsie' de Raymond Deniel." Afrique littéraire et artistique 43: 53-57.

1309 Miras, Claude de. 1982. "L'entrepreneur ivoirien, ou une bourgeoisie privée de son état." In Y.-A. Fauré and Jean-François Médard, eds. Etat et bourgeoisie en Côte d'Ivoire (Paris, Karthala).

1310 Raulin, Henri. 1957. Mission d'étude des groupements im-migrés en Côte d'Ivoire: Problèmes fonciers dans les régions de Gagnoa et Daloa. Paris: ORSTOM.

1311 Rouch, Jean. 1961. Second Generation Migrants in Ghana and the Ivory Coast. In Aidan Southall, ed. Social Change in Modern Africa (London: Oxford University Press), pp. 300-304.

1312 Ruf, François. 1979. "Travail et stratification sociale en économie de plantation: A propos du dynamisme allogène en pays Oubi." CIRES 23 (Dec.): 47-88.

1313 Saint-Vil, Jean. 1981. "Migrations scolaires et urbanisation en Côte d'Ivoire." COM 34 (133, Jan.-March): 23-41.

1314 Stavenhagen, R. 1975. "Commercial Farming and Class Rela-tions in the Ivory Coast." In Stavenhagen, ed. Social Classes in Agrarian Societies (New York), pp. 119-146.

1315 Touré, Abdou. 1983. La civilization quotidienne en Côte d'Ivoire: Procès d'occidentalisation. Paris: Karthala.

1316 _____. 1984. "La famille dans sa vie quotidienne selon les médias." In De Caracas à Kinshasa, pp. 355-370.

1317 _____. 1977. "Folklore, Politique et Culture en Afrique: L'exemple de la Côte d'Ivoire." Abidjan: ORSTOM.

1318 _____. 1982. "Paysans et fonctionnaires devant la culture et l'état." In Y.-A. Fauré and J.-F. Médard, eds. Etat et bourgeoisie en Côte d'Ivoire (Paris: Karthala).

1319 _____. 1985. Les petits métiers à Abidjan: L'imagination au secours de la conjoncture. Paris: Karthala.

1320 Tuho, Charles-Valy. 1984. J'ai changé de nom ... pourquoi? Abidjan: NEA.

1321 Vernière, Marc. 1973. "A propos de la marginalité: Réflexions illustrées par quelques enquetes en milieu urbain et suburbain africain." CEA 13 (51): 587-605.

1322 _____. 1966. "Monographie du centre semi-urbain d'Anyama (Côte d'Ivoire)." Abidjan: ORSTOM.

1323 Vidal, Claudine. 1979. "'L'argent fini, l'amour est envolé....'" L'homme 19 (3/4, July-Dec.): 141-158.

1324 _____. 1977. "Guerre des sexes à Abidjan: Masculin, feminin, CFA." CEA 17 (65): 121-153.

1325 _____. 1980. "Pour un portrait d'Abidjan avec dames." Cahiers internationaux de sociologie 69: 305-312.

1326 Zadi Zaourou, Bernard. 1974. "Rites funéraires et intégration nationale du pays Bété Sud." AUA:D 7: 67-104.

REGIONAL STUDIES

1327 Ancey, Gérard and Michel Pescay. 1983. Méthodologie: La planification à la base régionale en Cote d'Ivoire, le plan 1981-85 et ses antécédents. Paris: Ministère des relations extérieures.

1328 _____, et al. 1971. Problêmes posés par le développement à base régionale en Côte d'Ivoire. Aidjan: ORSTOM.

1329 Ivory Coast. Ministère du Plan. 1967. Côte d'Ivoire 1965: Etudes Régionales 1962-1965--Synthèse. Abidjan: Imprimerie Nationale.

1330 Paillet, Michel, Bertrand Maximin, and Sylvie Schaudel. 1976. Etudes sur le développement régional en Côte d'Ivoire. Bordeaux: Centre d'Etudes d'Afrique Noire.

Abengourou (Eastern Region)

1331 Ivory Coast. 1968. Departement de l'Est: Situation Economique, Sociale et Culturelle. Abidjan: Imprimerie Nationale.

1332 _____. 1967. Région du Sud-Est: Etude Socio-économique. Paris: Société d'Etudes pour le Développement Economique et Social.

Abidjan

1333 Antoine, Philippe and Claude Herry. 1981. Implications du déséquilibre de la structure par age et par sexe, le cas d'une métropole africaine: Abidjan. Abidjan: ORSTOM.

1334 Chegaray, Sophie. 1982. Abidjan. Abidjan: Société de presse et d'édition de la Côte d'Ivoire.

1335 Compagnie d'études économiques et de gestion industrielle. 1966. Etude socio-économique de la zone suburbaine d'Abidjan. Paris.

1336 Haeringer, Philippe, ed. 1983. "Abidjan au coin de la rue: Eléments de la vie citadine dans la métropole ivoirienne." Cahiers ORSTOM, série sciences humaines 19 (4): 363-592.

1337 Ivory Coast. Commission Interministerielle pour le développement de la région d'Abidjan. 1967. Rapport préliminaire sur l'urbanisation d'Abidjan. Abidjan.

1338 _____. Ministère des Finances, des Affaires Economiques et du Plan. Direction de la Statistique et des Etudes Economiques et Démographiques. 1962. Abidjan--Connaissance du milieu urbain: Méthodes et Résultats. Paris: Sociétés d'Etudes pour le Développement Economique et Social.

1339 _____. _____. 1962. Etude socio-économique du centre urbain d'Abidjan. Paris: Société d'économie et de mathématiques appliquées.

1340 _____. Ministère du Plan. 1965a. Etude socio-économique de la zone urbaine d'Abidjan, 6 vols. Paris: Société d'économie et de mathématiques appliquées.

1341 Liet-Veaux, G. 1977. "Commentaire du réglement d'urbanisme de l'agglomération d'Abidjan." RID 1/2: 4-20.

Agboville

1342 Grivot, R. 1955. "Agboville: Esquisse d'une cité africaine noire." Etudes Eburnéennes 4: 84-107.

1343 Simonet, M. 1968. Recensement d'Agboville. Abidjan: Cahiers ORSTOM, série sciences humaines 1 (5).

Bouake (Central Region)

1344 Ancey, Gérard. 1974. Relations de voisinage ville-campagne: Une analyse appliquée à Bouaké, sa couronne et sa région (Côte d'Ivoire). Paris: ORSTOM.

1345 Ancey, Gérard, J. Chevassu, and Jean Michotte. 1974. L'économie de l'espace rurale de la région de Bouaké. Paris: ORSTOM.

1346 Castella, P. and D. Baillon. 1970. Note de Synthèse sur l'Economie de la ville de Bouaké. Abidjan: ORSTOM, série sciences humaines 3 (7).

1347 Diambra-Hauhouot, Asseypo, Assa Koby, and Atta Koffi. 1983. De la savane à la forêt: Etude de migrations des populations du Centre-Bandama. Abidjan: Université Nationale de Côte d'Ivoire, Institut de Géographie Tropicale.

1348 Fride, B. 1964. "L'analyse démographique de la population actuelle." In Etude Régionale de Bouaké (Abidjan: Ministère du Plan).

1349 Ivory Coast. 1961. Enquête Socio-économique sur la ville de Bouaké, 2 vols. Paris: Société d'Etudes pour le Développement Economique et Social.

1350 Ministère du Plan. 1966. Etude Régionale de Bouaké 1962-64, 5 vols.

1351 Sirven, Pierre. 1972. "L'évolution des villages suburbains de Bouaké: Contribution à l'étude géographique du phénomène de croissance d'une ville africaine." Bordeaux: Centre d'études de géographie tropicale.

Daloa (Center-West)

1352 Ivory Coast. Conseil Economique et Social. 1967. Aperçu sur la Situation Economique, Sociale et Culturelle du Département du Centre-Ouest. Abidjan.

1353 _____. Ministère du Plan. 1967. Région de Daloa-Gagnoa: Etude Socio-économique. SECOBM.

Divo (South Central Region)

1354 Dobe, Lobognon. 1981. "L'organisation des espaces de vie: le cas de Divo." AUA:G 10: 5-91.

1355 _____. 1983. "La région de Divo: De l'espace vécu à aménagement régional." AUA:G 12: 147-223.

1356 Grivot, R. 1948. Le Cercle de Lahou. Paris: Larose.

1357 Schwartz, Alfred. 1970. "Le peuplement de la "zone" de Fresco: Présentation ethno-sociologique." Abidjan: ORSTOM.

Korhogo (Northern Region)

1358 Hinderink, J. and Tempelman, G. J. 1976-77. Etude Socio-économique du Bassin du Bou, Rapport Final. Utrecht: Department of Geography, State University of Utrecht.

1359 Ivory Coast. Ministère des Finances, des Affaires Economiques et du Plan. 1965. Région de Korhogo: Etudes de développement socio-économique, 8 vols. Paris: Société d'Etudes pour le Développement Economique.

1360 _____. Ministère du Plan. 1974. Le Nord Ivoirien en Mutation. Abidjan: DATAR/BNETD.

1361 _____. _____. 1965. Région de Korhogo, Etude de développement socio-économique. SEDES.

Man (Western Region)

1362 Allusson, M. 1967. Etude Générale de la Région de Man. Paris: Bureau pour le Développement de la Production Agricole.

1363 Gerardin, B. and Vo Quang Tri. 1965. Etude générale de la région de Man. Paris: Bureau pour le Développement de la Production Agricole.

1364 Ivory Coast. Conseil Economique et Social. 1969. Département de l'Ouest: Grande Potentialité Economique et Humaine à peine entamée. Abidjan: Imprimerie Nationale.

1365 _____. Ministère du Plan. 1965. Etude Générale de la Région de Man.

Odiénné (Northwest Region)

1366 Ivory Coast. Ministère du Plan. 1968. Région Odienné-Séquéla, 3 vols. Puteaux (France): IDET-CEGOS.

San Pedro (Southwest Region)

1367 Chevassu, Jean. 1971. "Effets d'un investissement massif dans une région sous-développée et sous-peuplée, San Pedro." Abidjan: ORSTOM.

1368 Haeringer, Philippe. 1973. "San Pedro 1969-San Pedro 1973." Cahiers ORSTOM, série sciences humaines 10 (2, 3).

1369 Ivory Coast. Autorité pour l'Aménagement de la Région du Sud-Ouest. n.d. Sud-Ouest Ivoirien. Abidjan.

1370 _____. Présidence de la République. 1978. Dixième Anniversaire: Opération San Pedro. Abidjan.

1371 Luzon, José L. 1985. "San Pedro: Nouveau port du sud-ouest de la Côte d'Ivoire." COM 149 (January-March): 81-87.

1372 United Nations Economic, Social, and Cultural Organization (UNESCO). 1977. "Le dynamisme pionnier dans le sud-ouest ivoirien, ses effets sur le milieu forestier (région de Soubré)." Paris.

Taabo

1373 Ivory Coast. Autorité pour l'Aménagement de la Vallée du Bandama. 1977. Taabo. Abidjan.

Toumodi

1374 DeBettignies, J. 1965. Toumodi: Etude Monographique d'un centre semi-urbain. Abidjan: Université d'Abidjan, Institut de Géographie Tropicale.